# The Emperor's Stargate

# *SUCCESS* ON ALL LEVELS

Albert Cheung Kwong Yin
&
Alexandra Harteam

OZARK
MOUNTAIN
PUBLISHING

For permission, serialization, condensation, adaptions, or for our catalog of other publications, write to Ozark Mountain Publishing, Inc., P.O . Box 754, Huntsville, AR 72740, ATTN: Permissions Department.

**Library of Congress Cataloging-in-Publication Data**

Cheung Kwong Yin, Albert – 1958 -

Harteam, Alexandra – 1954 -

1. Astrology  2. Chinese Astrology  3. Emperor's Stargate  4. Self-Help

5. Zi Wei Dou Shu  6. Success  7. Life Path  8. Career  9. Investment Strategy

I. Cheung Kwong Yin, Albert  II. Harteam, Alexandra  III. Chinese Astrology

IV. Title

Library of Congress Catalog Card Number:  2013943625

ISBN:  9781886940376

Cover Art and Layout: www.noir33.com
Book set in: Times New Roman, 18th Century
Book Design: Tab Pillar

Published by:

PO Box 754

Huntsville, AR 72740

WWW.OZARKMT.COM

Printed in the United States of America

# DEDICATION

We dedicate this book to all the people who have inspired us with new dimensions of thought that have made this book available to the destined readers.

# Table of Contents

# INTRODUCTION

## *The Life Path—Timing Is Everything*

The Chinese have a saying: "Success is 30% ability, 70% Yun Chi 運氣." Too often, Yun Chi has been loosely translated as *luck*. How irresponsible if we would study with only 30% effort and leave the rest to work itself out because, after all, that part is out of our control.

According to the Oxford dictionary, "luck" is "chance regarded as the bringer of good or bad fortune." In fact, Yun Chi has nothing to do with *chance* or *luck* at all. "Yun" alludes to "surrounding" or "encircling." And "Chi"—now, that's easier to understand! Chi is the aura, the electromagnetic field that surrounds us.

### Taking Control of Our Life Path

In this book we will be examining ways to recognize when that illusive percentage of fortuitous Yun Chi will come into our being. Thus, we are able to harness both hard work and effective timing to bring us success.

Mr. Bill Gates (founder and chairman of Microsoft, philanthropist, the planet's 2nd wealthiest person) has very often referred to himself as an extremely *lucky* person. However, is it just luck as we know it? We all know that surprising pleasure we all feel when things go smoothly, and we reach our goals seemingly effortlessly and without much ado. We call it *being lucky* or having good Yun Chi.

How do we grasp Yun Chi? Can we manifest it, quantify or change it? How do we know when it will come into our being, so we can take it by the horns and make it work for us?

Let us first look at the obvious reward of Yun Chi—SUCCESS. A common denomination to measure success is a person's wealth. The more money a person makes and accumulates, the wealthier and, therefore, more successful that individual is believed to be. However, there is a limit as to how wealthy we can become in this lifetime, and this limit is unique for each of us.

When a tremendously wealthy person's net worth exceeds a certain range, this wealth will have very little influence over his basic lifestyle. Conversely, an excess of wealth will create the obvious problems, such as fear of harm, burglary, or kidnapping or the loss of freedom, loneliness, etc. Then there's the problem that we might become a slave to our own wealth and become overly concerned with how to invest and reinvest it to make it grow even larger. We all know or have heard how a sudden change of fortune or a windfall created more problems than pleasure for some individuals.

Basically, we are all created equal. Every living being gets twenty-four hours to the day. The seas and skies are ours to enjoy. Although we all walk our vastly different paths through this journey called life, each of us experiences youth, old age, sickness, and ultimately death.

The limitations of wealth should be clear to all of us. Wealth can cover some or all medical expenses, depending upon what we can afford; however, it will never buy health. Success, therefore, cannot be measured by wealth alone.

For some, success is achieved when they have reached their goals. These goals might be to find a steady job with a steady income, buy a home and perhaps a car, marry the person they love, and eventually be able to enjoy a comfortable retirement. Goals for others might be building a brilliant career or business empire, which, in turn, would reap tremendous or unlimited wealth. Then again, for others success may lie in innovation and invention and be about leaving a legacy of some type, like having one's name forever forged in stone.

Borrowing from the famous line of the late John F. Kennedy, "And so, my fellow Americans, ask not what your country can do for you; ask what you can do for your country," we are reminded of the vastly diverse ways we can contribute towards mankind. Billionaire philanthropists, led by Bill Gates and Warren Buffett, make huge donations towards humanitarian causes. However, the relentless dedication and self-sacrifice of nameless soldiers, nurses, social workers, or others are by no means less.

In the context of this book, success is defined as "total dedication to one's life path." If each of us would apply our total energy towards our life's work, then success would be the inevitable outcome for our loved ones, the world at large, and us.

So the next question begs, "How? How do we find our life path? Where do we start?"

We start right here. Between the covers of this book, we will be guided through ways to recognize our life's purpose, what we are here to do. Stamped within our DNA is the perfect job for us. It is obvious that Yao Ming at 7'6" has all the right height to be an outstanding basketball player. A sharp-tongued critic with a quick mind and argumentative nature might make a brilliant barrister-at-court or debater. A helpful, caring personality may want to follow a career in nursing or social work.

All of us have heard people complaining that no matter how long and hard they have toiled, luck seemed to have eluded them. They have met with nothing but disaster. Here the obvious might be that they had chosen the wrong path. It follows that in the wrong field, the doors would be shut for any success to enter.

Having discovered our life path, i.e., the career that would best serve us, we must learn how to time our moves. For timing is everything when it comes to Yun Chi. The twenty-eight major stars in The Emperor's Stargate (Zi Wei Dou Shu) will not only be the tool to calculate our life's work but will guide us throughout life, prompting us when to start something, when to apply the brakes, when to wait, and when to go full throttle.

The same also holds true for our investment strategies. We shall find out what the stars have to say about risk tolerance with regard to investing. Timing one's success is what it's all about!

> Step One: The Emperor's Stargate reveals our best Career and Investment Strategies.
>
> Step Two: The Emperor's Stargate helps us learn when to make all the right moves with regard to Yun Chi.
>
> Step Three: Then the Emperor's Stargate shows us how to work realistically with our worst and best years.

Amazing, right?

# THE TAO

—✦—

*Development of virtue*

*is one's chief task.*

*The Three Jewels*

*to be sought are*

*compassion, moderation,*

*and humility.*

# Chapter 1

# To Live by Success

The oldest records of The Emperor's Stargate (Zi Wei Dou Shu 紫微斗數) date from the Tang Dynasty (619-907 CE). There are many divination schools of Old China dating to the present. These include palmistry, physiognomy (the art of judging character and destiny from facial characteristics), I-Ching, Joss Sticks (not to be mistaken with *incense*), as well as Animal Signs and Birth Hour calculations, which include the 4-Pillars and 8-Character Systems. Traces of many of the above divination tools can be found within Stargate, especially where intricate birth calculations are concerned. All these come under the Tao (The Way) of ancient Chinese philosophy.

Taoism (or Daoism) refers to a variety of related philosophical and religious traditions that have influenced Eastern Asia for more than two millennia and have had a notable influence on the Western world since the 19th century. The word 道, Tao (or Dao), literally translates as *path* or *way* although in Chinese folk religion and philosophy, it carries more abstract meanings. The founder of Taoism is believed by many religious historians to be Lao Tzu 老子or Lao Zi (604-531 BCE), whose life overlapped that of Confucius (551-479 BCE).

Over the centuries across the Northern Song (960-1279 CE), Yuan (1271-1368 CE), Ming (1368-1644 CE), and Qing (1644-1911 CE) dynasties, more and more records of Stargate surfaced. However, because they span over a thousand years, interspersed by civil wars, invasions, and natural catastrophes, records are far from complete. Where near-complete records were found, these seem to contradict one another. It is an impossible task to discern the true records from the fake, the right from the wrong. It is a fact that many Chinese textbooks deal with Stargate. Each professes its version to be the closest to the original with many copying from one another.

Let us not be overly taken with history. At its core, The Emperor's Stargate is an intricate calculation system that enables one to build an extremely accurate birth chart. Based on this chart, the whole life is laid out, explained, and understood, and thus we are guided to be the best we can be.

The first part of The Emperor's Stargate deals with the thirty-two major stars that tell us about our self, our life's work, our loves and family. Depending upon the positions of the various stars, one is shown each year in each ten year period the highest and lowest one can expect to reach throughout one's lifetime.

In this second section, we delve more deeply into the meanings of groups of stars in certain chambers and learn how to recognize our life mission and time our moves so that we can be and achieve our best in our lifetime.

Further, it should be noted that the Emperor's Stargate should be used as a tool and guide for self-discovery. It is not the intention of the writers to instill absolute belief or superstition in the system. Stargate provides a tool that is one of countless ways to achieve a rich, meaningful life, based on the teachings of the ancients.

The stars act as a gauge, showing us our strengths and where we may be off-balance. It is in knowing where we stand that will help us ultimately to arrive at our goals.

**Taoist Concepts, Beliefs, and Practices**

*Tao is the first-cause of the universe. It is a force that flows through all life. It surrounds everyone, and, therefore, everyone must listen to find enlightenment. To harmonize themselves with the Tao is the goal of all believers.*

*Taoism has provided an alternative to the Confucian tradition in China. The two traditions have co-existed in the country, regions, and generally within the same individual.*

*The priesthood views the many gods as manifestations of the one Dao, "which could not be represented as a [single] image or a particular thing." The concept of a personified deity is foreign to them as is the concept of the creation of the universe. Thus, they do not pray as other religions do: there is no God to hear the prayers or to act upon them. They seek answers to life's problems through inner meditation and outer observation.*

*In contrast with the beliefs and practices of the priesthood, most of the laity believes as follows:*

> *Spirits pervaded nature . . . The gods in heaven acted like and were treated like the officials in the world of men; worshipping the gods was a kind of rehearsal of attitudes toward secular authorities. On the other hand, the demons and ghosts of hell acted like and were treated like the bullies, outlaws, and threatening strangers in the real world; they were bribed by the people and were ritually arrested by the martial forces of the spirit officials.*

*Taoists believe that time is cyclical, not linear as in Western thinking. They also strongly promote health and vitality. Each person must nurture the ch'i/chi (spirit) that has been given to them, and development of virtue is each individual's chief task. They believe that one should plan in advance and consider carefully each action before making it.*

*The five organs and six orifices of the body correspond to the elements: metal, water, wood, fire, and earth.*

*Taoists believe that there are Three Jewels to be sought: compassion, moderation, and humility. They believe "people are compassionate by nature; left to their own devices, [they] will show this compassion without expecting a reward." In addition, Taoists follow the art of "wu wei," which is to let nature take its course. For example, one should allow a river to flow towards the sea unimpeded and never build a dam or anything that would interfere with its natural flow.*

# CHINESE PROVERB

— ✦ —

SUCCESS

is

the total dedication

to our life path.

*Chapter 2*

# Playing by the Rules of Destiny
# Yun Chi 運氣

審時度勢, 知所進退 - *"Analyze timing and circumstance.*
*Know when to ebb or flow."*

L et's say we all want to find the key that unlocks the door to success. Countless books have been written on this subject with a large percentage chronicling the rise of the rich and famous. Others offer "tried and tested" investment formulas or strategies on how to climb the corporate ladder, jump the queue, and/or beat the system.

One has only to drop into the neighborhood bookstore or click onto the Internet to find countless publications on the Golden Rules of Success. Concurrently, the 21st Century has seen the introduction of many new schools, covering subjects like management consulting, team building, positive thinking, life coaching, and/or Neuro-Linguistic Programming (NLP) that includes the use of anagrams. The list is endless. Their intention is to lead others towards self- development, growth, and ultimately success.

In the past, we believed that IQ was the best measure of human potential. During the past twenty-five years, however, researchers have found that this isn't necessarily the case. In fact, our emotional intelligence quotient (EQ) might be a greater predictor of success. Since 2000, we are now embracing MQ—Multiple Intelligence Quotient. All this has to do with our quest to find the key that opens that elusive door to success.

While it is fair to say that given time and effort, all the above will work for us and pay dividends, it seems we have been all too occupied with trying to change who we are or how we are doing or being. As yet, no one has come up with a solution on how to employ birth-given elements (those ingrained in us from birth) and STILL attain success. Until now . . .

Let's take a look at those birth elements. They include the following:

1. Intelligence quotient;
2. Personality;
3. Emotional quotient;
4. Stress/volatility tolerance;
5. Linguistic skills;
6. Logical ability;
7. Bodily or kinesthetic control;
8. Spatial and artistic inclination, and
9. Yun Chi—the harmony of Heaven, Earth and People

Let's say you have devoted several hundred hours to working on your IQ, EQ, and MQ, attended more than enough self-development workshops, and read all the books on success. So why aren't you there yet? To this end, you might like to check your Stargate charts to see if you made all your moves at the wrong time—when your Yun Chi hadn't come in yet. One or more element/s of the Harmony Equation (天时, 地利, 人和) might have been missing.

To the Chinese, every great outcome has to do with that precise moment when this is formed—when heaven, earth and people are in accord.

- Heaven 天时 is in accord when all the right stars are gathered together. This is heavenly timing or your Success Triangle of the moment;

- Earth 地利 is circumstantial or the environmental empathy. This is when the Earth sustains us;

- People 人和 are the third element. This is human touch in its myriad ways: through diligence, intervention, or just lending a helping-hand.

This Harmony Equation has been discussed at length, notably, in *The Art of War* by Sunzi Bing Fa – 孫子兵法 . Sunzi 孫子 (544 – 496 BCE) who was a Chinese military general and strategist who is traditionally believed to have authored this influential book on military strategy that is considered to be a prime example of Taoist thinking. *The Art of War* has continued to influence both Asian and Western culture and politics to this day.

**Sunzi listed the Five Principles for Success:**
**Ethics, Heaven, Earth, Leadership, and Discipline.**

*Below is a quotation of Sunzi's words:*
*The Art of War* is critical to the State.
In a life or death situation, the road leads to salvation or perdition.
This is, therefore, a subject of inquisition that on no account [should] be neglected.
*The Art of War* comprises The Five Principles for determining tactics according to field conditions.
These are Ethics 道, Heaven 天, Earth 地, Leadership 將 and Discipline 法.
Ethics 道 binds complete accord with the Leader, following him into battle unquestionably, regardless the threat of injury or death.
Heaven 天 signifies yin and yang—night and day, cold and heat, the time of the day, and the seasons.
Earth地 encompasses great or short distances, safety or danger, open fields or narrow passes, survival or death.
Leadership 將 accounts for wisdom, sincerity, benevolence, courage, and austerity.

Discipline 法 is in the marshaling of the army and its subdivisions, the graduation of rank and file, the maintenance of roads for supplies, and military expenditure.

Every General should familiarize himself with these Five Principles.
He who abides by them shall be victorious. He who lives by them shall not fail.

## Applying This Ancient Knowledge Today

If we conduct ourselves with and Heaven and Earth in compliance and add leadership and discipline, SUCCESS WILL BE OURS.

## Yun Chi 運氣

It cannot be stressed enough that Yun Chi is the crucial ingredient in the success equation. On several occasions, Bill Gates has referred to himself as "a lucky man." Perhaps so. However, in Chinese, we would call it "having extraordinary Yun Chi." In the pages that follow, we will see how the stars are placed in the chart of this pioneering philanthropist, the wealthiest person on earth. [As of March 2010, *Forbes* placed Bill Gates as the 2nd wealthiest person by just over $5 billion. However, the countless billions he has donated to medical research and various charities are not taken into account.]

The Chinese have the saying 謀事在人，成事在天 : *People toil towards their goals, but Heaven bestows.* In this context, NASA comes to mind. No matter how scientifically advanced and intricate the space exploration plans are, if there is bad weather, take-off will be delayed.

If Heaven and Earth do not agree, our lives and plans will be swept around and carried off by circumstances totally beyond our control. If we learn to read the stars and know when and how our best times will present themselves, we can control our Yun Chi instead of having Yun Chi control us.

Before we begin, let's stop and look at the Chinese adage at the beginning of this chapter: 審時度勢，知所進退 "Analyze timing and circumstance. Know when to ebb or flow." It is of vital importance that we heed this advice. In Stargate, the procedure is to plot the stars in the heavens using our exact time of birth (year, month, day, and time) according to the Western calendar. The Life Chart thus generated will give all the clues regarding IQ, personality (EQ), linguistic skills, and other inclinations and abilities, as defined in the Birth Elements. From these, the most suitable careers or Life Path can be deduced.

Further star formations will reveal one's overall Yun Chi throughout life and at various specific years. Therefore, it is easy to pinpoint when to lie low and wait and when to forge ahead and let our Yun Chi carry us to the success that's rightfully ours.

# CONFUCIUS

--✦--

不 知 命, 無 以 為 君 子 也

*To ignore one's mission*

*is to renounce*

*GREATNESS.*

# LEO BURNETT

--✦--

When you reach for the stars,

you may not quite get one,

but you won't

come up with

a handful of mud either.

# Chapter 3

## Charting the Stars, Symbols and Their Meanings

It's hard to imagine the Emperor's Stargate *(Zi Wei Dou Shu)* in the days before the computer. It would take a whole separate instruction book, months of practice with finger and knuckle counting, committing to memory a multitude of rules and exceptions, and an hour or so to manually plot just one chart. During the 1990s, Stargate masters in China, Taiwan and Hong Kong began developing their own programs in Chinese DOS. Then came *The Emperor's Stargate* book and software on CD-ROM in the English language. So then the rules changed.

*The Book of Success on All Levels* continues to extend Stargate's plotting tool, providing professional readers and students alike capabilities that a few years ago were the sole realm of the masters.

What's more, the complete volume of all the major stars, Catalysts, Auspicious and Killing Stars, obstructions, and milestones, and the full list of phenomena in the different houses are now all accessible with a mouse click. Explanations for the minor stars in the chart are now also included here. This makes the total of 108 stars, all digitally accessible.

With its theme of success, this book is not only an introduction for the student new to Stargate, but also its software is so comprehensive that even the professional reader would find it an invaluable tool.

**Prerequisites**

To make the most of this course, you should understand basic computer terminology. This book isn't designed to teach you anything more than Stargate interpretation. Other than that, as long as you can turn a computer on and off, you'll be a great candidate for learning this system.

## Getting Started

The CD-ROM included with this book includes a trial version of The Emperor's Stargate program, all the charting files, calendars and time charts, and explanations of the total 108 stars as they appear in the various Chambers. Alternatively, you may download this at www.iching-tarot.com

| SPOUSE 2042-2051辛 103-112 巳 | PEERS 2052-2061壬 113-122 午 | THE SELF 1942-1951癸 3-12 未 | ELDERS 1952-1961甲 13-22 申 |
|---|---|---|---|
| ✗ CRMSN<br>✗ OPPOR<br><br>FIRE<br><br>*LITE* | ⦿ MESGR | ▲ MIROR<br><br>DELI SPIN VOID | ⦿ WAIF ■<br>✗ SCHOL<br>COMP<br><br>ARTS |
| T C G<br>K 7 C<br>B  DH  HQ JS | T J T T T F<br>f L X Y Y G<br>S  FB SM ZS | K T<br>W S<br>M  GF  GS  TS | T Y L E<br>W S C G<br>J  BS  Gf  ZB |

Life Analysis

Name: LiXiaoLong

Date of Birth (yyyy/mm/dd): 1940/11/27     Time (hh:mm:ss): 8:00:00 A     ⦿ Male   ◯ Female

Life | Ten Years | Years | Month | Day | T.Z+1 / T.Z-1 | Record | Print

Lunar B.T. (庚辰)Y( X )M( II VIII)D(辰)T

Solar B.T. (庚辰)Y(丁亥)M(甲戌)D(辰)T

陰陽五行 陽男 木三局 龙人

■ Obstacle  ◯ Fame  ↗ Power  $ Wealth
■ Life  ■ 10 year  ■ Year  ■ Month  ■ Day

| MINORS 2032-2041庚 93-102 辰 | | KARMIC 1962-1971乙 23-32 酉 |
|---|---|---|
| ▲ MOON | | ⦿ COMDR↗<br>▲ GENRL<br>*RAM* |
| S J H<br>T S G<br>A  BF  SJ  HG | | C Y<br>32 D<br>T  LS  XH  D46 |

| PROSP/L 2022-2031己 83-92 卯 | | PROPERT 1972-1981丙 33-42 戌 |
|---|---|---|
| ▲ VAULT ◇<br><br>PUNI | | ✗ SUN  $ |
| DW  XS  Xs  BF | | B C T T<br>Z 20 x g F<br>Y  QL  SP  Ys |

| HEALTH 2012-2021戊 73-82 寅 | TRAVEL 2002-2011己 63-72 丑 | STAFF 1992-2001戊 53-62 子 | CAREER 1982-1991丁 43-52 亥 |
|---|---|---|---|
| HORS BELL | ◯ EMPER<br>⦿ PNEER<br>STAR LEFT RIGT | ◯ INTEL | |
| T T t<br>c k s<br>LG  FL  SY  DK | G P T<br>S S D<br>GD  Zs  PA  TD | T<br>s<br>MY  JJ  JX  BH | T C T<br>G 31 C<br>CS  XH  LD  WS |

Heaven Stem ⎯⎯⎯
Earth Branch ⎯⎯⎯

This program runs on Windows Vista, XP, 7, and higher. It is not suitable for Apple or Mac. Screen resolution must be at least 1024 x 768. You may use the software free for 30 days. To purchase a license to continue using this software, you must purchase either the basic version which includes the Life Chart, 10 Year Charts, and Current Year for $30.00. Information for interpreting these is contained in this book.

If you desire the software for the advanced version which includes the month and day charts, there is an additional $30.00 charge. The interpretation of these charts will be in a forthcoming book. Details for purchasing these will be provided on www.iching-tarot.com website or by email billland@netvigator.com The registration process is simply with payment being made through PayPal.

Please follow these directions.

- If you are using the CD, insert it into the computer. Follow the instructions that appear on the screen to install the **Stargate program** onto the hard drive. A box will appear titled "This 8-star Divination System is provided by HongKong Holistic Centre, V 2.e." If you are using the website to access the Stargate program, follow the directions there. Both programs with open with "This 8-star Divination System is provided by HongKong Holistic Centre, V 2.e" and will continue as follows.

- The birth chart of actor Bruce Lee (LiXiao Long), the chart by default, will appear.

- Click once on the button titled "Life" to see Bruce Lee's Life Chart. To see another Life Chart, key in your or someone else's Name, Year, Month, Day, Time of Birth and Gender, and the Life Chart (Life Analysis) will automatically appear.

- NOTE: For the Birth Time, it is *not necessary* to convert to China's time zone. You must, however, make adjustments if you were or the individual whose chart you wish to see was born at a location that was observing Daylight Savings Time. Many countries in the northern hemisphere observe DST, but not all. Daylight Saving Time begins in the northern hemisphere between March–April and ends between September–November. Standard time begins in the northern hemisphere between September–November and ends between March–April. Thus, if the person was born in June in the Illinois (United States), then you would subtract an hour from the birth time. Not all states in the United States observe DST, so be sure to check. Northern and Southern hemispheres are different, as are various countries.

- NOTE: For those whose chart you are studying who are unsure of their birth time or were born at the cusp of two time slots (2 hrs. = one slot in the Chinese clock), try this approach. Examine each time slot to see which seems most accurate. To study the next Time Slot (TZ), hit "TZ+1" or "T.Z-1" for the earlier or later chart. Those born close to midnight who are unsure should try the next day's first hour.

- An explanation of the Chambers, Calendar/Time, their relationship to each other, plus a list of the 108 stars are on the following pages. Click on each *star* in the chart for a complete in-depth explanation of how the whole spectrum of the 108 stars affect each house. NOTE: By *click on each star*, I mean to click on basically everything in each box— EMPER, GENRL, INTEL, MIROR, PUNI, STAR, etc. (abbreviations for the actual words), as well as the abbreviations that run vertically like GS, C32, Gf. Just play for a bit and see what's there.

- If you wish to save a birth chart, click on "Record." In the "History" sub-screen which appears, choose "Add." Then "Save."

- In order to save more details, go to "History" and highlight the name of the person whose chart you are examining. Then choose "Details." In the "Person's Details" section, a sub-screen appears. Enter the address, telephone number and e-mail, plus other notes. Save and then close both screens.

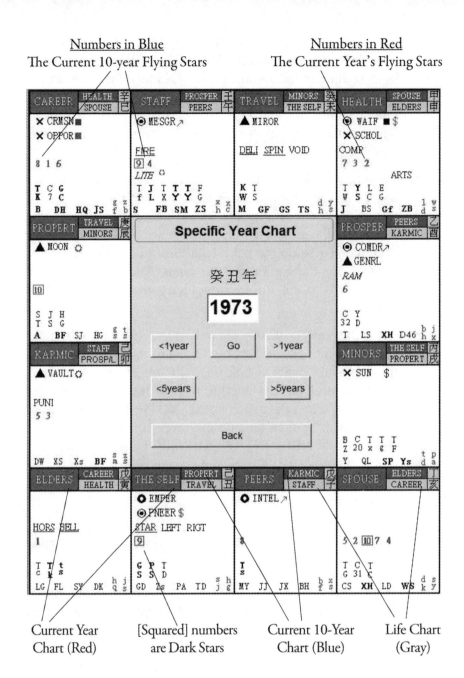

Numbers in Blue
The Current 10-year Flying Stars

Numbers in Red
The Current Year's Flying Stars

Current Year
Chart (Red)

[Squared] numbers
are Dark Stars

Current 10-Year
Chart (Blue)

Life Chart
(Gray)

- To delete an entry, click on "Record." In the "History" sub-screen, click on a name to highlight it. Then hit "Delete," followed by "Save."

- To save an on-screen chart, move the mouse to the "Lunar B.T." area in the middle. Click on the "arrow and file-save" icon which appears. In the "Save As" sub-screen which appears, key in your file name and choose the file-type to save as appropriate.

- For the 10-Year Chart (all headings and elements colored blue), click once on "Ten Years" and choose a specific 10-year phase to look into. (Always refer to the overall Life Chart when making predictions.)

- The numbers in blue represent the Flying Stars of the current 10-year phase. Numbers in red represent those in the current year. Click on any of these to show the sub-screen "Stars of Current Time Zone." The squared numbers/numbers in squares are stars that are dark.

- Keep in mind this One-Way Flow of Influence:
    o The Life ▶ 10 Years ▶ Year ▶ Month ▶ Day
    o The year, therefore, cannot have or has very little impact on the 10-Year or Life. The Life impacts all.

- For the "Year" chart, it is the opposite—all headings and elements are colored red. Click once on "Years" and key in a specific year you wish to examine. Always refer to the overall Life Chart, as well as the 10-Year Chart, referring to the above One-Way Flow of Influence.

- The Stars, Catalysts and Flying Stars (because they "fly" to their different locations with each time span) and their consequential influence on our Success Triangle—The Self, its opposing chamber (Travel), Career, Karmic and Prosperity—are explained in Chapter 5.

- Chapters 7 and 8 are in-depth explanations on how to read the Life, 10-year, and specific year charts with special emphasis on the Success and Challenges of the subjects during specific times of their lives.

- The Success of a Triangle is determined by the various groupings of Auspicious Stars and the lack of the Dark or Killing Stars and the Obstruction Catalyst. Refer to Chapters 7 and 8 for interpreting these.

- After 30 days, you will not be able to run the progam until you register.

- NOTE: If you wish to purchase the license or password to continue to work with the program, you will need to send an email with the SN to billland@netvigator.com You will then receive payment instructions. You will receive the password within 48 hours after you have sent the payment.

| | | | |
|---|---|---|---|
| | | | |
| *Snake* | *Horse* | *Goat* | *Monkey* |
| *Dragon* | *The Animal Chambers refer to* **TIME** *This means The Life, 10-year, Year, Month, Date or Hour Chart* | | *Rooster* |
| *Rabbit* | | | *Dog* |
| *Tiger* | *Ox* | *Rat* | *Pig* |

# First Layer: Birth Time/Animal Chambers

In simple terms, the basic Birth Chart is a map of the heavens at an individual's time of birth. Picture the Stargate chart as a mansion in the sky with a courtyard in the middle and twelve dwellings all around. This base layer, which is comprised of the twelve "Earth Branches," is invariable and does not change, move, or rotate.

To simplify matters, we shall call these Earth Branches by their animal representations. You are probably familiar with Chinese Animal Signs. For example, if you were born in 2010, you would be a Tiger person. These earthly branches are also time sensitive. They pertain to the hours, days, months, and years. (Because of this variable, only the animals are referred to in the following pages. The reader may apply the meanings of the stars in them according to the time frame he is referring to).

This layer, much like the face of a clock, is stationary. If read as TIME as in Birth Time, the hours would be as follows:

| Branch 1 | Rat | 11 p.m.-1a.m. |
| Branch 2 | Ox | 1-3 a.m. |
| Branch 3 | Tiger | 3-5 a.m. |
| Branch 4 | Rabbit | 5-7 a.m. |
| Branch 5 | Dragon | 7-9 a.m. |
| Branch 6 | Snake | 9-11 a.m. |
| Branch 7 | Horse | 11 a.m.-1 p.m. |
| Branch 8 | Goat | 1-3 p.m. |
| Branch 9 | Monkey | 3-5 p.m. |
| Branch 10 | Rooster | 5-7 p.m. |
| Branch 11 | Dog | 7-9 p.m. |
| Branch 12 | Pig | 9-11 p.m. |

## The Second Layer—The Houses or Chambers

Superimposed is the second layer with the "Houses" or "Chambers," which are the twelve important aspects of our lives. A house or chamber is literally a 30-degree portion of the entire universe, viewed from where we are at the time of birth.

The houses represent the people and things that we hold dear. Rotating clockwise with each passing year, the Self, the people, and events surrounding us take on the characteristics of the stars sprinkled onto our chart at the precise time of our birth.

When reading a chart, it is important to consider the major stars at the Opposing Chamber, as well as those at 120°, which affect us to a lesser degree. Here are the twelve Houses or Chambers.

|  | Opposite | @ 120° Clockwise | @ 120° Counter - clockwise |
|---|---|---|---|
| Self | Travel | Career | Prosperity |
| Elders | Health | Staff | Minors |
| Karmic | Prosperity | Travel | Spouse |
| Properties | Minors | Health | Peers |
| Career | Spouse | Prosperity | Self |
| Staff | Peers | Minors | Elders |
| Travel | Self | Spouse | Karmic |
| Health | Elders | Peers | Properties |
| Prosperity | Karmic | Self | Career |
| Minors | Properties | Elders | Staff |
| Spouse | Career | Karmic | Travel |
| Peers | Staff | Properties | Health |

For determining the personality, 10-year, and current year analyses, we need only consider grades A & B stars, (a total of 28 stars). Most C & D stars pertain to the month and day charts.

## The Third Layer—The Stars

The placements of all the major stars on the third layer remain constant, never changing throughout the individual's whole lifetime. Only the Catalysts (attachments) and the "Flying Stars" (Auspicious, Killing Stars, and Milestones) move around with time. As we (the second layer—The Houses or Chambers) move through time with each passing year, 10-years, month, or day, we come under the stars' influence.

The Stars that are present in each House exert the greatest influence over that particular sphere of our lives, whether it be our Self, Career, or Prosperity. However, Stars at the opposing chamber also play a significant role. If a sector is devoid of any major star, the opposing house is where we look for these. Still further, stars at 120° also influence. It should be noted that the influence of stars at 120° is weak. The stars are, however, crucial in detecting powerful constellations and alignments.

| A STARS (14) | | B STARS (14) | |
|---|---|---|---|
| Brightness Levels: ●◎▲✖ | | Bright; Neutral; *Dark* | |
| Emperor | (EMPER) | Left Minister | (LEFT) |
| Intelligence | (INTEL) | Right Minister | (RIGT) |
| Sun | (SUN) | Literary Minister | (LITE) |
| Commander | (COMDR) | Arts Minister | (ARTS) |
| Waif | (WAIF) | Stardust | (STAR) |
| Crimson | (CRMSN) | Delight | (DELI) |
| Vault | (VAULT) | Winged Horse | (HORS) |
| Moon | (MOON) | Completion | (COMP) |
| Opportunity | (OPPOR) | Ram | (RAM) |
| Messenger | (MESGR) | Spinning Top | (SPIN) |
| Mirror | (MIROR) | Fire | (FIRE) |
| Scholar | (SCHOL) | Bell | (BELL) |
| General | (GENRL) | Void | (VOID) |
| Pioneer | (PNEER) | Punishment | (PUNI) |

# C STARS (33)
Brightness levels are Neutral and **Dark**

| | | | | | |
|---|---|---|---|---|---|
| Riser | (TF) | Pedestal | (Fg) | Opposition | (TX) |
| C31 Lover | (HL) | C7 Happiness | (Tx) | Vantage | (EG) |
| C32 Pond | (XC) | C20 Encounter | (Ty) | Solver | (JS) |
| Sorcerer | (TW) | Malady | (TY) | Three-Storey | (ST) |
| Eight-Seater | (BZ) | Divine Fortune | (TXS) | Malice | (YS) |
| Elite | (Tg) | Phoenix Hall | (FG) | Buster | (PS) |
| Governor | (TG) | Divine Blessing | (Tf) | Clear Sky | (TK) |
| Griever | (Tk) | Dragon Pond | (LC) | Rebel | (Txu) |
| Loner | (GC) | Divine Chef | (Tc) | Recluse | (GS) |
| Tabloid | (FL) | Virtuoso | (TC) | Longevity | (TS) |
| Sage | (HG) | Benevolence | (YD) | Ethics | (TD) |

# D STARS (47)
Brightness levels are Neutral and **Dark**

| | | | | | |
|---|---|---|---|---|---|
| Verve | (CS) | Green Dragon | (QL) | Bitterness | (HQ) |
| Robe | (GD) | White Tiger | (BH) | Joyous | (XS) |
| Silence | (Xs) | Aura of the King | (DW) | Calamity | (ts) |
| Sloth | (A) | Open Letter | (Zs) | Mourning | (DK) |
| Disease | (B) | Courthouse | (GF) | Buried | (B) |
| Bath | (MY) | Severance | (J) | Embryo | (T) |
| Rope | (GS) | Academic | (BS) | Strength | (LS) |
| Officer | (JJ) | Careless Spender | (XH) | Great Loss | (Ts) |
| Gossip | (FL) | Affliction | (BF) | Scourge | (Ys) |
| Saddle | (PA) | Big Spender | (DH) | Morgue | (S) |
| Pause | (XZ) | Commandant | (JX) | Roadblock | (Jl) |
| Blank | (KW) | Ride of the Year | (SY) | Subpoena | (Gf) |
| Robber | (JS) | Nemesis | (ZS) | Slanderer | (ZB) |
| Bane | (TS) | Lord of Death | (WS) | Nurture | (Y) |
| Funeral | (SM) | Base of the Year | (SJ) | Ambush | (FB) |
| Arrival | (LG) | Grace of the Dragon | (LD) | | |

# THE CHAMBERS

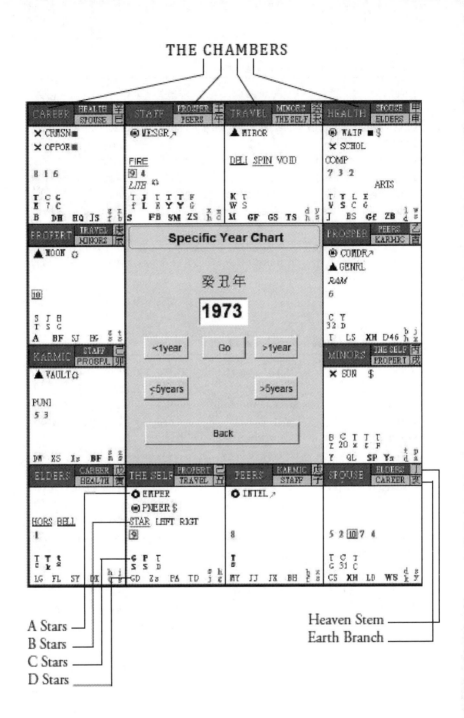

A Stars
B Stars
C Stars
D Stars

Heaven Stem
Earth Branch

# Star Brightness

Just as there is sunrise and sunset and the moon waxes and wanes, the hours affect brightness and are crucial in determining strength or weakness. The following are the brightnesses of the stars and their meanings.

## *Brilliant*: A Stars (O)

A Brilliant is a star at its best, giving forth its most positive energy. It has the ability to avert the evil influences of the obstruction catalyst (■) or dim the detrimental powers of the Killing Stars. In the presence of other Brilliants, a strong and auspicious house will be created.

## *Bright*: A Stars (⊙); **B Stars** are shown underscored.

This is an Auspicious Star, possessing all the strong, positive qualities. However, watch out for the obstruction catalyst (■) in the same or opposing chamber. Depending on the influence of the Killing Stars in the same or opposing house, positive qualities may become weakened or neutralized.

## *Twinkling*: A Stars (▲); **B, C & D Stars** are shown as neutral

In its weak state, a twinkling star would try but can only manage to deliver equal amounts of its strengths and weaknesses. A twinkling star will incline toward the negative, and the obstruction catalyst (■) or any of the Killing Stars will wreak considerable destruction. A twinkling major star will be rendered useless against these and may even turn dark.

B, C & D Stars will be in their neutral state here with their influence also being neutral.

## *Dark*: A Stars (✖); B Stars: *italicized*; C & D Stars: **Bold**

This is a star in retrograde, whereby all of its challenges have come to the foreground. It is neutralized at its best by surrounding positive stars. A dark star will have the negative enhanced by the obstruction catalyst (■) or any of the Killing Stars. Look for redeeming qualities (always at opposite or 120°). At any rate, this is a time to lie low and wait it out.

**B, C & D Stars** will also have these dark powers. However, being lesser, their influence can be controlled by the Brilliants and other positive stars and Catalysts.

# DAVID BRINKLEY

Eighty percent

of

SUCCESS

is

showing up.

# Chapter 4
# The Journey Begins

## The Birth Time

The Emperor's Stargate specifies the Birth Time as being the precise moment when the umbilical cord is severed. This is an important criterion to understand. Stargate with its records dating back to the Sung dynasty (960—1279 CE) does not deviate from the scientifically accepted fact that life begins at the time of conception. However, as long as we are still snugly nurturing inside the womb, our entire existence is still very dependent upon our mother. The bond between the developing, unborn child and its mother is only broken when the umbilical cord is cut—the moment that we begin to exist as a separate entity and so set out on our own journey through this lifetime.

Also, in Stargate, in contrast with other astrological systems, we do not gradually morph into the next "sign," "birth chart," or "time zone." There is no gray area. One has only to compare the Life Charts (of two hours' difference) before and after to notice the vast disparity of the placements of the major stars.

## The Life Chart—Our Blueprint

With the year, month, date, and time of birth specified through an intricate placement system, all positions of the major and minor stars of The Emperor's Stargate are determined. The cosmos and the person become integrated to form the first basis of all charts— the Life Chart, the blueprint of our life.

From this Life Chart we can see all the indications as to character and personality and relationships with superiors, friends, lovers, and family. We can see our dispositions towards responsibilities, risk tolerance, and what career we are likely to be attracted to and would follow. As we go through the yearly or 10-year charts, we can determine when, how, and where we will shine or lose our bearings. All of these are indicated by the different star placements inside the 12 Chambers that make up the elements in our life.

# The 12 Chambers

## The Self

This is who we are and who we will become. This encompasses the whole spectrum of what makes up the person: character, personality, physical traits, our outlook or perspective of our surroundings. The various stars here are our components; in turn, these will tell what kind of life, career, and spiritual path we are likely to follow. In general, our life's path is revealed here.

## Elders

This chamber tells of one's relationship with parents, mentors (teachers) or employers (including the corporation you work for), superiors and business owners, the (government) officials who will cross your path. Here are also revelations regarding clients if you are a business owner. In other words, all those whom you hold above yourself are explained herein.

## Karmic Wealth

Here is the window through which we take a glimpse into your mental and spiritual well-being. Whether or not one possesses a quick and agile mind is deduced by looking at the stars here. This is an important place to look at how one looks at his own quality of living—more so than in the Prosperity or Career Chambers. This house also sheds light on our emotional self—in general, our ability to appreciate what we have. Is one contented and happy with life's lot or emotionally unstable and miserable in the midst of great physical wealth? This is the chamber that rules spiritual, not physical, wealth.

## Properties/Business

This chamber tells of one's home or living conditions, the properties that you own and ultimately, the state of affairs in the company if you are a business owner. Inheritance is also dealt with here. On a day-to-day level, one can deduce the general environment in which one works and resides. Neighbors and the relationships with these people are also revealed. Contemplating starting your own business? The stars in here will tell how you will fare.

## Career

Herein lies the answer to probably the most asked question in one's life path: what career would give the most joy and abundance? What are the pitfalls to be avoided? Check out what the stars have to say about your working environment. Comparing the Property and Career houses reveals whether one's success lies in being a business-owner or a salaried staff. The stars say much about your earning power here. Pay close attention to the Career house if you are employed.

## Staff

These are the people who support you—employees and all those working under you. Note this distinction: this sector deals with general or support staff. The devoted right-hand men and women in our life and our relationship with them, their situations, etc., are disclosed by stars in the Minors Chamber.

## Travel/Relocation

What would happen should we migrate to another country? Checking out this sector will indicate whether migration is viable or not. Happenings when in a foreign land, indeed, travel of any kind, including interactions with foreigners at home or abroad, are all disclosed here.

## Health

The Sickness or Health Chamber outlines one's general physical well-being at various stages. The stars here give warnings as to hidden illnesses one may be prone to, physical impairments, and internal disorder.

## Prosperity

This House deals with profit and liquidity. The stars in the chamber reveal the nature and the platforms through which we can make our wealth. For example, some of us will do well in finance or investments; others can only accumulate their savings through steady employment. However, it's important that we don't waste precious years chasing that illusive pot of gold. Discover your life's work, business, and investment strategies here.

### Minors

This sector deals with another group of the important people in our life—our children, students, and the very close, trusted right-hand men and women in whom we place our trust. The relationship with these and what is going on with these people are revealed. This sector covers all those whom you take under your wing, including, the family pet.

### The Spouse

We should probably have named this sector The Lover—for this is how modern China calls our "other half," the person we are in love with and with whom we share our life and dreams. However, The Lover is the name of a (romance) star here. In keeping with how this sector is called in Stargate, this section will retain the name "The Spouse." This Sector tells of the trials and tribulations of the person you consider "your other half" at any given time and the state of the relationship. For the unattached, the stars here, together with those in the Self Sector, will indicate if romance is in store and where it will all lead.

### Peers

Your Siblings are discussed here, e.g., the number of siblings, the quality of the relationship, their fortunes, etc. This is also the sector of our business partners, best friends, colleagues, fellow students, etc.,—everyone on our own level. It is here also that we discover what is going on with "the competition." You assess the strengths and weaknesses of your rivals by studying the stars in this chamber.

### The "Floating" Life Chamber

Depending on the birth hour, "Life" will share house with one of the following: Self, Spouse, Prosperity, Travel, Career, Karmic. It sheds extra insight regarding Life Path and lets us know where our heart will lead us if we let it. "Life" shows us what truly is important. We have a choice. Whether we walk in darkness and fear or with light and joy is completely up to us. Given the backdrop, here is where we are free to write our Karma. Look at the table on p.23

## The Self/L

With the Life and Self in the same chamber, we will see the personality traits of the stars here being emphasized. Being the most self-assured of the lot, we will have our well-defined outlook on just about everything and will not be swayed into accepting another's point of view.

## Spouse/L

Life sharing the same chamber with Spouse will have us putting emphasis on family and home. We will also see the most romantic of personalities here. Our days will be spent caring and sharing, and our efforts will be about achieving conjugal bliss and harmony, home and family.

## Prosperity/L

Our days will either be about having Wealth, embroiling in it, or chasing after it. Whatever the reason, our karma with Wealth will become our driving force and a heavy burden because of this psyche.

## Travel/L

Sharing house with the Travel Sector, our Life will involve constant moving about, whether it be home, country, or job. No matter what we do, it seems that constant change is inevitable.

## Career/L

Being the most career-minded of all, those of us with Life and Career in the same house will spend most of our time and energy climbing the corporate ladder or building a business. The driving force is Achievement.

## Karmic/L

Our spiritual development is important with Karmic and Life together. A peaceful, idyllic environment is necessary for these people because they will be spending much time in quiet contemplation. These are the most idealistic.

# WARREN BUFFETT

Rule #1:

Never lose money.

Rule #2:

Never forget Rule #1.

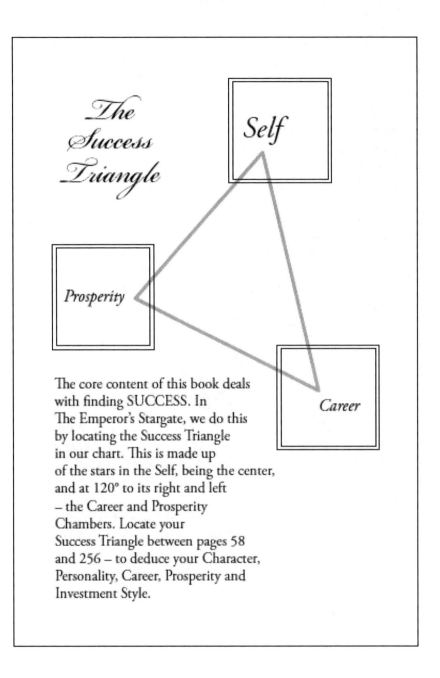

_The Success Triangle_

**Self**

**Prosperity**

**Career**

The core content of this book deals with finding SUCCESS. In The Emperor's Stargate, we do this by locating the Success Triangle in our chart. This is made up of the stars in the Self, being the center, and at 120° to its right and left – the Career and Prosperity Chambers. Locate your Success Triangle between pages 58 and 256 – to deduce your Character, Personality, Career, Prosperity and Investment Style.

# THERE ARE NO 'GOOD' OR 'BAD' STARS

If we were to believe that we all have a unique mission in life, then it is well for each one of us to get clear on this mission before embarking in this adventure called Our Life. In aid of this mission, we are given tools. These tools are the unique traits in our character and personality. Stargate is the key that unlocks the door towards our mission.

In *I-Ching* – The Book of Change – of which The Emperor's Stargate also encompasses, we should not look at the stars that form our character and personality as good or bad, lucky or unlucky. The *I-Ching* is based on the Taoist concept of the Universe. This cosmology starts with The Tao (pronounced "Dao"), which in English is translated as "The Way." The Tao is represented by the symbol called the *Tai Ji Tu* 太極圖 :

Forever evolving, complete opposites are in fact, the two sides of a whole. At the zenith, the seeds of the opposite are germinating – and so the cycle begins again. The concept of *yin* and *yang* is about understanding polarity, dualism and complementarity. Everything is comprised of both aspects in varying proportions. Nothing is solely a *yin* or *yang* thing, it is always some relative combination. Every thing or activity has an opposite polarity, every *yin* has its *yang*.

The ever-changing positions of the stars tell a story. It is up to us – at any given time – to grasp their meanings and use them as beacons to light our way towards our goals.

# Chapter 5
# The Stars & Catalysts

*The following pages contain*

*The 14 Major, Auspicious and Killing Stars,*

*the Catalysts and how they influence us.*

*With the Stargate program open,*

*click on each symbol*

*to find what it does to the chamber*

*it chooses to reside within.*

*Nearby Auspicious Stars and Catalysts*

*(in the same house, opposite, or at 120 degrees)*

*will enhance the strengths of the Majors*

*whereas the Killing Stars and the Obstruction Catalysts*

*will obliterate these and release their challenges.*

# The Emperor

The Emperor in the Self enhances longevity. At its zenith, a Brilliant Emperor would bestow prosperity and banish evil. In fact, it is so strong that it accommodates rather than eradicates. For example, the Killing Stars (Ram, Spinning Top, Fire, Bell, Void, Punishment) can all be altered and become strengthening forces by the presence of a Brilliant Emperor. It displays power and elegance and commands respect.

Having all the qualities of self-confidence and leadership, many will be mesmerized by this personality. Therefore, this magnetism can also manifest itself as sexual attraction.

However, this is not a stand-alone star. As an emperor needs his ministers and warlords, this star, alas, will not shine alone. Supporting The Emperor, preferably, should be the presence of General, Commander and Pioneer, and his Left and Right Ministers, as well as Literary and Arts Ministers. Also, to keep things light, let's call in Stardust and Delight, the angelic beings. These would make up the perfect court–The Emperor surrounded by his entourage. A strongly supported Emperor will become a formidable wealth star, shining on business and investments. Alone in his financial dealings, a dark Emperor's personality, alas, will fall prey to his emotions and pride. If used unwisely, the public veneration that he is capable of attracting might also result in liaisons he would live to regret.

**Challenges: Totalitarian, Proud, Arrogant, Frustrated, Angry, Isolated, Tyrannical, Erratic, Bad-tempered, Low EQ**

# Intelligence

> **Strengths: Pioneering, Quick Witted, Strong Convictions, Agile, Strategist, Kind, Meticulous, Multi-tasker, Hard Working, Lateral Mover**

A balanced, strong mind breeds a kind leader who is calm yet motivated. Intelligence here would ensure a quick mind and agility. His thirst for knowledge is contagious, and many will be intrigued by his unique thoughts and ideas. His strength lies in being challenged by obstacles and not felled by difficulties. Alas, intrigued by anything that's a challenge, he may be stalled by minute details. This star is a strategist and is mechanically inclined. Because of this nature, he may be perceived as blunt and insensitive. Once he overcomes this challenge, success will be easy. Easily distracted, Intelligence may find his powers dimmed or have his negative qualities surfaced should he meet up with such Killing Stars as Void or Punishment. Under dark influences, fear, self-doubt, and despair will set in. This negative star combination bodes ill for an entrepreneur. At its best, Intelligence shines on steady employees, not entrepreneurs or business owners. Take care that Intelligence does not become a Jack-of-All Trades and Master-of-None. They will thrive if given autonomy and trust. As an employee, Intelligence can look to apply all his positive traits to good use and will rise to great heights. Its appearance would indicate lateral movements—changeability or much travelling, a change of job or duties as opposed to moving up the corporate ladder. This is one of the drawbacks of having Intelligence in Self. A career which entails planning of any kind would suit them, as in corporate, strategic planning or public works.

> **Challenges: Delays, Fear, Pride, Self-doubt, Stinginess, Despair, Inconsistency, Distractions, Bluntness, Calculating Personality, Out of Control, Jack-of-All-Trades, Low EQ**

# Sun

> **Strengths: Elegance, Popularity, Visionary, Benevolence, Chivalrous, Fair, Straightforwardness, Charitable, Caring, Honest, Leadership**

The Sun stands for everything that is positive and life-giving. His position is second only to the Emperor with his traits of leadership, farsightedness, sociability, compassion, and fairness. He sees the good in everyone and will not hesitate to fight for the underdog. He doesn't care about earnings but will work hard and, therefore, attain success.

With this star in the Self house, the accumulation of wealth would be the least of The Sun's desires who would unquestionably give this away if someone else needed it more. Sun's mission, therefore, is in the relief of the ills and suffering of humanity. So the best place for The Sun would be a career in education, medicine, or the public sector where all of Sun's most positive qualities would be able to shine. The brighter the star in this house, the better. At Brilliant, this person will rise to great heights.

A Brilliant Sun would be able to transform the powers of any of the six Killing Stars: Ram, Spinning Top, Fire, Bell, Void or Punishment, and turn them into assets. Under the circumstance, only the males around the Self would be affected. The Self would encounter certain difficulties, but the Sun is a strong enough influence to counteract any serious damage. The best pairing up for Sun would be with Scholar and/or Literary Minister. If joined by Completion, the perfect but very rare quadrangle star combination of good looks, brains and outstanding accomplishments will be formed. Such a combination would be in the birth chart of star-quality, high-profile personalities (Bill Gates' & Princess Diana's life charts).

> **Challenges: Impatience, Fiery Personality, Arrogance, Gullibility, Spendthrift, Over-trusting, Emotional, Somewhat Low EQ**

# Commander

> **Strengths: Wealth, Metals, Finance, Honesty, Investments, Leadership, Pioneer, Confidence, Farsightedness, Decisive, Business-minded, Charitable, Cool Exterior**

This is a major wealth star that is best found in the Prosperity Chamber. Likewise, there will be huge prosperity issues should it become obstructed, which would result in an individual chasing wealth but never attaining it or having fortunes tend to come and go. The Commander is an action-packed leader who charges forward. Strong and determined, this star will lead us to success if found in our Career sector.

If aided by other positive stars, such as Completion and the Wealth $ catalyst, we can expect entrepreneurial triumph. We would be encouraged to start our own business with this star in our Properties/Business sector! However, with the Obstruction Catalyst ■ attached, it would be well to give up any such hope as the circumstance is an indication of great losses.

Look for the Power↗ Catalyst, which enhances The Commander. This makes for an outstanding partnership, which is conducive to a career in the armed forces. Chiefs of units and military commanders will usually have this star combination in their charts.

Fiercely independent, the Commander would make for a menacing guest if found in the Spouse sector. This star indicates a strong-willed and forthright person who likes to walk alone.

> **Challenges: Soft-hearted, Overly Generous, Fiery, Over-spender, Sharp-tongued, Thoughtlessness, Impatience, Gullible, Greed, Remote, Friendless, Low EQ**

# *Waif*

Contented by nature, The Waif goes through life as a happy-go-lucky little child. There isn't a streak of competitiveness in her. She would be happiest letting those around her take all the credit. Therefore, if we're looking for advancement and found this star in our Career house, that would be very aggravating. If present in the Self or Career houses with the absence of any of the Killing Stars to prod her on, Waif may become too complacent and maybe even slovenly. It is apparent this star would do little for career advancement.

The Waif in the Self House will bring in emotional volatility and a hard childhood. Those with The Waif in the Self will be fair, have a square-roundish face, and round shoulders. She will be gracious—a learned, gentle soul leaning towards the arts. She will spend much time in idealistic contemplation and is likely to remain a contented dreamer.

Her saving grace, though, is her very nature. Her presence counteracts evil and averts disaster! This lucky, twinkling star silences Bell and cools Fire and sweeps out the forces of the other four Killing Stars. Indeed, these Killing Stars will do a world of good for Waif. If awakened by their presence, this star will move forward with creativity and aplomb!

She possesses the ability to build wealth from nothing. So, watch out for this one—especially if zapped by the fires of the Killing Stars.

# Crimson

Being spontaneous and friendly, this star will soar above the rest whether it is in PR or politics. Just put Crimson among the crowd. Everyone will love it! Crimson will do well easily and naturally in situations which require constant communication/ dealings with the opposite sex; e.g., a man in cosmetics or fashion; a woman in finance or in any sector traditionally dominated by men. If there are other Auspicious Stars around, their career can expect a lift-off!

Powered by drive and the urge to achieve, Crimson will, however, closely guard her privacy. She will be strong emotionally and have above average intuition. This person is an artist by nature and just loves being surrounded by art, music, theatre, and the like. She can deftly weave her influence and reach her goals with dexterity. She's also splendidly munificent and has a good backbone. If needed, support is all around. This is because everyone just warms to her genuinely friendly nature.

A point to note, however, is the presence of Crimson could mean very different things, depending on its position and the presence of other stars and Catalysts. Grouped with Auspicious Stars, Crimson can rise to great heights, especially in politics. The Killing Stars around Crimson could spell disasters of the life-threatening kind, having to do with blood. In this situation, great care should be taken with interpretation.

# *Vault*

**Strengths: Trustworthy, Proprietary, Abundance, Acceptance, Benign Leadership, Problem-solver, Wealth-saver, Guardian, Benevolence, Longevity**

Vault is a major prosperity star from the conservative faction. As The Emperor rules the North, so the Vault governs the South. As the Emperor pioneers, so the Vault guards. Safely trekking paths hewn and hacked by others before it, Vault quietly builds and amasses its fortunes.

This star would shine on careers having to do with administration and management. And who could say that these people with tenacity and hard work will not reach as high or higher than their more daring sisters?

The Vault in the Self sector produces outstanding and high-ranking administrators and government officials who lead with prudence, groundedness, and caution. If free of any Killing Star, these individuals will become the pillars of the earth. They live by honesty and integrity.

The Self will be careful and detailed. Parents and guardians will play an important part in forming its character and personality and ultimately its success later in life. It is a characteristic of the Vault to never lack for earthly possessions.

The Vault would benefit from being surrounded by Bright, positive stars and Catalysts (opposite and at 120°). Otherwise, the negative or Killing Stars would bring about its negative traits, including the loss of revenue.

**Challenges: Pride, Over-conservativeness, Lack of imagination, Faint-hearted, Stress, Pickiness, Narrow-mindedness, Somewhat low EQ**

# Moon

Strengths: Loving, Supportive, Cooperative, Soft, Kind, Calm, Stillness, Wealth Management, Meticulous, Insightful, Homemaker

The Moon is at the most brilliant during the hours 9 p.m.-3 a.m.. Outside of these, she is in darkness. It is a point to note that the hours of influence of a Brilliant Moon is the direct opposite to that of The Sun.

Because of this, whereas a Brilliant Sun promotes grace and elegance—the spiritual qualities, Moon adorns with the physical qualities. Together these make up the Chinese characters for Opulence.

A woman with a Brilliant Moon in the Self sector will be beautiful, romantic, a home-maker and very supportive of her spouse and family. Whether male or female, Moon in the Self sector makes for a strong, mature person who is also clever and introspective.

With Moon in darkness, Self usually takes on the qualities of a Brilliant Sun. The Moon Self will be concerned with benevolence rather than wealth (Bill Gates' Life Chart).

If found in the male Self sector, this star would indicate heightened positive female qualities. For example, this individual may display gentle strength, be supportive and encouraging, intuitive, and excel at or at least be very good with what is traditionally labeled female domain, e.g., homemaker and caregiver of children. This male self will also find empathy more with female than male colleagues and friends.

Challenges: Conservative, Sluggish, Timid, Secretive, Suspicious, Depression (Females), Emotional Bondage

# Opportunity

Opportunity in the Self house will be refined and conversant in the arts, as well as a trendsetter. However, in the seemingly never-ending rounds of meetings and partying, Opportunity may suddenly realize the need to pull away from a few shady characters that have become attached. Opportunity has many friends from the highest echelons of society right down to the underworld. Opportunity lives and breathes excitement and challenges. Life is great and meant to enjoy!

Opportunity in Self, if coupled with one or more positive stars, denotes a long life. This person will have otherworldly spiritual leanings while also busily enjoying all the sensual pleasures of life: the finest culinary fare, the arts, people who would pander to him and indulge him.

Where Opportunity appears in Self, his two brothers, General (in Career) and Pioneer (in Prosperity) will also be there, forming their Success Triangle. Where these three stars appear together is an indication for great changes and dynamic outcome. Opportunity would make this possible without the throes or hard lessons of the other two.

The Completion-Winged Horse duo (in Self or reflecting) will ensure even greater achievements without much effort. This is all fine, for Opportunity is much too busy enjoying life!

# Messenger

**Strengths: Articulate, Persuasive, Clever, Spontaneous, Outgoing, Conviction, Confident, Resolute, Meticulous**

Messenger in the Self sector indicates outstanding rhetoric abilities. Coupled with sharp diplomatic skills that are associated with the star, this is surely an obvious prompt for any career path! Alas, much controversy surrounds such a prominent personality.

The one who has Messenger in Self will also always be on the go. However, we're not talking about smooth sailing here. Not born with a silver spoon in the mouth, the struggle uphill will have begun early in life. This one can anticipate a long, exciting road ahead.

An eloquent speaker, Messenger is best suited to be in any career that entails selling, marketing, speaking for or promoting issues close to its heart. For here is where it excels and will find satisfaction. Messenger will shine in any career that makes its voice heard.

Messenger in the Self indicates someone who is careful and detailed. Also, Messenger denotes events developing under the surface, undercurrents where things may not be what they appear to be. Depending on adjacent stars, Messenger may eradicate bad influences or bring dissatisfaction to the surface. Before you know what's hit you, it's a done deal.

**Challenges: Gossip, Boisterousness, Regretful, Careless, Suspicious, Depressed, Doubtful, Financial Negligence**

# *Mirror*

> **Strengths: Professional, Authoritative, Loyalty, Integrity, Impartiality, Responsible, Righteous, Gracious, Meticulous, Dependable, Thorough, Second-in-Command Strategist**

Bearing the seal of the Emperor, Mirror endorses every edict that is passed down. Therefore, the outstanding feature for Mirror is Responsibility. Here, if ever, is a responsible person—be it to himself or to those around him. He sees himself as totally answerable to everything that he puts his seal on. He is a just and impartial leader. When and only when he is satisfied with the details, will he carefully endorse it with his seal. And no smudges, please!

Mirror in the Self will be recognized by the care and detail he applies to his attire, home, and office. Here is a careful personality. Where everyone else has already jumped in, he would still be busy plugging up the holes. Upright and blessed with a big heart, he just fits right into everyone's ideal of the big brother. He will not hesitate to go out of his way to fight for what he believes in (Bruce Lee's Life Chart).

He will rise above the rest. Heads of large organizations will benefit from having the loyal Mirror by their side. Ministers, secretaries, or anyone who is second-in-command will have this star in their Self/Career House.

If surrounded by the Killing Stars without the help of the positive ones, the Mirror's positive energy will diminish, making him self-protective and suspicious.

> **Challenges: Overly Conscientious, Conservative, Suspicious, Burnout, Loneliness, Unimaginative, Hesitant, Stubborn, Missed Opportunities**

# Scholar

Any time that Scholar appears in the Self, Career, or Prosperity Sector is not a good sign for business transactions. Not one to toil and struggle for gains, Scholar will emanate a certain degree of elegance as he pursues his goals. This star in the Self sector indicates a long but lonesome existence. Scholar will have a high opinion of himself. He has his own set of rules and cannot be easily swayed. In the presence of the Killing Stars or the Obstruction Catalyst, Scholar may become self-righteous or vain. A friendly, Auspicious Star on the whole, but even at Brilliant, its strengths would reach only the twinkling level. It should not be confused with the Brilliant powers of Mirror, and its elegance is but a glow when compared with that of The Sun. An alliance with the Sun would, therefore, benefit Scholar in everything, especially professional pursuits like medicine, law, or teaching and administration. Clutching its lofty ideals, Scholar is positively unsuited for any entrepreneurial pursuits, for business entails monetary transactions, and money goes against Scholar's opinion of what is right. In the presence of the Killing Stars or the Obstruction Catalyst, if in business, Scholar will get entangled in a few curious "incidents" involving money because money or the involvement with it is Scholar's life lesson.

The best pairing for Scholar would be with Sun and/or Literary Minister. If joined by Completion, the perfect but very rare quadrangle star combination of good looks, brains and outstanding accomplishments would be formed. Such a combination would be in the birth charts of star-quality, high-profile personalities, like Bill Gates and Princess Diana.

**Challenges: Business Transactions, Distant Personality, Dogmatic, Narrow-Minded, Hermit, Loss, Dispassionate, Overly Generous, Money Issues, Tactlessness, Disillusion, Loneliness**

# General

> **Strengths: Commands Respect, Formidable, Disciplinarian, Independent, Self-Assured, Leadership, Heroic, Fighter, Fair-Minded**

Whereas Pioneer is out there at the front line, General is the brains behind the scenes. He is a cool-headed strategist—and one to be reckoned with. He commands respect and can hold court alone in any sector. If ever, here is one star that will shine if left utterly alone.

Whether male or female, General in the Self or Career sector is a sure indicator of a brilliant career. One of the General's outstanding traits is that he jealously guards his independence.

This person has great tenacity, will set goals and overcome any obstacle in order to succeed. Where General appears in Self, his two brothers, Pioneer (in Career) and Opportunity (in Prosperity) will also be there, forming their Success Triangle. Where these three stars appear together is an indication for great changes and dynamic outcome. Not unlike Pioneer, General will have his share of turbulence but to a slightly lesser degree, for both immediately respond to the beckoning of adventure, even danger. This trio indicates great strides but hard work.

General is silent and powerful and likes to walk alone. Blessed with fortitude, he is strong and independent. However, little does he know he needs all the help he can get. Few words fall from his lips, but nothing escapes his sharp gaze. A sharp blow early on in life comes with General in the Self. With supporting stars behind him, he will ride the waves and emerge the better for it.

> **Challenges: Upheavals, Harshness, Anger, Loneliness, Cruelty, Low EQ, Rebellious, Ruthless Associates**

# *Pioneer*

**Strengths: Commands Respect, Great Confidence, Extremely Positive, Brave, Revolutionary, Action-Packed, Comradeship**

Supporting and protecting the Emperor, this star fighter is constantly in the thick of battle. He charges forward with total disregard for his own safety, fighting for and protecting his turf. The Pioneer, one of the tri-star formation (the other two being Opportunity and General), stands for great changes, uprooting, tearing down, and new beginnings.

The time that Pioneer appears will see the greatest upheavals with life-shattering consequences. At this point, it is well to remember that change is only change. It forces your car down another, albeit unexpected road. Remember Opportunity (in Career) and General (in Prosperity)—forming the Success Triangle—will always be there to meet Pioneer,so take the reins and embark on this exciting journey!

Many will find fault with Pioneer. He is angry, headstrong, and overbearing, but we suspect they all secretly admire this hero who charges on regardless. They see the pioneering spirit and brave heart, and didn't they walk through the many doors that he opened for them?

Quick to anger, Pioneer benefits with having the Emperor around—the highest authority and the only one who can subdue him. The Emperor lessens the upheavals caused by Pioneer and ensures a smooth transition. Let this fantastic energy flow toward new ideas and challenges. This will be a hard-working professional or craftsman of the highest order.

**Challenges: Volatile, Opinionated, Tyrannical, Low EQ, Pride, Emotional, Upheavals, Great Changes, Difficult Life Lessons, Wicked Associates**

# The Auspicious Pairs of Stars

**Left & Right Ministers**
In support of the Emperor, this pair is best found to his left and right—straddling his chamber. The same applies to any chamber at any moment in time. Note this is in contrast to the Triangle of Influence (in the same house, opposite and at 120 degrees).

If found in the Self Chamber, either of the Left or Right Ministers will be handsome, beautiful or distinguished looking. The personality will be easy going, gracious, supportive, understanding and kind.
Present in the Self or Career, they will be working in service to their fellows. Therefore, they will be in supportive roles, e.g., as assistants or secretaries or in counseling as in management training. Clever and hardworking, these stars are an asset to any chamber.

Generally and especially from the finance point of view, these Auspicious Stars would boost positive energy and curb surrounding Killing Stars. With these two in support, helpful friends would always appear at the most critical moments for you. The Right Minister would lean towards attractions leading to romantic alliances.

**Stardust & Delight**
These two stars usher in helpful people first of all and also surround us with an artistic aura. Either Stardust or Delight in the Self will wrap us in an air of regality and sophistication. When faced with obstacles, the right people would always seem to appear out of the blue with a helping hand. This is, therefore, not one to remain in dejection for long. Delight will carry strains of sensual attraction or romance—i.e., help would come from a member of the opposite sex.

If found in the Self or Career, in the work environment Stardust or Delight should be surrounded by as many people as possible in order to shine. They are, therefore, effective in PR and/or marketing, the entertainment or service industries, or education or management consultants where they would be facing an "audience" would also be suitable.

As regards prosperity, Stardust & Delight would shine on investments or business endeavors. There will always be helpful people making their appearance at just the right moment to help brush away any obstacle.

**Literary & Arts Ministers**
As their names imply, these strengthen literary achievements and artistic pursuits. The Literary Minister helps with success in academic qualifications and public examinations. Arts Minister would have us excel as artists or stage performers, as well eloquent speakers.

As can be imagined, physical beauty is the hallmark of those with Literary or Arts in the Self. None would fail to notice their elegance and refinement, as well as their capacity for learning and honing their craft. Apart from artistic pursuits, Arts Minister in Self would suggest physic abilities as well, and we may see them dabbling in other worldly, spiritual matters. This person would also be overflowing with sensuous charm.

If found in Career, we would see them immersed in cultural activities, theatre, and dance or be involved with the promotion or teaching of these. As such, they would be leaders or trendsetters in their chosen fields.

Their ability to reap in the cash may not be as powerful as the foregoing two pairs of stars. However, the FameR Catalyst will give it the booster shot necessary to help propel it to dazzling heights (Donald Trump's Life Chart).

The best pairing up for the Literary Minister would be with The Sun and/ or Scholar. If joined by Completion, the perfect but very rare quadrangle star combination of good looks, brains and outstanding accomplishment will be formed. Such a combination would be in the birth chart of star quality, high profile personalities like Bill Gates, Princess Dianna, Barack Obama, Michael Jackson, and Oprah whose charts reflect this characteristic.


**Completion**
Conservative, independent, steadfast and wealthy describe Completion. Moreover, because of its abilities to untangle misfortune and enhance the Brilliants, it is considered an exceptionally propitious star to have around. Completion in the Self people are gracious, kind-hearted and confident. They are born into wealth and will be wealthy throughout life. No matter where Completion settles in the Life Chart, it would be between Ram and Spinning Top. Therefore, being alone in the chamber is an indication of aloofness and solitude. For this reason, it is best that Completion is housed with the Wealth $ catalyst and Winged Horse.

If Completion is found in Career, Completion would do well in finance or banking. Working independently would also suit this personality, e.g., accountant/CPA, investments, or design. A wealth star in its own right, Completion would indicate strong financial aptitude if found in Prosperity. It also stands for movement and liquidity and, therefore, would be made stronger with the Winged Horse in the same chamber. If not met up by any of the three pairs of Killing Stars, Completion would soar to great heights and make huge gains (George Soros' 10-year Chart 1982-1991).

**Winged Horse**
This star represents strength, dexterity, and change. If Winged Horse is found in the Self, these people are full of energy and aliveness. They will not and cannot be tied down. However, this

isn't a stand-alone star and is best found together with Completion at the same house or opposite. The pair is the perfect wealth enhancement for each other.

In the Career sector, the Winged Horse would be seen in the transportation industries, airlines, tour operation, or just about in any capacity where constant travel or moving around is involved. The Winged Horse is not a prosperity star. However, if linked up with Completion in Prosperity and free of any Killing Stars, the pair would have the ability to bring in unlimited wealth (Soros' 10-year Chart 1982-1991).

Note that the Winged Horse can be dragged down by the Killing Stars. In this case, the road ahead will be fraught with obstacles, and the Winged Horse-Completion duo may see many of its hopes dashed. In that circumstance, any business or investing endeavor should be avoided.

## The Killing Stars

**Punishment & Void**
Punishment would bring in robbery while Void would sustain losses and foreclosure. If found in any of the relationship sectors, our romantic aspirations would be dashed. However, there are definite positive qualities the pair delivers life-changing thoughts and pioneering ways. Suitable careers should involve high levels of creativity, change and experimentation or even spiced with a certain degree of danger (Bruce Lee's Life Chart).

Also, Punishment in Self pushes toward a brilliant career in politics (Barack Obama's Life Chart). We are advised not to venture into any kind of business undertaking should our Self or Prosperity Chamber be afflicted with Punishment or Void. However, Punishment indicates Finance. A careful, non-speculative and medium- to long-term span in investing is therefore suitable, e.g., real estate, gold.

The Void's contradictory streak would come to the fore if met up by Fire. This pairing-up would ignite an explosive development which would create a tremendous up-lifting effect on one's life work.

**Fire & Bell**
In the Self Chamber, this pair hones a tough, relentless personality. They bring in catastrophes. These people are basically kind-hearted but can be angry, blunt, and unyielding. Faced with difficulties of which there will be many, they will not give up and will plod on fearlessly. However, Fire or Bell will be able to conquer by breaking down barriers and opening new doors. In Career, their relentless bravery would lead them towards success in anything that is goal-oriented and requires a high level of optimism and enthusiasm. Explosives or firearms would work well with Fire or Bell in Self (e.g., Armed Forces) as would a career in the creative industry (e.g., journalism or advertising). If straddling Prosperity, Fire and Bell would work against any gains or add difficulties and delays. When paired with Ram, a Brilliant Fire is a good sign as they would go on to manifest extraordinary results. However, much hard work will be involved. The best combination with Fire and Bell would be with a Brilliant Opportunity. The force thus created will see an explosive power for prosperity. A lone Fire in the Self sector indicates an outstanding achiever.

**Ram**
Albeit a Killing Star representing anger and destruction, Ram also stands for righteousness and bravery. The Ram in the Self sector or directly opposite indicates a serious accident at an early age which affects one for a lifetime. Healing will be lengthy, or the individual would just have to learn to live with this shadow. Blessed with great bravery, people with Ram in the Self will conquer whatever great difficulties life may toss at them early on and emerge stronger. These brave pioneers will hew a path for others to follow. We would do well working with this element in Career because Ram's element is metal. Weaponry and protection would be

suitable, e.g., counter-terrorism, the Armed Forces, security, or in any situation which would need the Ram's charging abilities.

In Prosperity, Ram points to gains coming from gaming or gambling. However, it should be remembered that such winnings would be hard to come by and perhaps even harder to keep. With Fire, Bell, or Punishment in obstruction■ in the same house, any investment endeavor would sustain losses. The long-term investments into the metals or the equities as such would be suitable.

**Spinning Top**
This star's energy spins round and round without going anywhere. Its other name is, therefore, Delay. Secretive and unnoticeable, much time would be lost before we notice something isn't right. Spinning Top in the Self notes they are patient, conscientious, observant, highly analytical, and persistent. Being opinionated, they are not business-minded and would do well in employment or being in service to others.

A career in large multinational organizations would suit them, e.g., lab work, as administrative assistants, repetitive or intrinsic work, as in drafting or IT programming, clockwork, or cultural activities.

If found in the Prosperity Chamber, its nature would cause delays or going around in circles and the weakening of the Brilliants or Completion if found in the same chamber with these.

Expect losses, setbacks, and delays to come before any success. In the end, we would see that working patiently with metals (its element) would put us on the road to accumulating wealth. The long-term investments in metals would, therefore, be suitable.

# The Catalysts

Always look for these symbols first. The placement of these four attachments allows us to foretell at a glance the exact Yun Chi of any particular moment.

## The Wealth Catalyst $

The Wealth Catalyst attached to any major star carries the implication of income or gain. Specifically, this would bring in additional wealth or possessions. From where the wealth comes, when, or how would depend on the major (A) star it is attached to. However, the Obstruction■ catalyst in the same house or opposite would bring on problems associated with such gains.

## The Power Catalyst↗

The power catalyst is most positive of the Catalysts. Its appearance indicates a highly energized sector. It has been given the go-ahead. Relevant issues would be supported with obstacles fading away. Power gives extra strength to a Brilliant, Bright, or twinkling star to suppress whatever Killing Star that may be in the same or opposite house. It enhances positive traits, and this is the only Catalyst that can weaken the destructive powers of Obstacle■ in the same house, opposite, or at 120 degrees.

## The Fame Catalyst ✿

Prominence would shine in the House where Fame comes to rest, and there would be recognition for one's life work. However, depending on surrounding stars, this could also mean unwanted attention. A house with positive stars would indicate success gained through honest, hard work. Watch out for the inauspicious or Killing Stars. Surrounded by these, Fame may usher in bad press!

## The Obstacle Catalyst ■

This catalyst would strike a blow to any House or Star it gets attached to. Expect to work extra hard and be prepared to be put to the test during this time. Obstruction is the most obvious indication to put a stop to any afflicted activity. Take a break and lie low for the time being. Unfortunately, Obstacle taints the Wealth $ and Fame ✿ Catalysts if found attached to the same star or house, bringing on wealth loss or reputation disasters.

# HEAVEN

T I M I N G

天时

# Chapter 6

## The 14 Major Stars

## In

## The Self

## At Each Animal Chamber


Each Animal Chamber affects the quality of the stars in it. In the following pages, we will discuss in detail each major star as it comes to rest in the Twelve Animal Chambers.
We'll find the clues that tell us why we are who we are, the careers we're likely to follow, plus our risk tolerance and suitable investment strategies.

# The Self as Emperor in the 12 Chambers

| | | | |
|---|---|---|---|
| | | | |
| Snake | Horse | Goat | Monkey |
| | LARRY KING | | |
| Dragon | ✦ | | Rooster |
| | *Try not to be* | | |
| | *a man of SUCCESS* | | |
| | *but rather try to become* | | |
| Rabbit | *a man of VALUE* | | Dog |
| | | | |
| Tiger | Ox | Rat | Pig |

# EMPEROR in Self in the Rat or Horse Chamber

## The Self—Emperor

Alone in Rat, the Emperor's brightness will be twinkling. Look for support from Pioneer, General, and Commander, and the four Ministers from opposite and at 120°. Otherwise, any Killing Star in his path would unleash all the Emperor's weaknesses and challenges.

At the Horse chamber, our Emperor is Brilliant and will display all its positive strengths. Enhanced by the Ministers and the lucky stars, such as Completion, his rise will be even more dramatic. At its zenith, he enriches and banishes evil. In fact, he is so strong that he accommodates more than eradicates.

The Killing Stars (Ram, Spinning Top, Fire, Bell, Void or Punishment) can all be positively altered by the presence of a Brilliant Emperor. A leader in every sense of the word, he displays power and elegance and commands respect.

## Career—Crimson & Vault

The Emperor at both the Rat and Horse will have Crimson and Vault in Career. With popular Crimson in Career, the Emperor will do famously well in positions that require constant change and sociable contacts with the opposite sex. Being delightfully sociable and accommodating, Crimson will aid the careful and but rather staid Vault in many work or play situations. Therefore, the climb up the career ladder will entail some patience but will surely pay off.

## Prosperity—Commander & Mirror

Commander here dispenses direct prosperity, i.e., through sheer, hard work; however, if stricken with the dreaded Obstruction Catalyst nat any moment in time (included the Life Time!), do not engage in any business or investment venture.

Mirror is also here. This person will deal with his finances in a principled, responsible manner. Depending on influencing stars, good things come in doubles. However, the same goes for bad influences. Other stars in the same or opposite sector will give insights. Remember that when the stars turn retrograde, it is time once again to take the profit and wait.

# SELF: EMPEROR
## CAREER: CRIMSON & VAULT   PROSPERITY: COMMANDER & MIRROR

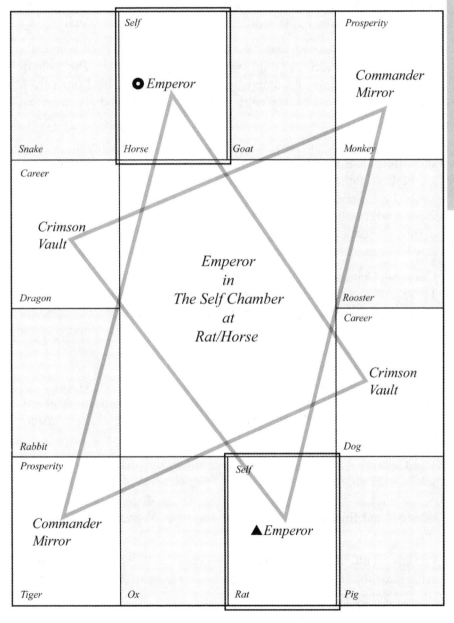

| | Self | | Prosperity |
|---|---|---|---|
| | ⦿ *Emperor* | | *Commander Mirror* |
| *Snake* | *Horse* | *Goat* | *Monkey* |

Career

*Crimson Vault*

*Dragon*

Emperor
in
The Self Chamber
at
Rat/Horse

*Rooster*

Career

*Crimson Vault*

*Rabbit*

Dog

Prosperity

*Commander Mirror*

Self

▲*Emperor*

*Tiger*   *Ox*   *Rat*   *Pig*

# EMPEROR in Self in the Ox or Goat Chamber

**The Self—Emperor & Pioneer**

Whether in the Ox or Goat chamber, our Emperor will be Brilliant and will display all of his positive strengths. Enhanced by the ministers and the lucky stars, such as Completion, his rise will be even more dramatic. At its zenith, it enriches and banishes evil.

In fact, he is so strong that he accommodates more than eradicates because the Killing Stars (Ram, Spinning Top, Fire, Bell, The Void or Punishment) can all be altered by the presence of The Emperor. A leader in every sense of the word, he displays power and elegance and commands respect.

With a Brilliant or Bright Pioneer here, our Emperor is well supported. The Pioneer benefits with having the Emperor around— the highest authority and the only one who would be able to subdue him. The Emperor will lessen the throes of upheaval caused by The Pioneer and ensure a smooth transition. The Pioneer of the dynamic tri-star formation (the other two being Opportunity and General) stands for great changes, uprooting, and tearing down.

**Career—Crimson & Opportunity**

These two sociable and accommodating stars will be outstanding in positions that require constant change and contact with the opposite sex. Look for where you can bask in attention, for therein your success lies.

**Prosperity—Commander & General**

Commander and General here make up a dynamic Triangle of Success. However, if stricken by the dreaded Obstruction (n) in any moment in time (including the Life Time), do not engage in any business or investment venture.

The General will set goals and overcome any obstacle in order to achieve his goals. Like The Pioneer, The General will have his share of turbulence although to a slightly lesser degree. Therefore, in business and finance, they are at the forefront of great turbulence and change.

Persons with this constellation in Self will attain exceptional achievements at the helm of large, multinational corporations, e.g., George Soros.

# SELF: EMPEROR & PIONEER
## CAREER: CRIMSON & OPPORTUNITY
## PROSPERITY: COMMANDER & GENERAL

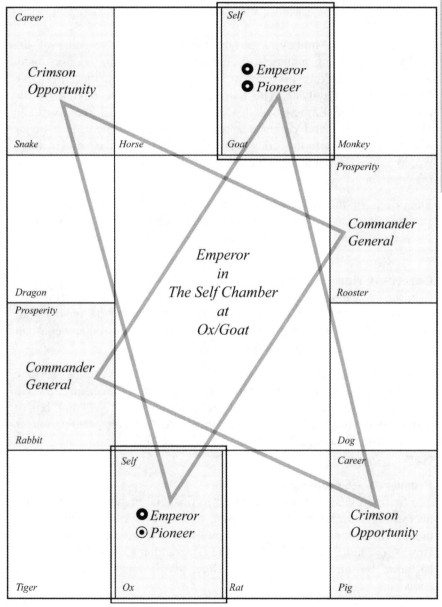

# EMPEROR in Self in the Tiger or Monkey Chamber

## The Self—Emperor & Vault

Our Emperor is Brilliant here and will display all of his positive strengths. Enhanced by the ministers and the lucky stars, such as Completion, his rise will be even more dramatic. At its zenith, it enriches and banishes evil. In fact, he is so strong that he accommodates more than eradicates.

Alternatively, in Monkey, a Bright Emperor will have most of the qualities of a strong monarch. Preferably, there shouldn't be too many Killing Stars blocking his way to success. Look for support from the Bright stars or Catalysts. The Killing Stars can all be altered by the presence of The Emperor. A leader in every sense of the word, he displays elegance and commands respect. Vault, also here, is a major prosperity star from the conservative faction. This star, at Brilliant, would shine on careers having to do with administration and management.

The Vault in the Self sector produces outstanding and high-ranking administrators and officials. However, at twinkling, its dark features may surface. If free of any Killing Stars, they will live by honesty and integrity.

## Career—Crimson & Mirror

Crimson in Career will find itself basking in attention and, ultimately, success. This person will soar above the rest whether he is in PR or politics and will do famously well in situations which require constant communication/dealings with the opposite sex.

Blessed with great tenacity, the Mirror in Career points to one unswerving career (or employer) throughout the whole working life. He will rise above the rest. Heads of large organizations will not fail to benefit by having the loyal Mirror by their side. Ministers, secretaries, or anyone who is second-in-command will have this star in their career chart.

## Prosperity—Commander

The Self will deal with or have power in financial matters. This does not necessarily indicate a prosperous Self, e.g., careers in financial control, money management, etc. Surrounding stars will give a fuller picture. However, should he meet up with the Obstruction Catalyst n here, then he must be forewarned to steer clear of all business or financial endeavors.

# SELF: EMPEROR & VAULT

## CAREER: CRIMSON & MIRROR    PROSPERITY: COMMANDER

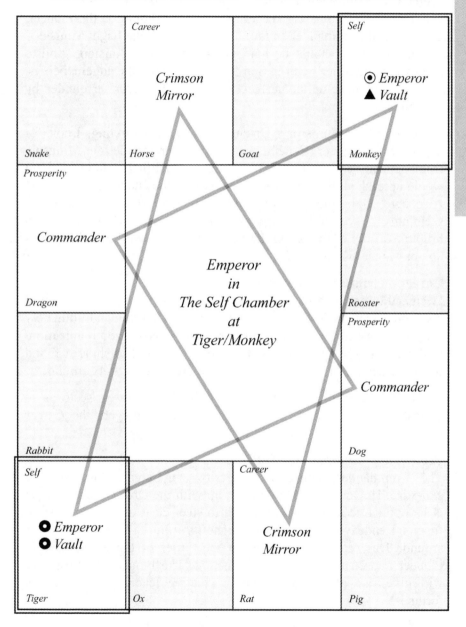

| | Career | | Self |
|---|---|---|---|
| | *Crimson* *Mirror* | | ⊙ *Emperor* ▲ *Vault* |
| *Snake* | *Horse* | *Goat* | *Monkey* |
| Prosperity | | | |
| *Commander* | | *Emperor in The Self Chamber at Tiger/Monkey* | |
| *Dragon* | | | *Rooster* — Prosperity |
| | | | *Commander* |
| *Rabbit* | | | *Dog* |
| Self | | Career | |
| ◐ *Emperor* ◑ *Vault* | | *Crimson* *Mirror* | |
| *Tiger* | *Ox* | *Rat* | *Pig* |

# EMPEROR in Self in the Rabbit or Rooster Chamber

## The Self—Emperor & Opportunity

A Bright Emperor has most of the qualities of a strong monarch. Preferably, there shouldn't be too many Killing Stars blocking his way to success. To assist The Emperor, there should be the Pioneer, General, and Commander and preferably his Left and Right Ministers. Further on, there should be his Literary and Arts Ministers. And to keep things light, let's call in Stardust and Delight, the angelic beings. These would make up the perfect court—The Emperor surrounded by his entourage.

At Rooster, the Emperor's Brightness will be twinkling. Look for support from Pioneer, General and Commander and the four Ministers from opposite and at 120°. Otherwise, any Killing Star in his path would unleash all the Emperor's weaknesses and challenges.

Also here, Opportunity truly relishes the interest he creates in the seemingly never-ending rounds of meetings. However, with brightness only at twinkling, he must take care that the Killing Stars do not trigger his vices.

## Career—Crimson & General

Designed or destined for social activities, the person with Crimson in his Career sector will find himself basking in attention and ultimately success. Look for situations which require constant communication/dealings with the opposite sex. Crimson can expect to shine if found in the Career sector, especially with other Auspicious Stars around.

Whether male or female, the General in the Self or Career sector is an indicator of a Brilliant career. The General empowers the Career sector.

## Prosperity—Commander & Pioneer

The Commander, being a prosperity star, commands financial expertise. However, should he meet up with the Obstruction Catalyst ■ here, then he must be forewarned to steer clear of any business or financial endeavors. The Pioneer benefits from having the Emperor around. This regal star will lessen the throes of the ever-changing Pioneer and ensures a smooth transition. The Pioneer in Prosperity will give rise to an exceptionally creative leader in finding his fortunes.

# SELF: EMPEROR & OPPORTUNITY
## CAREER: CRIMSON & GENERAL
## PROSPERITY: COMMANDER & PIONEER

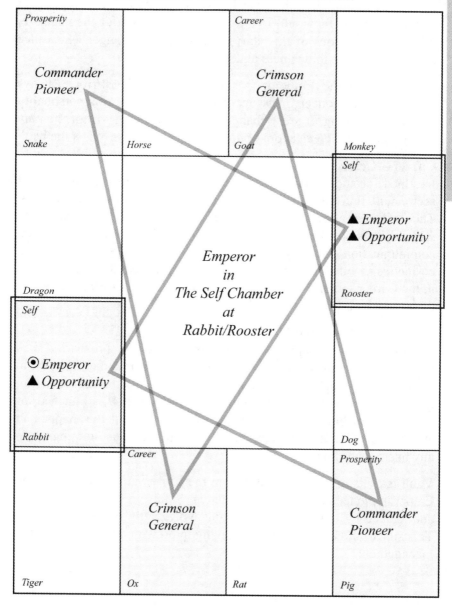

# EMPEROR in Self in the Dragon or Dog Chamber

## The Self—Emperor & Mirror

Emperor at Dragon will be dark. In his financial dealings, a dark Emperor personality will very often fall prey to his emotions and pride. The public adoration that he is capable of inviting might also result in liaisons he would live to regret. Watch out for the negative, detrimental qualities of this star: pride, frustration, anger, etc., since all are destructive to business and investment conduct.

Together with the Emperor in the Self House is Mirror. Always reflecting The Pioneer in its opposite Travel sector, this personality will strive to bring in great changes. However, being Mirror, he may tend to repeat past endeavors or duplicate the good as well as the bad!

## Career—Crimson

Destined for social activities, the person with Crimson in his Career sector will find himself basking in attention and ultimately success. They will soar above the rest whether they are in PR or politics. They will do famously well in situations that require constant communication/ dealings with the opposite sex, e.g., a man in cosmetics; a woman in finance. Crimson can expect to shine if found in the Career sector. Should there be other Auspicious Stars around— this career can expect a lift-off!

## Prosperity—Commander & Vault

Commander is a major star that dispenses direct prosperity, i.e., through sheer, hard work. To have a prosperity star come in to rest in the Prosperity Chamber of our chart is undoubtedly the best scenario, unless, of course, the dreaded Obstruction Catalyst ■ is attached, or Void or Punishment make their appearance. Should this happen in any moment in time (included the Life Time), he must not engage in any business or investment venture.

Vault is a major prosperity star from the conservative faction. As the Emperor pioneers, so the Vault guards. Safely trekking paths hewn and hacked by others before it, Vault will quietly build its fortunes. This star would shine on careers having to do with administration and management.

# SELF: EMPEROR & MIRROR
## CAREER: CRIMSON    PROSPERITY: COMMANDER & VAULT

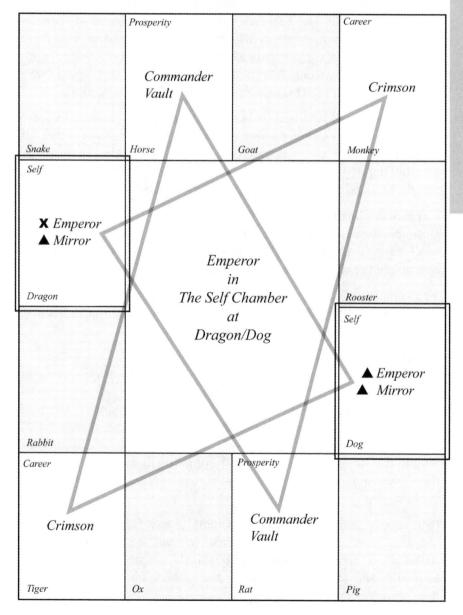

# EMPEROR in Self in the Snake or Pig Chamber

### The Self—Emperor & General
At Snake, a Bright Emperor will have most of the qualities of a strong monarch. Preferably there shouldn't be too many Killing Stars blocking. In aid of The Emperor, should be the presence of Pioneer, General, and Commander and his Left and Right Ministers, also there should be his Literary and Arts Ministers. Then, to keep things light, let's call in Stardust and Delight, the angelic beings. This would make up the perfect court—The Emperor surrounded by his entourage.

General, also here, will set goals and overcome any obstacle in order to succeed. Like The Pioneer, General will have his share of turbulence but to a lesser degree. At twinkling only, be wary of surrounding Killing Stars igniting his dark side. Whether male or female, General in Self is a sure indicator of a Brilliant career.

### Career—Crimson & Pioneer
Destined for social activities, Crimson in the Career sector will find itself basking in attention and ultimately success. This person will soar above the rest whether he is in PR or politics.

The Pioneer in Career will indicate inventiveness and success. He will be out there at the forefront of any new industry, perhaps wearing different hats as befitting the circumstance.

### Prosperity—Commander & Opportunity
Commander is a major star that dispenses direct prosperity through sheer, hard work. To have Commander, a prosperity star, come in to rest in the Prosperity Chamber of our chart is undoubtedly the best scenario, unless, of course, the dreaded Obstruction Catalyst (■) should become attached or Void or Punishment make an appearance. Should this happen in any moment in time (including the Life Time), the Commander should not engage in any business or investment venture.

Opportunity here relishes the seemingly never-ending rounds of meetings and partying. Its success comes with entertainment, socializing, sports, and other physical activities. Opportunity, General, and Pioneer together are indication for turbulence, innovation, and great change.

## SELF: EMPEROR & GENERAL
### CAREER: CRIMSON & PIONEER
### PROSPERITY: COMMANDER & OPPORTUNITY

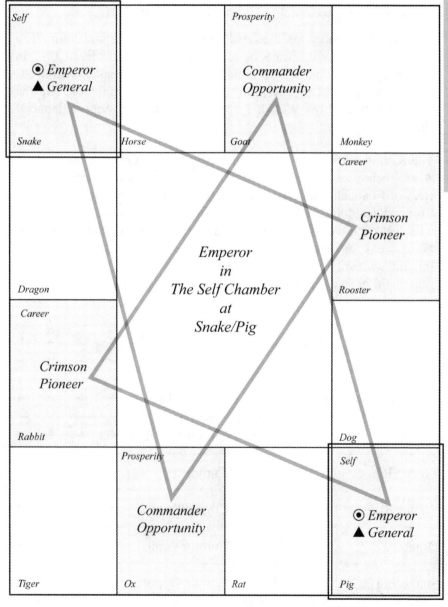

# EMPEROR in the Self House Investment Strategy

Investment Genius—Opinionated, willful, and confident are traits of Emperor in the Self. At its Brilliant state and helped by all the strong and positive stars, our Emperor's farsightedness will render him a financial wizard. His exceptional abilities to play and predict the financial market accurately will become legendary.

The Emperor represents the head, the CEO of an organization. The Emperor in Self will always be joined by his Commander at 120° in Prosperity. It is important to look for the Bright, Auspicious Stars— that is General and Pioneer, the four Ministers, Completion, and the Winged Horse or the Wealth $ catalyst for the true sign of financial success.

The Killing Stars (Void and Punishment) or the Obstruction Catalyst ■ will bring in financial loss. It cannot be stressed enough to steer clear of financial transactions or starting your own business if you are Commander dragged down by Obstruction ■. Also the Killing Stars will destroy a weak Emperor and thwart the road to success. A dark ✖ or weak ▲ Emperor, surrounded by the Killing Stars, will be fraught with difficulties in his financial endeavors, i.e., he may be successful in finance, but success will be hard to grasp.

| HOURS | SELF HOUSE | PROSPERITY | LONG | SHORT | DIVERSE | FOCUS |
|---|---|---|---|---|---|---|
| Rat/Horse | Emper | Comdr/Miror | ✦ | ✦ | ✦ | ✦ |
| Ox/Goat | Emper/Pneer | Comdr/Genrl | ✦ | ✦ | ✦ | ✦ |
| Tiger/Monkey | Emper/Vault | Comdr | ✦ | ✦ | ✦ | ✦ |
| Rabbit/Rooster | Emper/Oppor | Comdr/Pneer | ✦ | ✦ | ✦ | ✦ |
| Dragon/Dog | Emper/Miror | Comdr/Vault | ✦ | ✦ | ✦ | ✦ |
| Snake/Pig | Emper/Genrl | Comdr/Oppor | ✦ | ✦ | ✦ | ✦ |

# The Self as Intelligence in the 12 Chambers

| Snake | Horse | Goat | Monkey |
|---|---|---|---|
| Dragon | NAPOLEON HILL ✦ *The jack-of-all-trades seldom is good at any. Concentrate all of your efforts on one definite chief aim* | | Rooster |
| Rabbit | | | Dog |
| Tiger | Ox | Rat | Pig |

# INTELLIGENCE in Self in the Rat or Horse Chamber

**The Self—Intelligence**

Intelligence at Rat or Horse will be Brilliant. As such, these will be hard workers with an insatiable thirst for knowledge. The Self in Intelligence will be quick-witted with an agile balanced, strong mind that is calm, motivated, and prone to change. These individuals will thirst for knowledge and be blessed with agile bodies also. Alas, intrigued by anything that is new and pioneering they may spread themselves too thin and become a Jack-of-all-Trades but Master of None. Intelligence is a strategist by nature, mechanically inclined, and tends to move laterally pursuing new or challenging duties as opposed to moving up the corporate ladder.

**Career—Moon**

Moon here represents careers that involve tranquility, caring, and supportive roles in the servicing sectors like hotels, hospitals, or jobs involving with women or feminine interests, nursing, or finance. More often than not, these individuals will be called upon to work shift duties and will be required to work into the night. The Moon is about detail and attending to small matters.

**Prosperity—Waif & Scholar**

Contented by nature, Waif is suited to an investment strategy which reflects her personality—long term and with less volatility. She has the ability to build from nothing; with the ignition of the (dormant) fire in her, she amasses great tenacity and could even regain fortunes lost.

Not one to toil and struggle, Scholar displays a certain degree of elegance. The presence of Scholar indicates a profession in teaching or administration. Possessing his own brand of pride, Scholar would be positively not suited to any entrepreneurial pursuits of his own, for high volatility is not for him.

The Waif-Scholar pair would do a world of good for Intelligence as these will cool his sometimes sudden instincts to take chances on high-risk ventures or investment positions.

# Self: Intelligence

## Career: Moon  Prosperity: Waif & Scholar

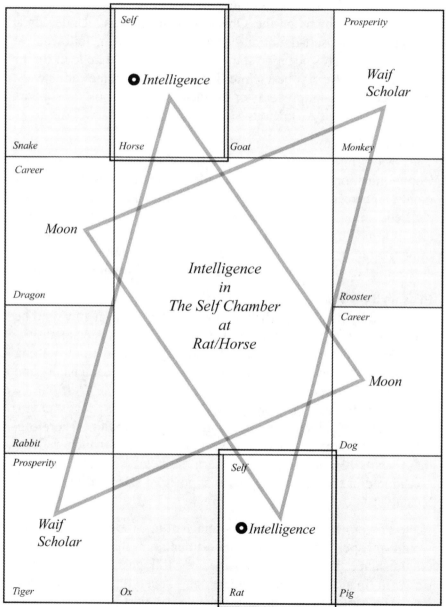

Chapter 6.2 – The Self as Intelligence in the 12 Chambers   81

# INTELLIGENCE in Self in the Ox or Goat Chamber

## The Self—Intelligence

Intelligence at the Ox or Goat would be in darkness. Easily distracted, it may find its powers being dimmed or have its negative qualities surface should it meet with such Killing Stars as Void or Punishment or the Obstruction ■ catalyst. Under dark influences, fear, self-doubt and despair would set in, followed by bad decisions. This negative star combination would bode ill for an entrepreneur. At its best, Intelligence would shine on steady employees, not entrepreneurs or business owners. Look for support from surrounding, Auspicious Stars.

## Career—Messenger

The Messenger at Bright or twinkling here, stands for Communication. The Intelligence-Messenger combination would point to a career in the communication of thoughts and knowledge, e.g., education, theatre, broadcasting, the arts, including culinary arts. If joined by the positive stars, this individual may find success in marketing or sales in the financial sectors, insurance, or perhaps at the most exciting platform of the century—Internet marketing.

## Prosperity—Waif

Contented by nature, the Brilliant or twinkling Waif here would be suited to an investment strategy that would reflect its personality—long term and steady. Waif has the ability to build from nothing and, depending on surrounding stars, could show great tenacity and even regain fortunes lost. Reflected by the Moon, the Waif will be helped along by her prosperity. Moon stands for caution, steadiness, and long-term accumulation of wealth. Therefore, Intelligence should adopt an investment strategy which reflects these traits. High risk, high return strategies should only be considered in the light of supportive, positive stars and the Wealth $ catalyst.

If the Power catalyst ↗ becomes attached to Moon, the individual would prosper with sizeable investments in their care. In the circumstance, it would be well then for this person to consider a career in finance or money management—everyone would stand to gain. The Moon, being yin, also indicates support from females.

# Self: Intelligence
## Career: Messenger    Prosperity: Waif

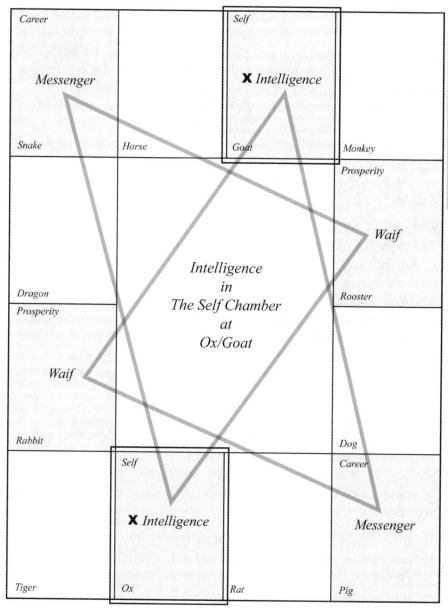

| Career<br><br>*Messenger*<br><br>Snake | Horse | Self<br><br>**X** *Intelligence*<br><br>Goat | Monkey |
| --- | --- | --- | --- |
| Dragon<br>Prosperity<br><br>*Waif*<br><br>Rabbit | | Prosperity<br><br>*Waif*<br><br>*Intelligence*<br>*in*<br>*The Self Chamber*<br>*at*<br>*Ox/Goat* | Rooster<br><br>Dog |
| Tiger | Self<br><br>**X** *Intelligence*<br><br>Ox | Rat | Career<br><br>*Messenger*<br><br>Pig |

Chapter 6.2 – The Self as Intelligence in the 12 Chambers    83

# INTELLIGENCE in Self in the Tiger or Monkey Chamber

## The Self—Intelligence & Moon

Intelligence at Tiger/Monkey would be Bright or twinkling. It will be a kind leader who is active and motivated. Intrigued by anything that's new and exciting, this star is a strategist by nature and mechanically inclined. Its presence indicates lateral movements—a change of job or duties as opposed to moving up the corporate ladder. A twinkling moon will also be here, adding care and support. The Intelligence/Moon combination makes for an unsullied servitude towards fellowmen. However, the pair could be overly careful, even miserly. Therefore, investments should be of low to medium risk. Higher risks should only be considered in the light of supporting, positive stars or the Wealth $ catalyst. Also, should Power ↗ become attached to Moon, it would be well to consider a career in finance or money management.

## Career—Scholar

The lofty Scholar is a friendly, auspicious star on the whole and is at Brilliant here. Being highly principled and disciplined, the Self may be drawn to a career in the professions—law, medicine or science. Since this star indicates a slow and steady development, patience will be the keyword, which points to the judiciary, religious, and social services. This star is about benevolence and charity work and will not shine on business owners. In the presence of the Killing Stars, Scholar may become self-righteous and vain.

## Prosperity—Waif

Contented by nature, The Waif is at twinkling here and thus suited to an investment strategy which reflects her personality—long term and steady. If prodded by the Killing Stars, she will gain the ability to build from nothing and even develop the tenacity to recoup fortunes lost.

High risk, high return strategies should only be considered in the presence of a positive Waif and Bright, positive stars. Always watch out for the dreaded Obstruction ■ in Prosperity, as any gains would eventually be lost again.

## Self: Intelligence & Moon

Career: Scholar    Prosperity: Waif

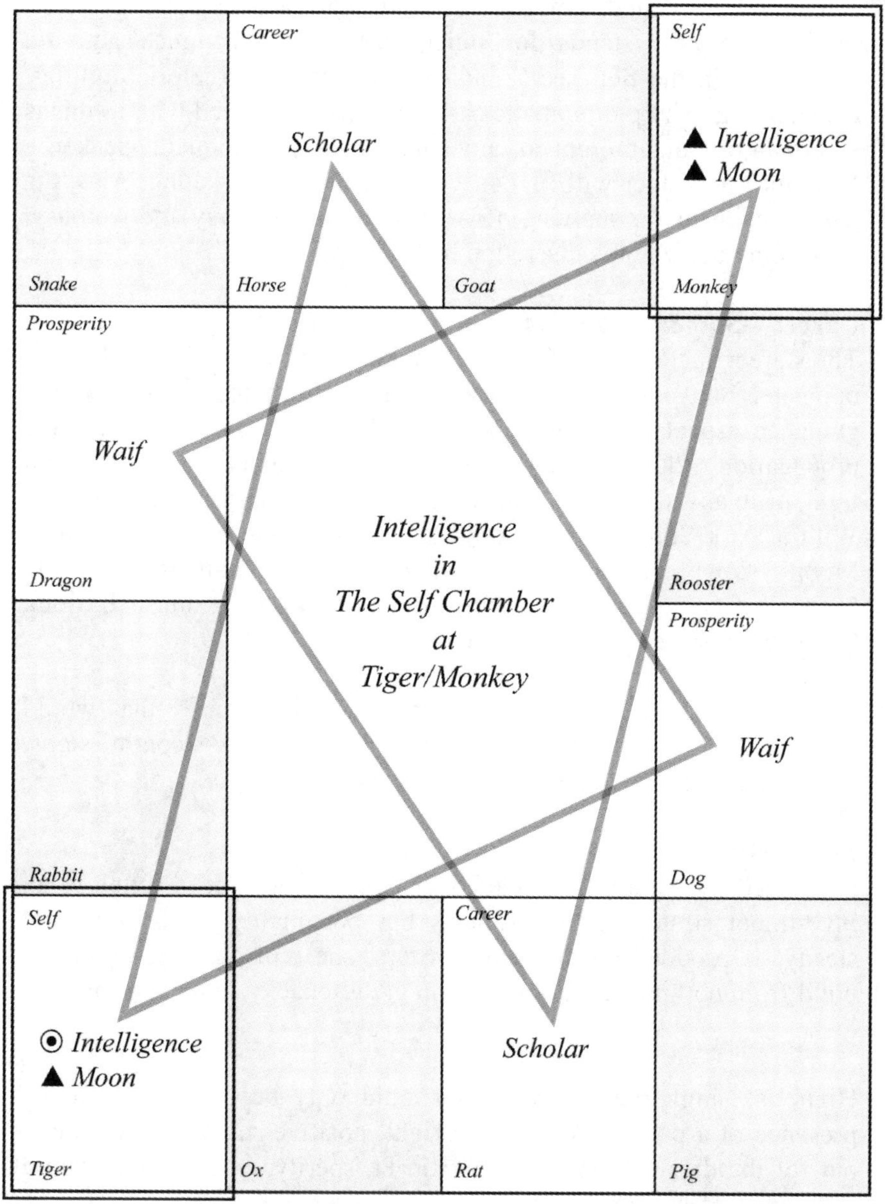

Career
Scholar
Horse
Self
▲ Intelligence
▲ Moon
Monkey
Snake
Goat
Prosperity
Waif
Dragon
Intelligence
in
The Self Chamber
at
Tiger/Monkey
Rooster
Prosperity
Waif
Dog
Rabbit
Self
⊙ Intelligence
▲ Moon
Tiger
Ox
Career
Scholar
Rat
Pig

# INTELLIGENCE in Self in the Rabbit or Rooster Chamber

**The Self—Intelligence & Messenger**

Intelligence at Rabbit/Rooster would be Bright—a kind leader who is active and motivated. Intrigued by anything that's new and exciting, Intelligence also stands for quick decisions and much activity. Messenger in the Self sector indicates outstanding rhetoric abilities. Coupled with sharp diplomatic skills that are associated with it, this is surely an obvious prompt for any career path. An eloquent speaker, a Brilliant Messenger will find success in sales or marketing. Alas, the pair's penchant for showing off will invite controversy and jealousy. Enhancing the Moon's discretion here will help.

**Career—Sun & Moon Opposite**

The Career sector being devoid of major stars, we shall read those at opposite. Sun and Moon in Career strengthens the leadership and guidance aspects of Intelligence and Messenger. Here we have the propagation of knowledge in lifestyle, entertainment, gourmet, health food, or in any supportive roles in the service industries (e.g. hotel).

With a Dark Sun, the Self would take on the qualities of a Brilliant Moon—slowly but surely accumulating wealth. Both the Sun and Moon in Career would entail shift duties or working unusually long hours, often spilling deep into the night.

Beware the Obstruction Catalyst attached to Moon ■ that would indicate problems from disputes regarding money—commissions, shares, etc., with a female colleague or friend.

**Prosperity—Waif**

Contented by nature, The Waif is at Brilliant here. It is suited to an investment strategy which reflects her personality—long term and steady. If prodded by the Killing Stars, she will gain the ability to build from nothing and even develop great tenacity to recoup fortunes lost.

High risk, high return strategies should only be considered in the presence of a positive Waif and Bright, positive stars. Always watch out for the dreaded Obstruction ■ in Prosperity, as any gains would eventually be lost again.

# Self: Intelligence & Messenger
## Career: (Sun & Moon Opposite)    Prosperity: Waif

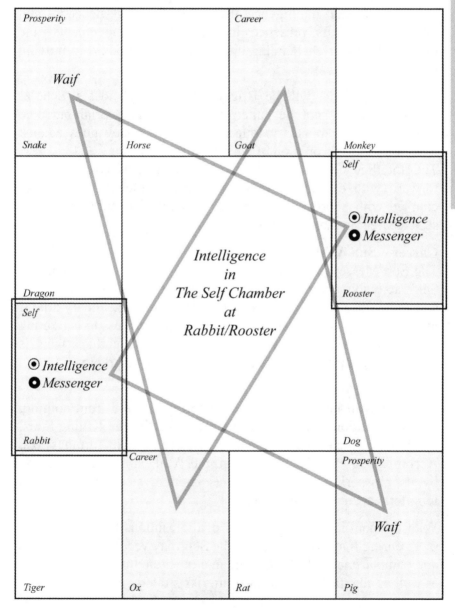

| Prosperity *Waif* | | Career | |
|---|---|---|---|
| Snake | Horse | Goat | Monkey |

(Self chamber at Monkey/Rooster)

Self
⊙ Intelligence
● Messenger

Dragon — Rooster

Self
⊙ Intelligence
● Messenger

*Intelligence in The Self Chamber at Rabbit/Rooster*

Rabbit — Dog

Career — Prosperity *Waif*

Tiger — Ox — Rat — Pig

# INTELLIGENCE in Self in the Dragon or Dog Chamber

**The Self—Intelligence & Scholar**
Intelligence at Dragon/Dog would be Brilliant. It will be a kind leader who is active and motivated. Intrigued by anything that's new and exciting, Intelligence also stands for quick decisions and much activity. Its presence indicates lateral movements—the pursuit of new or challenging opportunities as opposed to moving up the corporate ladder.

Scholar, also here, will be Bright. With its high ideals, Scholar would positively not be suited to any entrepreneurial pursuits. Business entails monetary transactions, and money goes against much of Scholar's opinion of what is lofty and right.

The Intelligence-Scholar combination here will have us going forward with caution. Distraction is Intelligence's weakness so coupled with Scholar's disinterest in wealth, it would be well to seek a career in management or teaching.

**Career—Sun & Messenger Opposite**
The Sun-Messenger combination here points to a career with the Self actively communicating thoughts and knowledge, e.g., education, theatre, broadcasting, the arts, including culinary arts. If joined by the positive stars, the Self may find success in marketing or sales, i.e., the financial sectors, insurance, or perhaps what is considered the platform of the century—Internet marketing.

**Prosperity—Waif & Moon**
A Bright Waif here would have the ability to build from nothing; with the ignition of the (dormant) fire in her by the Killing Stars, she would develop tenacity and might even regain fortunes lost. Accompanied by a Brilliant Moon, the Waif will be helped along by its prosperity. Moon represents caution, steadiness, and the long-term accumulation of wealth.

With the conflicting personalities of the cautious Scholar and the more daring Intelligence at play, the Self may veer between change and complacency. Working alone in a quiet environment will help, as well as adopting a low to medium risk strategy.

# SELF: INTELLIGENCE & SCHOLAR
## CAREER: (SUN & MESSENGER OPPOSITE)
### PROSPERITY: WAIF & MOON

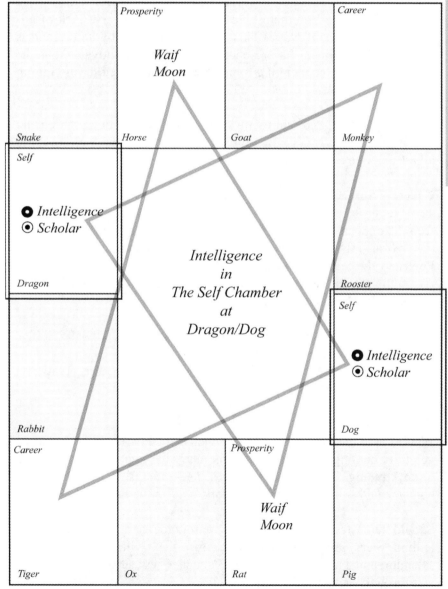

Chapter 6.2 – The Self as Intelligence in the 12 Chambers   89

# INTELLIGENCE in Self in the Snake or Pig Chamber

**The Self—Intelligence**

Intelligence at Snake/Pig would be twinkling. It will be a kind leader who is active and motivated. Intrigued by anything that's new and exciting, Intelligence also stands for quick decisions and much activity. Alas, intrigued by anything that is new and pioneering, these individuals may spread themselves too thin and become a Jack-of-all-Trades but Master of None. This star is a strategist by nature and is mechanically inclined. Its presence indicates lateral movements—the pursuit of new or challenging opportunities as opposed to moving up the corporate ladder.

At its best, Intelligence shines on steady employees, not entrepreneurs or business owners. As an employee, Intelligence can look to apply all his positive traits to good use and will rise to great heights.

**Career—Sun & Scholar Opposite**

The Career sector being devoid of major stars, we shall read those from its opposite. The Sun, if helped by the Power ↗ catalyst, carries the obvious trait of having the crowd or male supporters on your side. Power to the Sun makes for a highly independent mind which gives rise to the pioneering spirit. Scholar is also here, which would mean a slow development in which Patience will be the keyword.

The Sun-Scholar combination points to a career whereby the Self is actively communicating his thoughts and knowledge, e.g., education, broadcasting, guidance, and any field that would require creativity, new ideas, and planning.

**Prosperity—Waif & Messenger**

Waif at both the Snake and Pig chamber will be dark. With emotional volatility coming to the fore, it is not advisable to actively participate in any trading. The safe alternatives, i.e., savings, mutual funds, or bonds would suit someone with a Dark Waif in the Prosperity Sector.

Should the Messenger also be in retrograde here, beware of any Killing Stars or the Wealth $ catalyst that will strip away any splendor, and The Messenger with $ attached will subsequently bear a loss through slander or litigation.

# SELF: INTELLIGENCE
## CAREER: (SUN & SCHOLAR OPPOSITE)
## PROSPERITY: WAIF & MESSENGER

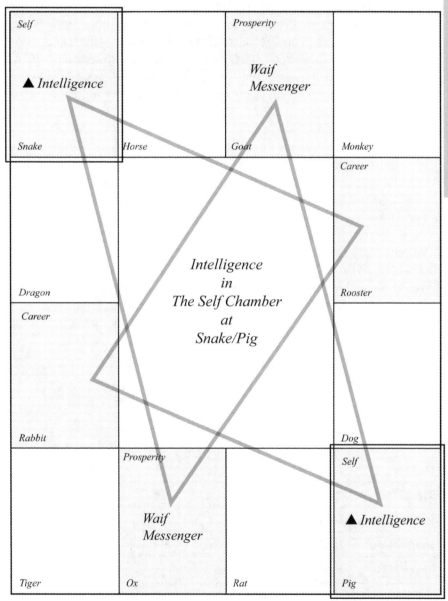

Chapter 6.2 – The Self as Intelligence in the 12 Chambers   91

# INTELLIGENCE in the Self House Investment Strategy

## A Natural Planner

Being a planner by nature, Intelligence will carefully plot his investment strategies down to the last detail. He prides himself in having an analytical mind. In this, however, he may find he is his own worst enemy. An overly careful personality may perhaps be just the excuse for procrastination. In the event of the Killing Stars being present, these will bring on unsteadiness and panic—the exact flip-side of the cool-headed strategist. A suitable investment plan, therefore, would be one that involved medium risk. Following through all his well-thought-out plans and strategies is also imperative.

## Prosperity—Waif

Waif is suited to an investment strategy which reflects its personality—long term and with minimum volatility. It has the ability to build from nothing; with the ignition of the (dormant) fire in it, it would show great tenacity and could even regain fortunes lost. Therefore, the liaison with a Killing Star would be good for Waif.

Reflected by Moon, Waif will be helped by this prosperity star. Moon stands for caution, steadiness, and the long-term accumulation of wealth. Also, if the Power catalyst ↗ becomes attached to Moon, it would be well to consider a career in Finance or Money Management. The Moon, being yin, indicates support from females. High risk, high return strategies should only be considered in the presence of a positive Waif.

| HOURS | SELF HOUSE | PROSPERITY | LONG | SHORT | DIVERSE | FOCUS |
|-------|-----------|------------|------|-------|---------|-------|
| Rat/Horse | Intel | Waif/Schol | ✦ | | ✦ | |
| Ox/Goat | Intel | Waif | ✦ | . | ✦ | |
| Tiger/Monkey | Intel/Moon | Waif | ✦ | ✦ | ✦ | ✦ |
| Rabbit/Rooster | Intel/Msgr | Waif | ✦ | | ✦ | |
| Dragon/Dog | Intel/Schol | Waif/Moon | ✦ | ✦ | ✦ | ✦ |
| Snake/Pig | Intel | Waif/Msgr | ✦ | | ✦ | |

CHAPTER 6.3

# The Self as Sun in the 12 Chambers

| | | | |
|---|---|---|---|
| | | | |
| *Snake* | *Horse* | *Goat* | *Monkey* |
| | COCO CHANEL | | |
| *Dragon* | ✦ | | *Rooster* |
| *Rabbit* | *Elegance is the prerogative of those who have already taken possession of their future* | | *Dog* |
| *Tiger* | *Ox* | *Rat* | *Pig* |

# SUN in Self in the Rat or Horse Chamber

### The Self—Sun
Sun at the Rat Chamber will be dark. A dark Sun would invite in recognition for any good work it does, and more often than not, this would come in the form of wealth. A dark Sun would have the ability to amass great wealth. Becoming a prosperity star, its elegance would then be taking second place. A dark Sun with Wealth $ attached is indicative of returns coming from investments, gaming, or secret sources.

Conversely, at Horse, the Sun will be Brilliant. A Brilliant Sun would just leave good fortune at his wake and wouldn't even notice he had done that, so he would not expect to be thanked. Independent, helpful, and FUN! Who could help but love him—even if he didn't reap vast fortunes, and very often he doesn't because he simply doesn't care for these.

### Career—Messenger
With the Sun at Rat/Horse, the Career House would have Messenger. Here the Self will hold down a career in public relations, marketing, or selling. It would be well to make use of the power of the voice.

The Sun stands for broadcasting. With Messenger also in Career, the pair would shine on anything having to do with teaching or the dissemination of knowledge, acting, or entertainment. The warmth of the Sun benefits us all with its generosity. We are, therefore, also looking at public service, management training, or facilitating in self-development programs. All these would be suitable for the Sun-Messenger pair.

### Prosperity—Intelligence & Moon Opposite
The Sun's Prosperity Chamber is devoid of any major star. We shall, therefore, look at its opposite where Intelligence (at Bright or twinkling) and Moon (twinkling) are housed. The energy of the much stronger Sun would, therefore, preside over these weaker stars.

Investments strategies are the Sun's domain. It will opt for the longer term holding of blue chips rather than the short-term trading of penny stocks. With the influence of Intelligence and Moon, some measure of daring speculation will be involved. This is all fine as long as we don't see the Killing Stars, e.g., Void and Punishment, around.

# SELF: SUN
## CAREER: MESSENGER
### PROSPERITY: (INTELLIGENCE & MOON OPPOSITE)

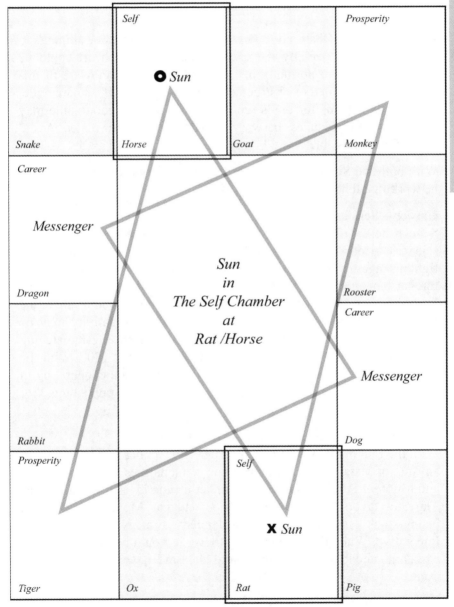

# SUN in Self in the Ox or Goat Chamber

**The Self—Sun & Moon**
A dark Sun would welcome recognition for any good work it does, and more often than not, this would come in the form of wealth. Becoming a prosperity star, its elegance would then be taking second place.

A dark Sun with Obstruction ■ would indicate injuries or ailments to the head area, especially the eyes. In addition, the heart could be affected. If you are normally insightful or intuitive, be aware of this power being dimmed or obstructed during the period. If you are male, the Sun also stands for one's reputation. Thus, your good name may be at stake. For females, be wary of partnerships with males. Avoid these if at all possible.

With both the Sun and Moon at Self, we will have someone who will be working all hours of the day or night.

**Career—Scholar**
Scholar here will pursue lofty career goals, e.g., medicine, law, or the sciences. A dark Scholar with Power ↗ especially will be definitely fighting against dark forces. For example, medical workers are forever engaged in fighting against disease; a lawyer would be litigating injustice. To the dark Scholar, power would have the implication of adding weight to Scholar's traits. Negativity may be enhanced but take these in stride because they are not life-threatening and look for redemption in the opposing houses or at 120°. With the Sun and Moon in Self, we would see these three stars cooperating in education and the social causes, medicine, publishing, or broadcasting.

**Prosperity—Intelligence & Messenger Opposite**
With the Sun in Ox or Goat, the Prosperity Chamber will be devoid of any major stars. Also, the conflicting personalities of both the Sun and Moon in Self may give rise to rather erratic investment decisions. The Sun favors long-term blue-chips whereas Moon is more of a penny-stock investor. A well-planned strategy is, therefore, imperative. When the Killing Stars arrive, it would be time to lie low, cash out, and put the winnings into the safe havens—gold or real estate.

# Self: Sun & Moon
## Career: Scholar
## Prosperity: (Intelligence & Messenger Opposite)

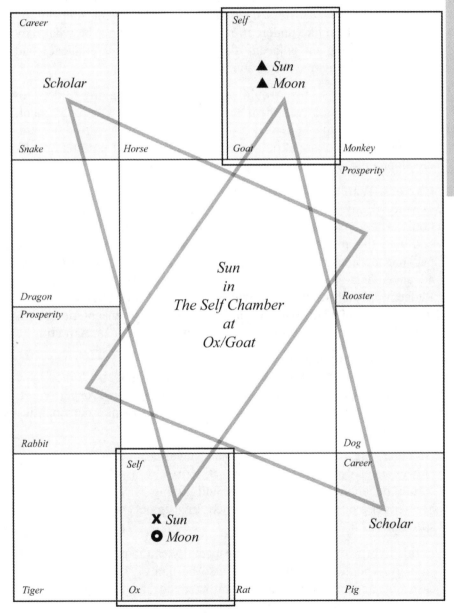

| | | | |
|---|---|---|---|
| *Career* | | *Self* | |
| *Scholar* | | ▲ *Sun*<br>▲ *Moon* | |
| *Snake* | *Horse* | *Goat* | *Monkey* |

*Prosperity*

*Dragon*
*Prosperity*

*Sun*
*in*
*The Self Chamber*
*at*
*Ox/Goat*

*Rooster*

*Rabbit*

*Dog*

*Self*
*Career*

✗ *Sun*
◉ *Moon*

*Scholar*

*Tiger*     *Ox*     *Rat*     *Pig*

# SUN in Self in the Tiger or Monkey Chamber

## The Self—Sun & Messenger
The Sun, which stands for broadcasting, is joined by a Brilliant Messenger here. Messenger in the Self indicates a person who is careful and detailed. Messenger also stands for events developing below the surface like undercurrents, so things may not be what they seem. Depending on adjacent stars, Messenger may eradicate bad influences or bring dissatisfaction to the surface.

The Sun-Messenger pair would shine on anything having to do with teaching, the dissemination of knowledge, acting, or entertainment. The warmth of the Sun would benefit with its generosity. We are, therefore, also looking at public service. Management training or self-development would alsobe suitable for the Sun-Messenger pair.

## Career—Waif & Moon Opposite
Devoid of any major stars in Career, we shall look to its opposite house where Waif and Moon are present. In the Self or Career houses and with the absence of the Killing Stars to prod her on, Waif may become too complacent. It is apparent this star does little for career advancement.
Redeeming qualities may be found in a Brilliant Moon where this pair may be working late into the night. They may be in entertainment, travel, or foreign corporations engaging in promotions or marketing.

## Prosperity—Intelligence & Scholar Opposite
Tiger and Monkey are the sunrise and sunset chambers. Joined by a Brilliant Messenger and devoid of the major stars in Prosperity, we will be seeing the Sun-Messenger investment personalities dominating.

At Tiger, the Bright Sun would make level-headed, wise decisions. However, at sunset if Obstruction ■ is in tow in Monkey, its rays would be about casting shadows and giving way to the Brilliant Messenger's doubting and negligence. Investments may soon become speculative.

In this light, we are advised to be especially cautious and adopt a safe strategy. Should the Killing Stars also be here, it is time to lie low, cash out, and put your winnings into the safe havens—gold or real estate.

# SELF: SUN & MESSENGER
## CAREER: (WAIF & MOON OPPOSITE)
## PROSPERITY: (INTELLIGENCE & SCHOLAR OPPOSITE)

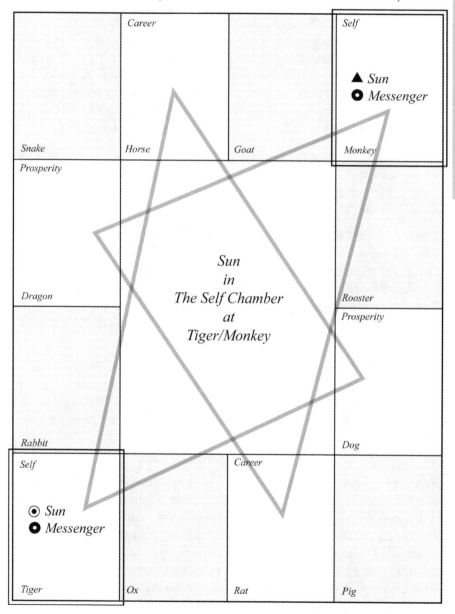

## SUN in Self in the Rabbit or Rooster Chamber

**The Self—Sun & Scholar**
The protective Scholar here joins the elegant, benevolent Sun. Being of similar nature, these two stars stand for broadcasting and teaching. However, note the different Catalysts attached to Sun:

- Obstruction ■ would indicate injuries or ailments to the head area, especially the eyes, as well as to the heart. If you are normally insightful or intuitive, be aware of this power being dimmed or obstructed during the period. If you are male, the Sun also stands for your reputation–your good name may be at stake. For females, be wary of partnerships with males, and avoid these.

- The Sun with the Power ↗ catalyst carries the obvious trait of having the crowd or male supporters on your side. Power to the Sun makes for a highly independent mind which gives rise to the pioneering spirit.

**Career—Waif & Messenger Opposite**
The Messenger is all about making the voice heard. If this sector is also filled with several Auspicious Stars and none of the bad ones, the Messenger with the Wealth $ catalyst attached would indicate fortunes being made by the voice. However, the Killing Stars will strip away any splendor and The Messenger with Obstruction ■ attached will suffer a loss through slander or litigation.

With Waif, having to do with enjoyment, the Sun-Scholar-Waif-Messenger constellation will shine on social work, teaching, or counseling. This star combination stands for being in service to mankind in religious or social undertakings (Princess Diana's Life Chart).

**Prosperity—Moon**
With the Sun already a benevolent star then joined by Scholar who is brimming with analytical sense, this creates a pair that can come up with just the right amount of detachment for investment success. However, there is weakness in the setting sun at the Monkey chamber. It should be noted that the rising sun in Tiger has a more positive energy for success when it comes to investments. The Moon in Prosperity is always an indication for savings and notes that any gains will be slowly accumulated.

# SELF: SUN & SCHOLAR
## CAREER: (WAIF & MESSENGER OPPOSITE)     PROSPERITY: MOON

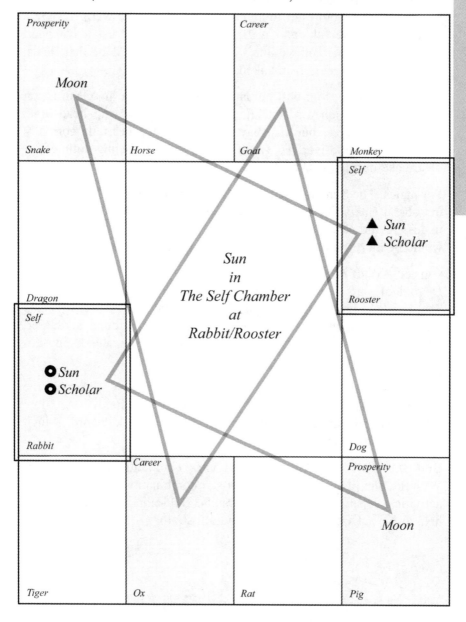

# SUN in Self in the Dragon or Dog Chamber

**The Self—Sun**
The Sun in Self will be basking in the limelight, so you won't fail to notice this person. He will love to give a helping hand, and at his brightest, none would fail to appreciative him and be warmed by his benevolent, powerful rays. A Brilliant Sun would just leave good fortune at his wake and wouldn't even notice he had done that. Thus, he would not expect to be thanked.

However, at Dog, Sun will be dark. If attached with the Obstruction Catalyst ■ , watch out for injuries or ailments to the head area, especially the eyes, but also pay attention to the heart. If normally insightful or intuitive, be aware of this power being dimmed or obstructed during the period.

For males, The Sun also stands for one's reputation—your good name may be at stake. For women, be especially wary of partnerships with males. Avoid these if at all possible. By the same token, females would be more sympathetic to you at this time.

**Career—Waif & Scholar Opposite**
Devoid of stars, we shall look at its opposite where the Waif and Scholar share house. The Waif is all about Fun and Leisure. It is also a lucky star. However, Waif does not bode well if found in Career. With the absence of the Killing Stars to prod her on, this happy-go-lucky star may become too complacent.

With a Brilliant Scholar, The Self will hold down a career in the traditional services, medicine, or medication fields. A slow development is indicated with patience being the keyword, which points to accountability.

Both the Waif and Scholar do not view competition as important. With the Sun in conjunction, this tri-star combination sees us in social activities, leisure, or religious pursuits. Self-empowerment or self-help group activities, as helpers or administrators, are also indicative.

# SELF: SUN
## CAREER: (WAIF & SCHOLAR OPPOSITE)
## PROSPERITY: MESSENGER

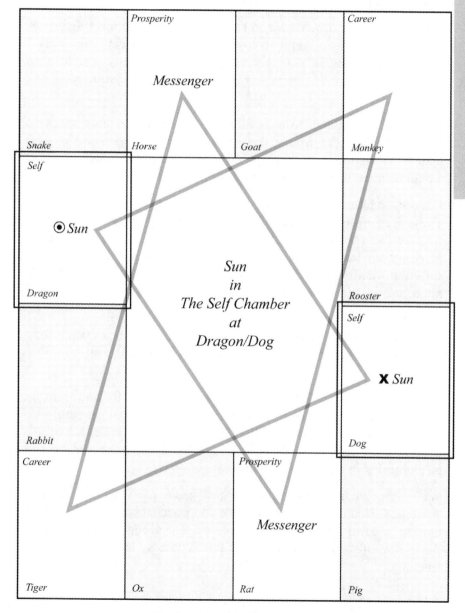

| | Prosperity | | Career |
|---|---|---|---|
| | *Messenger* | | |
| *Snake* | *Horse* | *Goat* | *Monkey* |
| Self | | | |
| ⊙ *Sun* | | | |
| *Dragon* | | | Rooster |
| | | | Self |
| | *Sun in The Self Chamber at Dragon/Dog* | | ✗ *Sun* |
| *Rabbit* | | | *Dog* |
| Career | | Prosperity | |
| | | *Messenger* | |
| *Tiger* | *Ox* | *Rat* | *Pig* |

# SUN in Self in the Snake or Pig Chamber

## The Self—Sun

The Sun in Self will be basking in the limelight, so you won't fail to notice this person. He will also love to give a helping hand. This will be a careful person who is also prone to extravagance.

However, should it be dark and carrying the Obstruction Catalyst ■, be wary of injuries or ailments to the head area, especially the eyes— also, pay attention to your heart. If you are normally insightful or intuitive, be aware of this power being dimmed or obstructed during the period.

For males, The Sun also stands for one's reputation—your good name may be at stake. For women, be especially wary of partnerships with males. Avoid these if at all possible. By the same token, females would be more helpful to you at this time.

## Career—Moon

These are helpful souls, quietly toiling away in service to others. We will see them working long hours and shift duties. They will happily give up their free time in order to help out. These are therefore long-suffering, hard-working givers rather than takers. Nursing comes to mind, as do social work, and attachments to religious groups and institutions.

A dark and obstructed ■ Moon would indicate problems arising from disputes regarding money, and a female will be behind it all.

## Prosperity—Scholar

Money goes against Scholar's opinion of what is lofty and right. In the presence of Killing Stars if in business, Scholar will get embroiled in some curious incidents involving money. Money or the lack of it is Scholar's life lesson. With the Killing Stars around Scholar, he will be embroiled in unrest or disputes brought on by earnings.

With Sun, we are looking at long-range, conservative investment strategies. This is the Sun's elegance and nonchalant outlook towards monetary gains. With Scholar here, we are seeing rewards earned through professional means, i.e., the sciences, law, medicine, or teaching.

# SELF: SUN

## CAREER: MOON    PROSPERITY: SCHOLAR

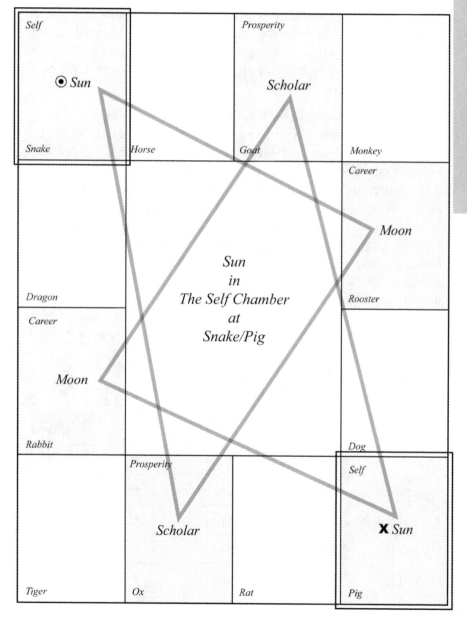

## Comfortable Sharing Information

Sun's position is second to none but the Emperor. He would love to be among the crowd, and so the careers he would most likely follow would be education and anything that would involve the propagation of knowledge or information, including broadcasting. At his brightest, all would appreciate him and be warmed by his benevolent, powerful rays. A Brilliant Sun would just leave good fortune at his wake.

## Prosperity—Intelligence-Moon-Messenger-Scholar

The Sun personality is not one to count the small change. His strategy or portfolio will reflect his long range and far-reaching plans. Even if he didn't reap vast fortunes—and very often he doesn't because he simply doesn't care for these—his name will be etched in stone—or at least be in the hearts of many.

Therefore, the Sun's prosperity house would either be devoid of stars or have different stars appear at the various hours. His fortunes are dependent on his association with these different energies. As with Emperor, the longer range, less volatile strategy would suit The Sun. Risk tolerance would depend on whether he has the support of the strong Brilliants, the Wealth Catalyst $, or the presence of Completion in the same house, opposite, or 120°.

| HOURS | SELF HOUSE | PROSPERITY | LONG | SHORT | DIVERSE | FOCUS |
|---|---|---|---|---|---|---|
| Rat/Horse | Sun | | ✦ | ✦ | ✦ | ✦ |
| Ox/Goat | Sun/Moon | | ✦ | | ✦ | |
| Tiger/Monkey | Sun/Msgr | | ✦ | | ✦ | |
| Rabbit/Rooster | Sun/Schol | Moon | ✦ | ✦ | ✦ | ✦ |
| Dragon/Dog | Sun | Msgr | ✦ | | ✦ | |
| Snake/Pig | Sun | Schol | ✦ | | ✦ | |

# The Self as Commander in the 12 Chambers

| | | | |
|---|---|---|---|
| | | | |
| Snake | Horse | Goat | Monkey |
| | INSPIRATION | | |
| Dragon | *Being decisive, being focused, committing ourselves to the fulfillment of a dream, greatly increases our chance for SUCCESS* | | Rooster |
| Rabbit | | | Dog |
| | | | |
| Tiger | Ox | Rat | Pig |

# COMMANDER in Self in the Rat or Horse Chamber

**The Self—Commander & Vault**
With the Commander's element being metal, this is a major action and wealth star. Vault also attracts and stores wealth. It is a characteristic of Vault not to lack for earthly possessions. The Commander-Vault pair combined will generate unlimited energy for business and career success. These will shine on business leaders, showering them with resourceful creativity and power to break down any barriers that may appear.

**Career—Emperor & Mirror**
Commander in Self would inevitably have Emperor here. Emperor careers would include high-end merchandise or managing global corporations.

The Emperor-Mirror pair here denotes insightful leadership. Any difficulties can be overcome by applying their outstanding management skills. The Commander-Vault-Emperor-Mirror constellation would, therefore, shine on decision-makers within large international institutions, as in banking and finance.

Mirror is also here. This person, therefore, will deal with any business in a principled, responsible manner. Depending on influencing stars, good things come in doubles. However, the same goes for bad influences. The nearby stars will give further insight. Remember that when the stars turn retrograde, it is time once again to take the profit and remain where you are until it leaves retrograde.

**Prosperity—Crimson**
With Crimson here, we are looking at highly diversified investment ventures. In partnership with the action-packed Commander but rather staid Vault, this combination would introduce just the right amount of caution to riskier speculations and vice versa.

Whether to be cautious or more adventurous would depend on whether we are seeing the Auspicious or Killing Stars around us (in the same house, opposite or at 120 degrees). The higher risk activities should only be performed when we are in a strong house with Wealth $, Completion, plus other Auspicious Stars and free of the Killing Stars. There will be major prosperity problems should Commander become obstructed ■ . Should that happen, you will be chasing wealth but it would never be in your grasp.

# SELF: COMMANDER & VAULT
## CAREER: EMPEROR & MIRROR   PROSPERITY: CRIMSON

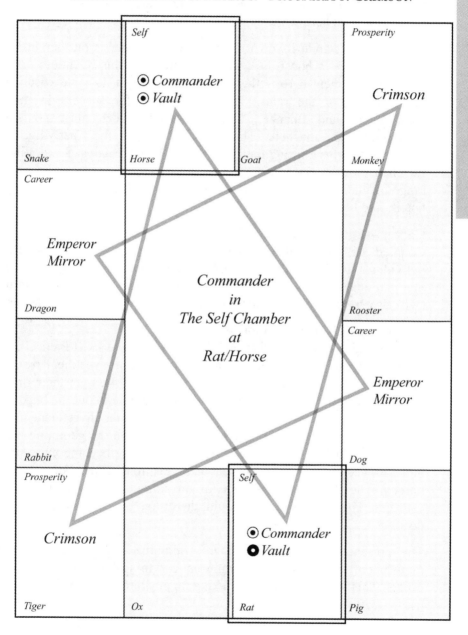

# COMMANDER in Self in the Ox or Goat Chamber

### The Self—Commander & Opportunity
The Opportunist here joins forces with the action-packed Commander. Our desires for fame and success are, therefore, realized through skill, socializing, and hard work.

A prosperous star in its own right, the Commander is our action hero. With Power ↗ to boost, he will be rewarded for his relentless efforts. Self-empowerment here is the key word. He must delegate wisely but never let go of the reins. This is the sign for success in money management and finance. Note that Commander must not have Obstruction ■ attached. The star for socializing, partying, and networking forms a fitting liaison with the Wealth catalyst $ and milks it for all it's worth. Such strong leadership points to successes in a wide range of glamorous businesses having to do with fine dining, lifestyle, hotels, and travel.

### Career—Emperor & General
Coupled with the Emperor-General pair in the Career house, these individuals would use decisive leadership or management skills in large multinational financial institutions. The Auspicious Stars would aid in a swift rise up the corporate ladder to become successful business leaders.

### Prosperity—Crimson & Pioneer
The delightfully diversified Crimson is joined by the swift Pioneer here. Together, these two may be just too daring on the investment front. In their enthusiasm to jump right in, the pair might often get their fingers burnt for lack of preparation and foresight. It is time to put the brakes on at this point and opt for a more conventional, safer investment mode. With the action-packed Pioneer here, together with the gambling-prone Opportunity in Self, chances for speculations may become excessively high. Pioneer with Power ↗, sees a bigger role to play or a heavier burden. The Pioneer also stands for the introduction of new ways or concepts. The Power Catalyst would, therefore, give him the authority to do so.

The presence of the Killing Stars (Spinning Top, Ram, Void and Punishment) may, therefore, bring in a win-all-lose-all sequence of events. This would be a call for taking no position at all until such times pass.

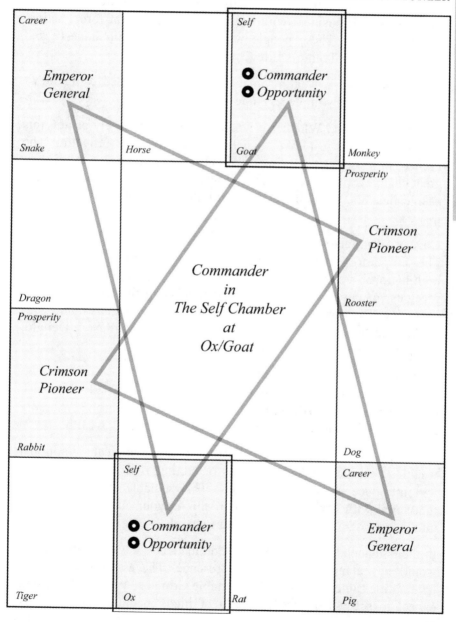

**SELF: COMMANDER & OPPORTUNITY**

CAREER: EMPEROR & GENERAL    PROSPERITY: CRIMSON & PIONEER

COMMANDER IN SELF

Career

*Emperor*
*General*

Snake | Horse

Self

○ *Commander*
○ *Opportunity*

Goat | Monkey

Prosperity

*Crimson*
*Pioneer*

Dragon | Rooster
Prosperity

*Commander*
*in*
*The Self Chamber*
*at*
*Ox/Goat*

*Crimson*
*Pioneer*

Rabbit | Dog

Self

○ *Commander*
○ *Opportunity*

Career

*Emperor*
*General*

Tiger | Ox | Rat | Pig

Chapter 6.4 - The Self as Commander in the 12 Chambers 111

# COMMANDER in Self in the Tiger or Monkey Chamber

## The Self—Commander & Mirror
The action-packed, Brilliant Commander joins forces with a Brilliant Mirror, the stabilizing force. This partnership ensures a smooth running of their business with just the right balance of force, action, and forethought. These people will forge ahead with honesty and integrity (Donald Trump's Life Chart).

The Commander is wealthy in its own right. If joined by Fame ✪ with wealth already in place, Fame will follow.

Mirror is also here. Whether it would influence positively or not, this individual would just love to get involved. Always reflecting The Pioneer in its opposite (Prosperity) sector, he would strive to bring in great changes. However, because of what he is, he may tend to repeat past endeavors. If he'll break out of the old cycle, he will move forward.

## Career—Emperor
The Emperor in career commands respect as the CEO of large multinational concerns. These would deal in high-end products, precious metals, jewelry, or the financial institutions, including insurance. The Emperor would deal in the exclusive niche markets. If well-supported by the Left & Right Ministers and Stardust & Delight, a brilliant career would be in place.

## Prosperity—Crimson & Vault
Crimson in Prosperity denotes highly diversified high-risk undertakings. We will see Crimson among the crowd, happily enjoying all the attention and at the same time, creating wealth.

If attached by Wealth $ here, Crimson would indicate emotional wealth—happiness. Close relations or siblings will bring wealth or will introduce propitious situations. This sociable star blesses this individual with her prosperity; so if this is your chart, put yourself into the crowd. You have everything to gain!

In their financial transactions, the Commander's adventurous instinct would be balanced by Mirror's presence. The Vault here is also lending the same weight to the excitable Crimson. We can, therefore, expect to see a balanced portfolio of high, medium, and low-risk products.

# SELF: COMMANDER & MIRROR
## CAREER: EMPEROR   PROSPERITY: CRIMSON & VAULT

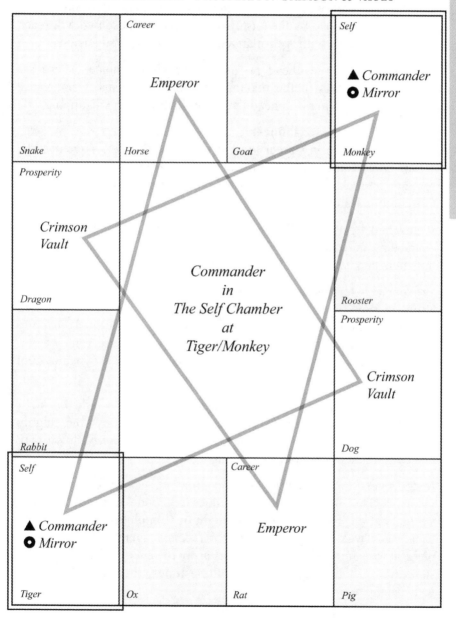

| | Career | | Self |
|---|---|---|---|
| | *Emperor* | | ▲ *Commander*<br>● *Mirror* |
| *Snake* | *Horse* | *Goat* | *Monkey* |
| *Prosperity* | | | |
| *Crimson*<br>*Vault* | | | |
| *Dragon* | | | *Rooster* |
| | *Commander*<br>*in*<br>*The Self Chamber*<br>*at*<br>*Tiger/Monkey* | | *Prosperity* |
| | | | *Crimson*<br>*Vault* |
| *Rabbit* | | | *Dog* |
| *Self* | | *Career* | |
| ▲ *Commander*<br>● *Mirror* | | *Emperor* | |
| *Tiger* | *Ox* | *Rat* | *Pig* |

# COMMANDER in Self in the Rabbit or Rooster Chamber

### The Self—Commander & General

With Commander, the action-oriented wealth star here, we are seeing a decisive leader who will lead his army to their goals under any circumstance. Joined by the unstoppable General, these two will reach their mutual goals with well-planned actions and swift decisions.

This pair will forge ahead no matter the circumstance. These are qualities of leaders in the making, and they will usually not waste much time in making it to head large multinational organizations.

### Career—Emperor & Pioneer

Joining them here in Career are Emperor and Pioneer. Together, the 4-star constellation of Commander-General-Emperor-Pioneer is a force to be reckoned with. CEOs of major organizations would have this combination of stars.

If attached by Power ↗, the Emperor—already a hot headed, fiery character—may become overburdened. Look for calmness from his ministers and advisors (the Auspicious Stars) to assist him to success.

### Prosperity—Crimson & Opportunity

Crimson in Prosperity denotes highly diversified high-risk undertakings. We will see Crimson among the crowd, happily enjoying all the attention and at the same time, creating wealth. Opportunity, if joined by Fire, will combine to make a dynamic duo. These two stars will create power and prosperity.

The highly synchronized Commander-General pair would be swift risk-takers in their investment strategy. Joined by the highly adventurous Crimson-Opportunity pair here in Prosperity, there may just be too much boldness and risk-taking.

In the event of the Killing Stars coming in, heavy losses may be incurred. This 4-star combination does not bode well for business ventures at all. Even in the benign light of Completion or the Wealth Catalyst, a well thought-out plan for risk management should be in place before any action is taken. This array of several powerful wealth stars may just be too volatile. At these times, they must keep to a well-balanced financial plan.

# SELF: COMMANDER & GENERAL
## CAREER: EMPEROR & PIONEER
## PROSPERITY: CRIMSON & OPPORTUNITY

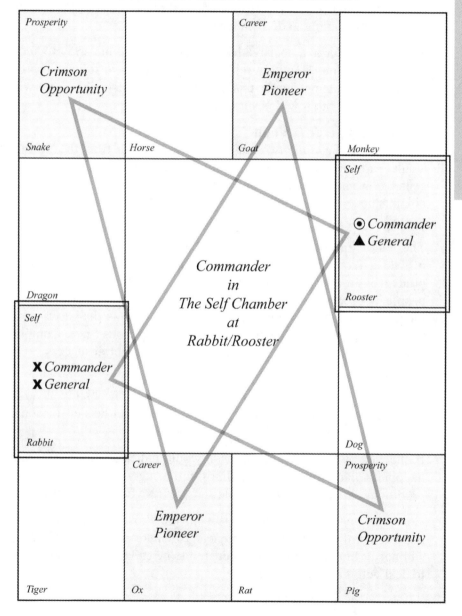

# COMMANDER in Self in the Dragon or Dog Chamber

### The Self—Commander
Alone in the Self chamber, this wealth star will rely on well laid-out plans and actions to attain its goals. Commander in the Self-sector people are often slightly built with strong, clear voices. This is a major star of action having to do with wealth.

The Commander is a decisive leader who will lead his army to success. If joined by Fame ↗, with wealth in place, Fame will follow. There will be money problems should this star be obstructed■. This one will be chasing wealth but it will never be in his grasp.

### Career—Emperor & Vault
In Career, we have the two major rulers—Emperor from the North, and Vault, ruler of the South—meeting up. The career, therefore, would center around exclusive, large-scale projects. Whatever the circumstance, we would see these individuals commanding respect all around.

The Vault produces outstanding and high-ranking administrators and officials. What they lack in pioneering savvy, they make up for in prudence, groundedness and caution. If free of any Killing Stars, these people will become the pillars of the earth. They live by honesty and integrity. This star combination would work well as the CEOs of large financial institutions. The presence of the Auspicious Stars, Completion or the Wealth Catalyst $ is indication of entrepreneurial success.

### Prosperity—Crimson & Mirror
The surging energy of Commander is met with the highly diversified Crimson here. Mirror balances it all with its level-headed personality. Controlled risk-taking is, therefore, the call of the day.

If attached by Wealth here, Crimson would indicate emotional wealth—happiness. Close relations or siblings will bring wealth or will introduce propitious situations. This sociable star blesses you with her prosperity.

However, an obstructed ■ Crimson in the Prosperity Chamber would point to conflicts arising from monetary disputes with or involving your siblings or blood relations. Be prepared to be called upon to put up funds to deal with these matters.

# SELF: COMMANDER

## CAREER: EMPEROR & VAULT   PROSPERITY: CRIMSON & MIRROR

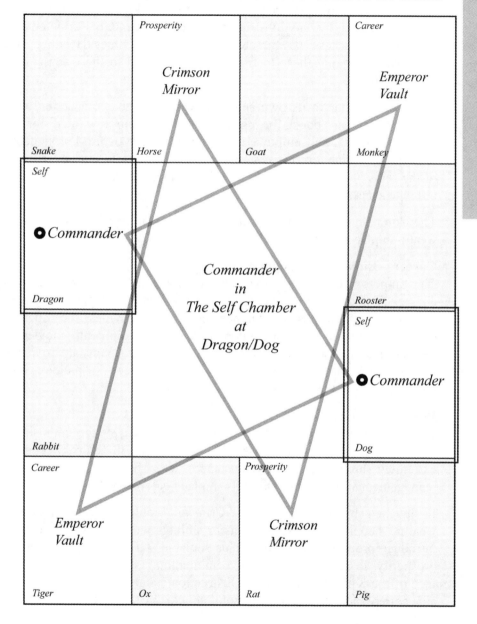

## The Self—Commander & Pioneer
These two action stars combine power, creativity, and adventure in their run for success. We are seeing craftsmen of the highest order who will not be daunted by any obstruction at any price. Goal-oriented and determined, success is, therefore, a matter of time. Heading new ventures and seeing these to fruition is best suited to the Commander-Pioneer pair.

A prosperous star in its own right, the Commander is our action hero. With Power↗ to boost, he can be sure of being rewarded for his relentless efforts. Self-empowerment here is the key word. For someone with this combination, it's essential to delegate wisely but never let go of the reins because only he can hold the power to his own destiny and ultimate success.

The Commander is wealthy in its own right. If joined by Fame✪, with wealth in place, Fame will follow.

## Career—Emperor & Opportunity
The Emperor here ensures that this individual will work for the high-end, exclusive, multinational kind of organizations. Opportunity also makes his glamorous appearance here and provides the opening ceremonies to anything having to do with entertainment—movies or casinos, perhaps? Opportunity in Career indicates a constant round of partying and entertainment. The addition of a few Auspicious Stars would then light the way to entrepreneurial success!

## Prosperity—Crimson & General
The surging of Commander and Pioneer is joined by the enthusiastic Crimson/General pair. The risk-taking energy is, therefore, becoming extremely high. In the circumstance, let's first ensure that risk management strategies are properly in place before anything else.

If attached by Wealth $ here, Crimson would indicate emotional wealth—happiness. Close relations or siblings will bring wealth or will introduce propitious situations. This sociable star blesses you with her prosperity. In retrospect, this star combination is extremely weak in the face of the Killing Stars and/or Obstruction Catalyst■. In this instance, any entrepreneurial, trading pursuits should be shelved until the stars turn.

# SELF: COMMANDER & PIONEER
## CAREER: EMPEROR & OPPORTUNITY
## PROSPERITY: CRIMSON & GENERAL

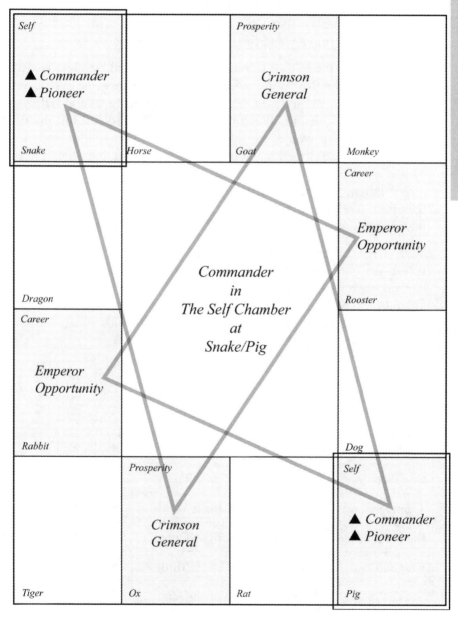

## The Physical Metal Industries

Its element being Metal, Commander would suit anything having to do with the physical metal industries—from copper and steel to gold and silver. Moreover, with honesty and decisiveness being its second-nature, The Commander is also very suited to working with jewelry or the finance sectors (money and finance being of Metal).

Commander in the Self or Career would be a natural business leader. As an extremely hard-working with a proactive nature, he would create exactly what he set out to do. With the Auspicious Stars and Catalysts to boost (e.g. Completion, Wealth$ and Power↗) and free of any of the Killing Stars, we would see these individuals enjoying success in the above Metals industries, including law enforcement, e.g., the Police and Military. Commander dispenses wealth within the Emperor constellation. It is also swift and impatient. Their decisive actions can, therefore, work for or against them. In the face of the Killing stars, when the market suddenly turns, we would see deep losses.

With Crimson in Prosperity, we are looking at highly diversified investment ventures. Whether to be cautious or adventurous would depend, therefore, whether we are seeing the auspicious or Killing Stars around us. The higher-risk activities should only be taken when we are in a strong house (with Wealth $, Completion, plus other Auspicious Stars) and free of the Killing Stars and Obstruction■.

| HOURS | SELF HOUSE | PROSPERITY | LONG | SHORT | DIVERSE | FOCUS |
|---|---|---|---|---|---|---|
| Rat/Horse | Comdr/Vault | Crmsn | + | + | + | + |
| Ox/Goat | Comdr/Oppor | Crmsn/Pneer | + | + | + | + |
| Tiger/Monkey | Comdr/Miror | Crmsn/Vault | + | + | + | + |
| Rabbit/Rooster | Comdr/Genrl | Crmsn/Oppor | + | + | + | + |
| Dragon/Dog | Comdr | Crmsn/Miror | + | + | + | + |
| Snake/Pig | Comdr/Pneer | Crmsn/Genrl | + | + | + | + |

CHAPTER 6.5

# The Self as Waif in the 12 Chambers

| | | | |
|---|---|---|---|
| | | | |
| *Snake* | *Horse* | *Goat* | *Monkey* |
| | | | |

JOSEPH ADDISON

✦

*A contented mind*

*is the greatest blessing a*

*man can enjoy in*

*this world*

| | | | |
|---|---|---|---|
| *Dragon* | | | *Rooster* |
| *Rabbit* | | | *Dog* |
| *Tiger* | *Ox* | *Rat* | *Pig* |

# WAIF in Self in the Rat or Horse Chamber

### The Self—Waif & Moon

Here the easy-going Waif would be sharing house with the helpful Moon. The Wealth part of the Chinese character for Opulence, a Brilliant Moon in The Self sector makes for a wealthy soul. However, in her dark hours or trailing Obstruction■, the Moon would take on the benevolence of the Sun. She would then be more concerned with helping humanity (Bill Gates' Life Chart). These rather similar sisters would, therefore, be engaging themselves in supportive roles and would not mind at all if they were doing these for very little or perhaps even for free. Also, they'd be happy to let the others enjoy the limelight or accolades.

### Career—Intelligence & Scholar

At its best, Intelligence shines on steady employees, not entrepreneurs or business owners. As a employee, Intelligence can look to apply all his positive traits to good use.

With Waif-Moon in the Self backed up by Intelligence and Scholar here, this constellation would shine on working tirelessly for the social causes without the need or want for monetary gains. Indeed, success lies in selfless support for/within religious groups and charities.

### Prosperity—Sun & Messenger Opposite

The above constellation shines on charities and the social causes. It is also for this reason that Prosperity is devoid of stars. Borrowing light from the Sun and Messenger opposite, we may see them reigning in public support for these plights.

These stars are not interested in any money-spinning activities at all. A long-term, safe approach to investments is, therefore, necessary. Moreover, should the Sun become obstructed■, a betrayal may undermine, resulting in loss. Otherwise, because of money or money invested, there may be a serious blow to the reputation. Be wary of males.

Moreover, with Moon in Self, the gradual accumulation of wealth is indicated, as in a long term savings or retirement plan. Lastly, any business venture or investment undertaking that would involve risk is strictly not advisable for Waif & Moon in Self.

# SELF: WAIF & MOON
## CAREER: INTELLIGENCE & SCHOLAR
## PROSPERITY: (SUN & MESSENGER OPPOSITE)

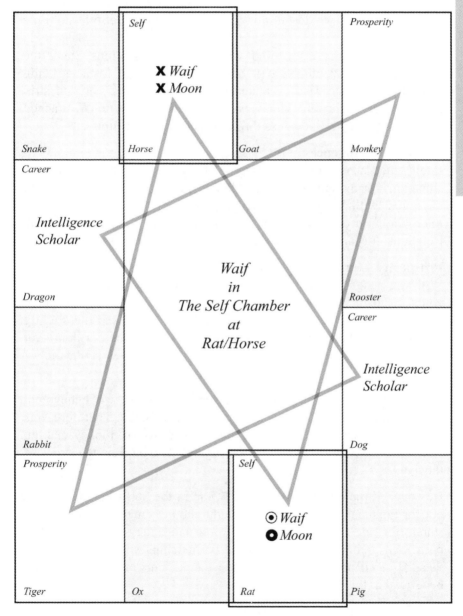

| Self | | | Prosperity |
|---|---|---|---|
| **✗** *Waif*<br>**✗** *Moon* | | | |
| *Snake* | *Horse* | *Goat* | *Monkey* |

*Career*

*Intelligence*
*Scholar*

*Dragon*

*Waif*
*in*
*The Self Chamber*
*at*
*Rat/Horse*

*Rooster*

*Career*

*Intelligence*
*Scholar*

*Rabbit*

*Dog*

*Prosperity*

| | | Self | |
|---|---|---|---|
| | | ⊙ *Waif*<br>● *Moon* | |
| *Tiger* | *Ox* | *Rat* | *Pig* |

Chapter 6.5 - The Self as Waif in the 12 Chambers  123

# WAIF in Self in the Ox or Goat Chamber

## The Self—Waif & Messenger

With enjoyment being the order of the day for Waif, when teamed up with Messenger, which stands for the propagation of news or knowledge, we have the pair in promotion or marketing. The wide range of products would fall under the umbrella of LifeStyle and Fine Dining.

In a sector that is also filled with several Auspicious Stars, the Messenger with Wealth $ will bear the meaning of fortunes being made by the voice. However, any surrounding killing star will strip away any splendor and The Messenger with Obstruction■ attached will subsequently strike a loss through slander or litigation.

## Career—Intelligence

Intelligence stands for wide-ranging interests. This star would also shine on steady employees in Management or Administration. In alignment with Waif and Messenger, we would see them promoting international products and services in the art of fine living or Public Relations or Marketing—the latest technologies of such.

## Prosperity—Sun & Scholar Opposite

With Messenger in Self, we would see more thoughts and questions, which need to be answered before any position in trading is taken. Instead of the happy-go-lucky Waif self, we would see the slightly more serious, thoughtful side emerging. This would be our dominant personality, especially since our Prosperity Chamber is devoid of stars.

With Sun and Scholar reflecting Prosperity, these two benevolent stars would rather see us engaging in the social issues. Therefore, this constellation will not shine on business deals or money-making ventures. If anything, long-term savings plans would be the order of the day.

However, if there is an Obstructed ■ Sun in the Self Chamber, watch out for financial woes or losses brought about by males. The Sun also stands for one's reputation—your good name may be at stake. For both men and women, be wary of partnerships with males. Avoid these if at all possible. By the same token, females would be more beneficial at this time.

# SELF: WAIF & MESSENGER
## CAREER: INTELLIGENCE
## PROSPERITY: (SUN & SCHOLAR OPPOSITE)

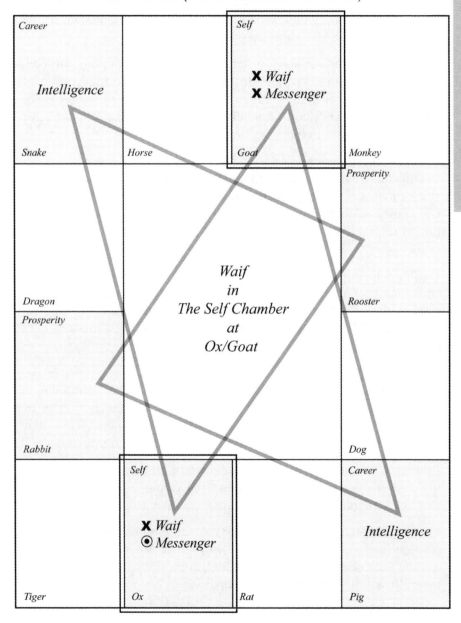

# WAIF in Self in the Tiger or Monkey Chamber

### The Self—Waif & Scholar

Waif is joined by the righteous and protective Scholar here. Scholar also shines on the professions like Medicine, Law, or the Sciences. This star, therefore, would prod our leisurely Waif into action, lifting her up to his lofty, humanitarian pursuits.

Note that Scholar stands for accommodation, protection, solitude, litigation and injury. Power↗ to the Scholar has the implication of adding weight to Scholar's traits. Negativity may be enhanced. Take these in stride. They are after all not life threatening and look for redeeming qualities in the reflecting house or at 120°.

### Career—Intelligence

Intelligence stands for wide-ranging interests. This star would also shine on steady employees. In alignment with Waif and Messenger, we would see them promoting international products and services in the art of fine living or PR and Marketing the latest technologies of such.

Wealth $ to Intelligence would have the Strategist maneuvering and collecting his due. However, if hemmed in by the killing or obstructed stars, especially The Moon obstructed ■ in the same or opposite sectors, Intelligence with Wealth may spell certain misfortunes, e.g., robbery.

### Prosperity—Moon

The Waif does not care much for investments. This sentiment is exacerbated with the addition of Scholar, who absolutely abhors or has issues with money and money-making ventures. This pair therefore, does not bode well for financial or business transactions.

Adding to the picture, we have Moon here in Prosperity, which points to the steady accumulation of wealth. If anything, a steady, non-risky savings or retirement plan is therefore recommended.

Moreover, Moon, being a prosperity star and feminine, also stands for dimness and secrecy. If trailing Obstruction ■, it would have us dealing with depression, economic loss, conspiracy, or ruin. Note that these ills will be brought on by a female.

# SELF: WAIF & SCHOLAR
## CAREER: INTELLIGENCE    PROSPERITY: MOON

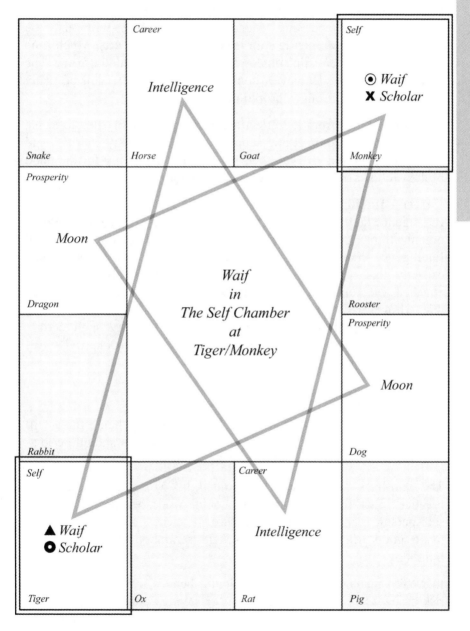

*WAIF IN SELF*

Chapter 6.5 - The Self as Waif in the 12 Chambers 127

# WAIF in Self in the Rabbit or Rooster Chamber

**The Self—Waif**
A lone Waif in the Self House will bring in emotional volatility and a hard childhood. Physical traits include being fair-skinned, having a square-roundish face and round shoulders. She will also be gracious—a learned, gentle soul leaning towards the arts. Much time will be spent in idealistic contemplation, and a contented dreamer she is likely to remain. However, being a lucky star, there will be many friends who will introduce propitious situations.

The Moon shines from its reflecting chamber. We will, therefore, see the pair creating comfort and support through the many charities and social organizations that are their base, working steadily for the good of their fellows without much expectations for reward.

**Career—Intelligence**
Intelligence here signifies diversified servicing in multinational organizations regarding global issues, humanitarian, or aid. Intelligence likes planning and administration, and it is in this capacity that it will shine. Should the Wealth catalyst $ become attached, we would have the Strategist maneuvering and collecting his due. However, if hemmed in by killing or obstructed ■ stars, especially The Moon, Intelligence with Wealth may spell certain misfortunes like Robbery. (Note this also alludes to charity – Bill Gates' Life Chart.)

**Prosperity—Messenger**
Messenger in Prosperity bears implications of slanders occurring from financial or money issues—Litigation. On the other hand, there will be a secret financial gain. Therefore, any investments should be low-risk. Business endeavors should also be avoided.

The laid-back Waif persona is joined by Messenger here. With practice, therefore, this person could well become a smooth salesperson reaping in some measure of success. They would also make good life coaches in self- help seminars and management training.

In wealth management, the Waif would benefit from a secure, low-risk strategy. Long-range retirement or savings plans would also be suitable.

# SELF: WAIF

## CAREER: INTELLIGENCE   PROSPERITY: MESSENGER

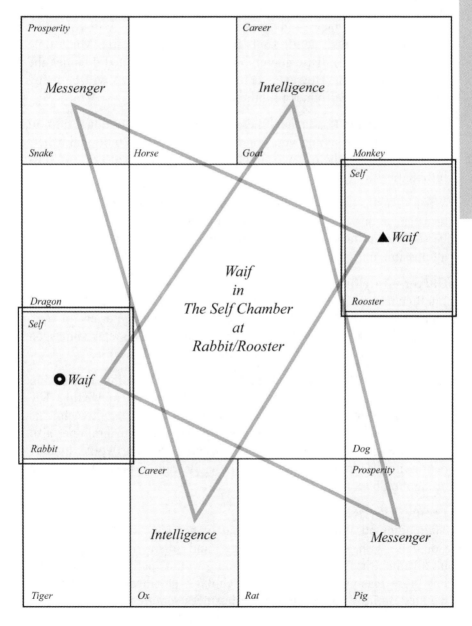

Chapter 6.5 - The Self as Waif in the 12 Chambers 129

# WAIF in Self in the Dragon or Dog Chamber

## The Self—Waif

A lone Waif in the Self House will bring in emotional volatility and a hard childhood. Physical traits include being fair-skinned, having a square-roundish face and round shoulders. She will also be gracious—a learned, gentle soul leaning towards the arts. Much time will be spent in idealistic contemplation, and a contented dreamer she is likely to remain. However, being a lucky star, there will be many friends who will introduce propitious situations.

With Obstruction ■ attached, there is likelihood of emotional turmoil and low self-esteem and yes, brace for a ride on the emotional roller-coaster. Would it help if we suggested most of this suffering is self-inflicted?

When this star for enjoyment is in retrograde, she must watch out for disasters at play. It is at times of fun that she will suddenly find herself face to face with danger. She must avoid the "fun" places if at all possible during this time.

## Career—Intelligence & Moon

Intelligence here signifies diversified servicing in multinational organizations in support of global issues, humanitarian or aid. Intelligence likes planning and administration. This star shines on employees, and it is in this capacity that it will find success.

However, the Moon is also here. This wealth star points to working with finance and the slow but steady accumulation of wealth. The Intelligence-Moon partnership would bring in diversified investments and multi-tasking. Moon, being a prosperity star and feminine, also stands for dimness and secrecy. Obstruction ■ here would include depression, economic loss, conspiracy, or ruin. These ills will be brought on by a female.

## Prosperity—Scholar

The contented Waif does not go out of her way to harness wealth. Coupled with Scholar's ideology and disinterest, any direct involvement in finance or stocks trading would spell certain disasters. For these reasons also, the Waif-Scholar's presidency in Prosperity would definitely not be suitable for business ventures of any sort.

# SELF: WAIF
## CAREER: INTELLIGENCE & MOON    PROSPERITY: SCHOLAR

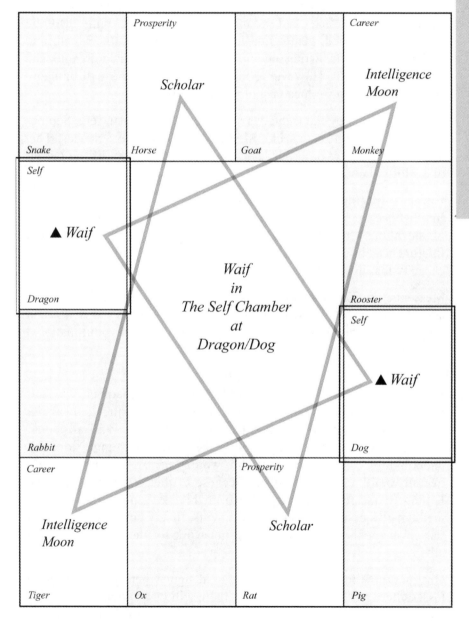

Chapter 6.5 - The Self as Waif in the 12 Chambers  131

# WAIF in Self in the Snake or Pig Chamber

**The Self—Waif**
A lone Waif in the Self House will bring in emotional volatility and a hard childhood. Physical traits include being fair-skinned, having a square-roundish face and round shoulders. She will also be gracious—a learned, gentle soul leaning towards the arts. Much time will be spent in idealistic contemplation, and a contented dreamer she is likely to remain. However, being a lucky star, there will be many friends who will introduce propitious situations.

Waif is opposed by the righteous and protective Scholar here. Scholar shines on the professions like Medicine, Law, or the Sciences. This star will, therefore, prod our leisurely Waif into action, lifting her up to his lofty, humanitarian ideals.

**Career—Intelligence & Messenger**
Intelligence signifies diversified servicing in multinational organizations regarding global issues, humanitarian, or aid. Intelligence likes planning and administration, and it is in this capacity that it will shine.

Messenger in Career always points to the use of the voice, i.e., Selling and Marketing. These two stars together with Waif in the Self could propagate lifestyle or leisure activities in large multinational organizations.

**Prosperity—Sun & Moon Opposite**
Without any major stars occupying the Prosperity chamber, we shall look to its opposite for indication. The Sun-Moon pair would ignite the interest for investing which has been lacking in Waif all along. Having said this, the Moon's influence is in long-range, low-risk undertakings. The Moon's wealth would also figure into Waif's overall wealth-creation abilities. Because of this, if we don't see the Killing Stars around, it may be worthwhile to venture into low- to medium-risk equities or other investments. In any circumstance, high-risk investments or ventures would not work for the Waif-Sun-Moon alliance.

Obstruction ■ to the Sun or Moon would signify betrayal, resulting in loss. Otherwise, because of income, there will be a serious blow to the reputation. Be wary of males for Sun ■ or females for Moon■.

# SELF: WAIF
## CAREER: INTELLIGENCE & MESSENGER
## PROSPERITY: (SUN & MOON OPPOSITE)

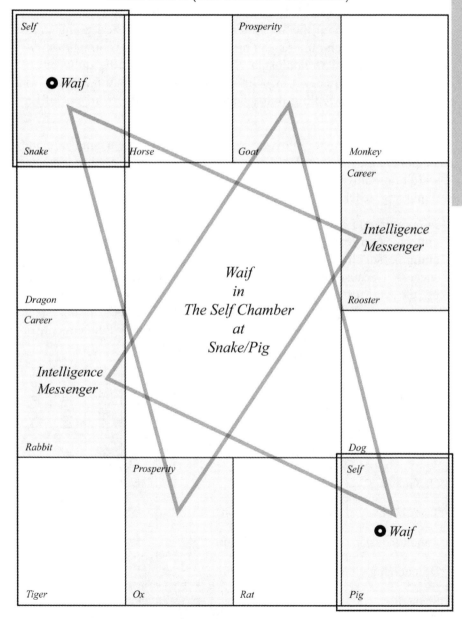

| | | | |
|---|---|---|---|
| *Self*<br><br>● *Waif* | | *Prosperity* | |
| *Snake* | *Horse* | *Goat* | *Monkey* |
| | | | *Career*<br><br>*Intelligence Messenger* |
| *Dragon*<br>*Career*<br><br>*Intelligence Messenger* | | *Waif in The Self Chamber at Snake/Pig* | *Rooster* |
| *Rabbit* | | | *Dog* |
| | *Prosperity* | | *Self*<br><br>● *Waif* |
| *Tiger* | *Ox* | *Rat* | *Pig* |

Chapter 6.5 - The Self as Waif in the 12 Chambers 133

# WAIF in the Self House Investment Strategy

**Low Risk Investments**

Being unassuming and modest, Waif people are easy to get along with. Because of this, they make friends easily. They are simply about enjoying the moment and the good, easy life. So please, let's not get all worked up about the world's economy or where it's going to go next. They'd much rather swap pressure, deadlines, or competition for afternoon tea at The Peninsula. Therefore, they will be quite out of place in any office setting, let alone business venture. Look for support from the Killing Stars, which would zap the Waif out of her dream world.

However, they would enjoy any role that calls for dispensing care and support, e.g., the board of prominent charities or the various social welfare organizations. Otherwise, working quietly behind the scenes in nursing, teaching, or the civil service would suit them.

In investments, as with most other matters, Waif would rather take the armchair and leave the role of investor to someone else. Their easy-going personality would obliterate the little desire, if any, for chasing success. Because of this, long-term and low-risk undertakings would be the call of the day. Unless we see the Auspicious Stars – Completion, Winged Horse or the Wealth Catalyst$ in the same chamber, opposite or at 120° – or Fire, Bell, Ram, Punishment, or Void – Waif will not be taking up the financial reins.

| HOURS | SELF HOUSE | PROSPERITY | LONG | SHORT | DIVERSE | FOCUS |
|-------|-----------|------------|------|-------|---------|-------|
| Rat/Horse | Waif/Moon | | ✦ | | ✦ | |
| Ox/Goat | Waif/Mesgr | | ✦ | | ✦ | |
| Tiger/Monkey | Waif/Schol | Moon | ✦ | | ✦ | |
| Rabbit/Rooster | Waif | Mesgr | ✦ | | ✦ | |
| Dragon/Dog | Waif | Schol | ✦ | | ✦ | |
| Snake/Pig | Waif | | ✦ | | ✦ | |

# The Self as Crimson in the 12 Chambers

| | | | |
|---|---|---|---|
| Snake | Horse | Goat | Monkey |
| Dragon | | | Rooster |
| Rabbit | | | Dog |
| Tiger | Ox | Rat | Pig |

### B.C. FORBES

✦

*The most important single ingredient in the formula of SUCCESS is knowing how to get along with people*

# CRIMSON in Self in the Rat or Horse Chamber

### The Self—Crimson & Mirror

This person will do famously well in situations which require constant communication/dealings with the opposite sex, e.g., a man in perfumery, cosmetics, or lingerie; a woman in finance, athletics or any sector of business traditionally dominated by men. With Wealth $ attached, success in terms of monetary gains is enhanced. Crimson's outgoing personality is matched by Mirror's reliability and carefulness—the perfect combination for success. The outgoing and vivacious Crimson is being toned down by Mirror's caution and stability. In any situation, you will see this person moving forward with hard work, determination, and integrity.

### Career—Commander

Commander, also a hard worker, will not be daunted by setbacks. We will see these at the forefront of the armed and uniformed forces. Together with Crimson and Mirror, this personality would best perform in planning, leadership, and people-oriented roles. If strengthened by the Auspicious Stars and Catalysts, we will see them rising to top ranking positions. With Fame ✿ attached, many will hear about this person's successes.

### Prosperity—Emperor & Vault

Working among the people is Crimson-Mirror's forte. It suits this personality to attain information from real-life situations, such as technical analysis, market surveys, the media, or just talking with like-minded friends. Crimson's adventurous personality indicates high risk tolerance. However, this is balanced by Mirror's prudence. Investment success, after all, is marked by research, strategy, skill, and action.

Emperor with Fame✿attached indicates strength, wisdom, and courage being enhanced and highlighted. However, if hemmed in or opposed by the Killing Stars, The Emperor with Fame, may gain notoriety through misguided or fraudulent channels.

With Vault, which is stable and conservative, another major investment star here in Prosperity, we are seeing investments into long-term, significant projects. Short-term, day-trading, or penny stocks, therefore, would not be of interest or benefit to this person.

# SELF: CRIMSON & MIRROR
## CAREER: COMMANDER     PROSPERITY: EMPEROR & VAULT

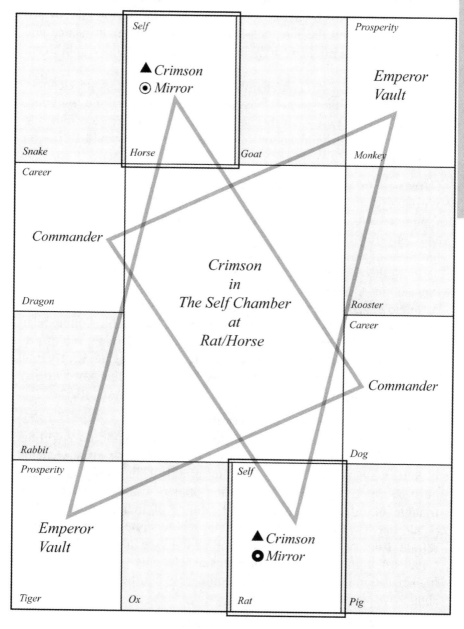

Chapter 6.6 - The Self as Crimson in the 12 Chambers 137

# CRIMSON in Self in the Ox or Goat Chamber

**The Self—Crimson & General**
Flirtatious and sociable, Crimson in Self will, however, closely guard her privacy. She will be strong emotionally and quite intuitive. Crimson is an artist by nature and just loves being surrounded by art, music, theatre and the like. She can deftly weave her influence and reach her goals with dexterity. Here we have a splendidly munificent personality.
Crimson in the Ox or Goat chamber would share house with General. The action-oriented General would lend power to the outgoing Crimson. These two, therefore, will join forces to create a dynamic duo that can withstand action and volatility. They would thrive on adventure.

**Career—Commander & Pioneer**
We have Commander and Pioneer here, which indicate hard work. Combined with the above, we are witnessing changeability, creativity, and physical challenges. This individual will be out there at the forefront of any new industry, perhaps wearing different hats as befitting the circumstance. The armed forces would suit Commander-Pioneer in Career, i.e., The Police, Army, Peace-Keeping, etc. Auspicious stars in the same house, opposite, or at 120° would aid career advancement. A prosperous star in its own right, Commander with Power ↗ can expect to be rewarded for his relentless effort. Self-empowerment is the key word. He must delegate wisely but never let go of the reins because only he can hold the power to his own destiny and ultimate success.

**Prosperity—Emperor & Opportunity**
Holding court are Emperor (ruling finance) and Opportunity (ruling investments, gaming and gambling). Coupled with Crimson-General in Self, we have someone who is not afraid of high risk-taking. He must be especially wary of the Killing Stars or Catalysts entering his triangle of influence. These will be times of major losses, and it would be wise for him to adopt a safe, secure strategy then. He must refrain from any business endeavor in the face of the Obstruction Catalyst■ in the same house or opposite. The only times to engage in high-risk trading or investments would be when he sees the strong, supportive stars returning.

# SELF: CRIMSON & GENERAL
## CAREER: CRIMSON & GENERAL
### PROSPERITY: EMPEROR & OPPORTUNITY

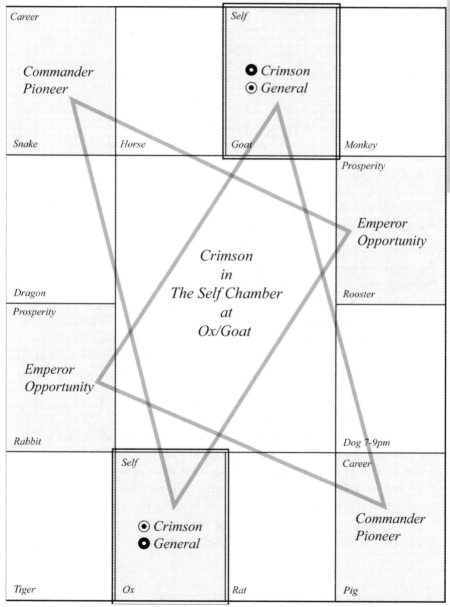

*Career*

*Commander Pioneer*

*Snake*

*Self*

**⦿ Crimson**
**⊙ General**

*Horse*　*Goat*　*Monkey*

*Prosperity*

*Emperor Opportunity*

*Crimson in The Self Chamber at Ox/Goat*

*Dragon*　*Rooster*

*Prosperity*

*Emperor Opportunity*

*Rabbit*　*Dog 7-9pm*

*Self*

**⊙ Crimson**
**⦿ General**

*Career*

*Commander Pioneer*

*Tiger*　*Ox*　*Rat*　*Pig*

Chapter 6.6 - The Self as Crimson in the 12 Chambers 139

CRIMSON IN SELF

# CRIMSON in Self in the Tiger or Monkey Chamber

**The Self—Crimson**

Crimson at Tiger or Monkey sits alone and faces Opportunity at its opposite. Driven by performance, Crimson in the Self Sector people will always take pride in being high achievers. Also, having to do with blood, Crimson with $ attached is splendidly munificent and indicates close, female relations bringing in propitious situations. This sociable star blesses with her prosperity.

With Opportunity reflecting the Self, we can expect the Crimson-Opportunity pair to be active and daring risk-takers. Of course, they must be especially wary of the Killing Stars or the Obstruction catalyst entering their Success Triangle. These will be times of major losses, and it would be well to adopt a safe, secure strategy.

It is important to refrain from any business endeavor in the face of the Obstruction Catalyst ■ in the same house or opposite. The only times when it is safe to engage in high-risk trading or investments would be when the strong, supportive stars come in.

**Career—Commander & Vault**

Commander shares this house with Vault. Commander is action-oriented whereas the Vault holds back and balances out with stability. These two prosperous stars shining in Career will, therefore, bring in successes through steady, hard work. A career in finance in the banking institutions is suitable. If helped by the Auspicious Stars (e.g., Completion and Winged Horse), the individual can expect to receive significant rewards. If Fame ✿ is attached, the success would bring eminence.

**Prosperity—Emperor & Mirror**

With Emperor here, The Self would have financial savvy. This does not necessarily indicate prosperity but will hold a Career in financial control, money management, etc. It important to look for support from the wealth and Auspicious Stars (Completion and Horse, etc.) With Mirror also here, depending on influencing stars, good things will arrive in doubles. However, the same goes for disappointments. Other stars in the same or reflecting sector will give further insight.

## Self: Crimson
### Career: Commander & Vault
### Prosperity: Emperor & Mirror

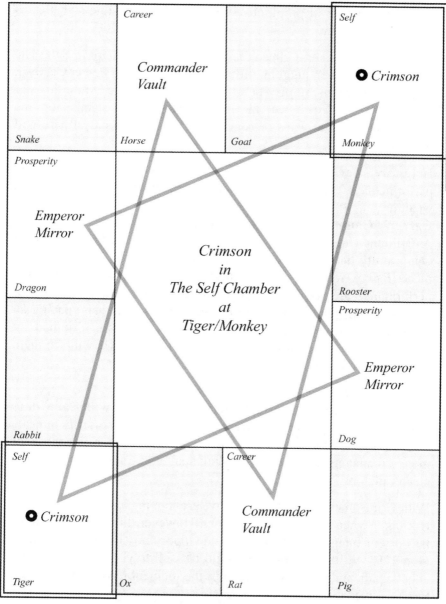

| Career | | | Self |
|---|---|---|---|
| **Commander Vault** | | | ● *Crimson* |
| *Snake* | *Horse* | *Goat* | *Monkey* |

| Prosperity | | | |
|---|---|---|---|
| **Emperor Mirror** | *Crimson in The Self Chamber at Tiger/Monkey* | | |
| *Dragon* | | | *Rooster* Prosperity |
| | | | **Emperor Mirror** |
| *Rabbit* | | | *Dog* |

| Self | | Career | |
|---|---|---|---|
| ● *Crimson* | | **Commander Vault** | |
| *Tiger* | *Ox* | *Rat* | *Pig* |

Chapter 6.6 - The Self as Crimson in the 12 Chambers 141

## CRIMSON in Self in the Rabbit or Rooster Chamber

**The Self—Crimson and Pioneer**

Crimson is an artist by nature and loves being surrounded by art, music, and theatre. She can deftly weave her influence and reach her goals with dexterity. Also, having to do with blood, Crimson with $ attached, is splendidly munificent and indicates close, female relations bringing in propitious situations. This sociable star blesses with her prosperity.

At Rabbit or Rooster, Crimson is joined by Pioneer here in Self. The Pioneer will be seen juggling different roles. With the Power Catalyst, we see a bigger role to play or a heavier burden in the House this star should come to rest within. The Pioneer also stands for the introduction of new ways or concepts. The Power Catalyst here will offer authority.

Here we have powerful innovation combined with brilliant performance. The outcome should equal propitious success and wealth!

**Career—Commander and Opportunity**

A Brilliant Commander with Fame shares house with the Brilliant Opportunity here. The Commander brings in wealth. With wealth in place, Fame ✪ follows. These four major stars of power, action, and performance are well-suited to be placed in a career of Politics or Acting. These personalities will be right at home on stage facing an audience, and this is where they will find success. If joined by Completion (or better still, Completion and Horse), we will see them rising to great heights in this arena.

**Prosperity—Emperor & General**

Presided by The Emperor and General here, The Self will deal with or possess financial prowess. However, this does not necessarily indicate a wealthy Self, for it could mean a Career in financial control or money management. The surrounding stars and Catalysts will give a clearer picture.

With Crimson and Pioneer in Self, we are looking at a highly versatile risk-taker when it comes to investing. However, this individual must be wary of financial downfalls should Opportunity become obstructed ■ at 120°. In this instance, it would be well to curb risk-taking and adopt a safe and secure strategy until the moment passes and the stars turn positive.

# SELF: CRIMSON & PIONEER
## CAREER: COMMANDER & OPPORTUNITY
### PROSPERITY: EMPEROR & GENERAL

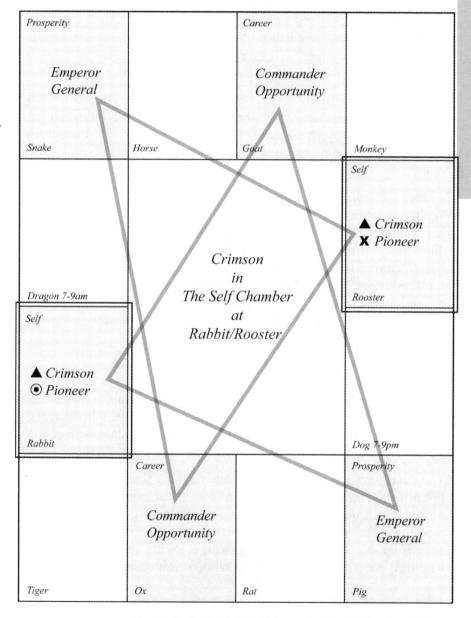

Prosperity

**Emperor**
**General**

Snake | Horse

Career

**Commander**
**Opportunity**

Goat | Monkey

Self

▲ Crimson
✗ Pioneer

*Crimson*
*in*
*The Self Chamber*
*at*
*Rabbit/Rooster*

Dragon 7-9am | Rooster

Self

▲ Crimson
⊙ Pioneer

Rabbit | Dog 7-9pm

Career

**Commander**
**Opportunity**

Prosperity

**Emperor**
**General**

Tiger | Ox | Rat | Pig

CRIMSON IN SELF

Chapter 6.6 - The Self as Crimson in the 12 Chambers 143

# CRIMSON in Self in the Dragon or Dog Chamber

**The Self—Crimson and Vault**
The outgoing Crimson gets a dose of care and precision from the conservative, careful, and detailed Vault. These two seemingly opposites are far from being at odds with each other. Vault takes pride in its work. Crimson cares about performance. Both aim towards the same commitment. If helped by the Auspicious Stars, we can expect outstanding achievements. It is a characteristic that they will never lack for earthly possessions.

Crimson is an artist by nature and loves being surrounded by art, music, and theatre. She can deftly weave her influence and reach her goals with dexterity. Also, having to do with blood, with $ attached, the wealthy Crimson indicates blood relations coming in with wealth or propitious situations. This sociable star blesses with her prosperity.

**Career—Commander & Mirror**
With Commander here, The Self will likely hold down a job that enjoys autonomy and has a say in the running of the business. Mirror duplicates, which indicates working in the printing or mass manufacturing industries. With Commander and Mirror, which stand for action and responsibility, combined with the above, we see a people-oriented career like the public sector and service industries, e.g., hotels. If enhanced by Fame✿, The Commander brings in wealth. With wealth in place, fame follows.

**Prosperity—Emperor**
Presided by The Emperor here, The Self will deal with or have financial prowess. However, this does not necessarily indicate a prosperous Self because it could also indicate a Career in financial control, money management, etc. The surrounding stars will give a better view.

The Vault-Emperor-Crimson combination in finance will incline towards the conservative. Because of this, we are seeing the steadiest of the Crimson-in-Self personalities with regard to finance and investing. The traditional values of Vault and Emperor are being spiced up by Crimson's daring nature. With the right stars in harmony, we will see a shrewd and successful investor.

# SELF: CRIMSON & VAULT

## CAREER: COMMANDER & MIRROR    PROSPERITY: EMPEROR

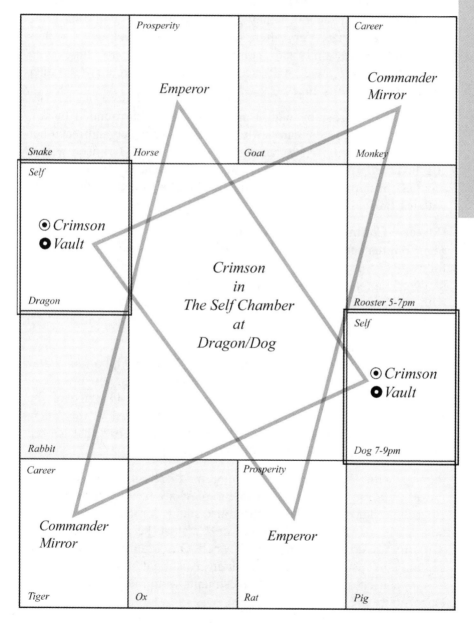

# CRIMSON in Self in the Snake or Pig Chamber

## The Self—Crimson and Opportunity

Here Crimson is joined by Opportunity. With both these popular and people-oriented stars in Self, we are seeing tremendous attraction surrounding them wherever they go. If anyone, they would have the power to mesmerize. Very often, movie stars, stage actors, as well as politicians, have this star combination. Adding to this, with Opportunity here, we will see them milling about in rather complicated circumstances.

Crimson is an artist by nature and loves being surrounded by art, music, and theatre. She can deftly weave her influence and reach her goals with dexterity. Also, having to do with blood, Crimson with $ attached, is splendidly munificent and indicates close, female relations bringing in propitious situations. This sociable star blesses with her prosperity.

## Career—Commander and General

The Commander brings in wealth. With wealth in place, Fame✪will follow. Commander is joined by General here. These are hardworking, pioneering people who will forge ahead of the pack with strategy and courage. This star combination indicates lucrative career success.

## Prosperity—Emperor and Pioneer

Here we have Emperor and Pioneer. The Crimson-Opportunity star combination would bring out the gambler in us. In investing, therefore, these individuals are high risk-takers. In the face of the Killing Stars (Ram or Top) or the Obstruction Catalyst ■, the roller-coaster ride is just not worth it! It is fortunate, therefore, that we see the Brilliant Emperor, aided by Pioneer in Prosperity.

Pioneer with Power ➚ will be juggling different roles. With the Power Catalyst, we see a bigger role to play or a heavier burden in the House this star rests in. The Pioneer also stands for the introduction of new ways or concepts. The Power Catalyst here gives him the authority to do so. Emperor will quell Opportunity's tendency to gamble and ensure shrewdness in their investment strategy. Adopting a more conservative strategy in investments would work for Crimson-Opportunity in Self.

# SELF: CRIMSON & OPPORTUNITY
## CAREER: EMPEROR & PIONEER
## PROSPERITY: COMMANDER & MIRROR

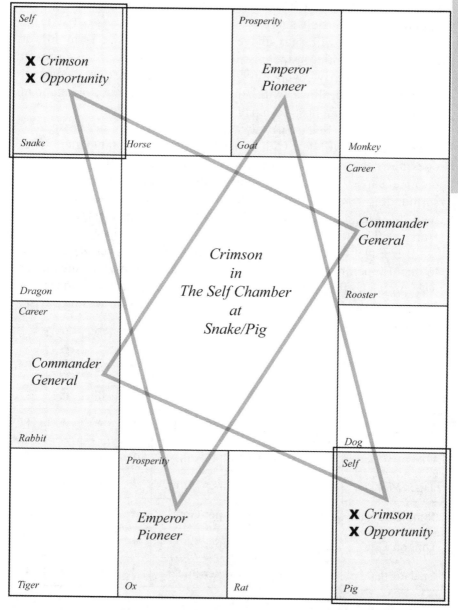

*Self*

**✗** *Crimson*
**✗** *Opportunity*

*Snake*

*Prosperity*

*Emperor*
*Pioneer*

*Horse*

*Goat*

*Monkey*

*Career*

*Commander*
*General*

*Crimson*
*in*
*The Self Chamber*
*at*
*Snake/Pig*

*Dragon*

*Rooster*

*Career*

*Commander*
*General*

*Rabbit*

*Dog*

*Prosperity*

*Emperor*
*Pioneer*

*Self*

**✗** *Crimson*
**✗** *Opportunity*

*Tiger*

*Ox*

*Rat*

*Pig*

**CRIMSON IN SELF**

# CRIMSON in the Self House Investment Strategy

**Prosperous Crimson**

An appealing number with a twinkle in its eye! Depending on supporting stars, the degree of success for career advancement can be gauged. Cut out for social activities, Crimson will strive for achievement. Crimson in the Self sector will find itself basking in attention and ultimately success.

This person will soar above the rest whether he is in PR or politics. Just put him in the crowd. The girls will love him! Crimson will do famously well in situations that require constant communication/dealings with the opposite sex; e.g., a man in perfumery or cosmetics; a woman in finance or athletics.

Crimson in Self will always have Emperor in Prosperity. Therefore, they will deal with or have power in financial matters. This does not necessarily indicate a prosperous Self, for it could simply mean a career in financial control, money management, etc. The surrounding stars will give a fuller picture. Rewards would come in with the Auspicious Stars, the Wealth $ catalyst or Completion and Horse at close range.

It is a fact that the Obstruction Catalyst ■ will never get attached to the Emperor. Given this, plus Emperor's ability to subdue or accommodate the Killing Stars, we are seeing good chances for investment success. The Crimson-Emperor partnership will be a wise, courageous, but shrewd investor.

| HOURS | SELF HOUSE | PROSPERITY | LONG | SHORT | DIVERSE | FOCUS |
|---|---|---|---|---|---|---|
| Rat/Horse | Crmsn/Miror | Emper/Vault | ✦ | ✦ | ✦ | ✦ |
| Ox/Goat | Crimsn/Genrl | Emper/Oppor | ✦ | ✦ | ✦ | ✦ |
| Tiger/Monkey | Crmsn | Emper/Miror | ✦ | ✦ | ✦ | ✦ |
| Rabbit/Rooster | Crmsn/Pneer | Emper/Genrl | ✦ | ✦ | ✦ | ✦ |
| Dragon/Dog | Crmsn/Vault | Emper | ✦ | ✦ | ✦ | ✦ |
| Snake/Pig | Crmsn/Oppor | Emper/Pneer | ✦ | ✦ | ✦ | ✦ |

# CHAPTER 6.7

## The Self as Vault in the 12 Chambers

| Snake | Horse | Goat | Monkey |
|---|---|---|---|
| Dragon | | | Rooster |
| Rabbit | | | Dog |
| Tiger | Ox | Rat | Pig |

**AL BERNSTEIN**

———— ✦ ————

*SUCCESS*
*is simple.*
*Do what's right,*
*the right way,*
*at the right time*

# VAULT in Self in the Rat or Horse Chamber

## The Self—Vault & Commander

Vault attracts and stores wealth. It is a characteristic that it will never lack for earthly possessions. The Vault-Commander pair combined will generate unlimited energy for business and career opportunities. These will shine on business leaders, showering them with resourceful creativity and power to break down any barrier that may surface.

Commander, being metal, is an action as well as wealth star. There will be major prosperity problems should this star become obstructed ■ because the individual will be chasing wealth but will never attain it.

## Career—Emperor & Mirror

Vault in Self would inevitably have Emperor here. Emperor careers would include dealing in high-end merchandise in global corporations.

The Emperor-Mirror pair here denotes insightful and wise leadership. Any difficulties can be overcome by applying their outstanding management skills. The Vault-Commander-Emperor-Mirror constellation would, therefore, shine on decision-makers within large, international institutions, as in Banking and Finance.

Mirror is also here, which indicates that it will deal with its business in a principled, responsible manner. Depending on influencing stars, good things will come in doubles. However, the same goes for disappointments. Other stars in the same or reflecting sector will give insights. Remember that when the stars turn retrograde, it is time to collect the profit and wait.

## Prosperity—Crimson

With Crimson here, we are looking at highly diversified investment ventures. In partnership with the rather staid Vault but action-packed Commander, this combination would introduce just the right amount of caution to riskier speculations and vice versa, which is fortunate.

Whether to be cautious or more adventurous would depend, therefore, whether the auspicious or Killing Stars are present around us (in the same house, opposite or at 120°. The higher-risk activities should only be taken when we are in a strong house (with Wealth $, Completion, plus other Auspicious Stars) and free of the Killing Stars and Obstruction ■.

# SELF: VAULT & COMMANDER
## CAREER: EMPEROR & MIRROR   PROSPERITY: CRIMSON

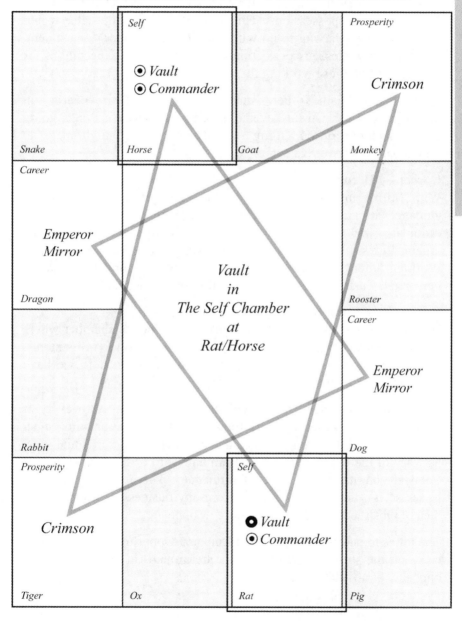

| Self | | | Prosperity |
|---|---|---|---|
| | ⊙ *Vault* | | *Crimson* |
| | ⊙ *Commander* | | |
| *Snake* | *Horse* | *Goat* | *Monkey* |
| Career | | | |
| *Emperor* | | *Vault* | *Rooster* |
| *Mirror* | | *in* | *Career* |
| *Dragon* | | *The Self Chamber* | *Emperor* |
| | | *at* | *Mirror* |
| | | *Rat/Horse* | |
| *Rabbit* | | | *Dog* |
| Prosperity | | Self | |
| *Crimson* | | ● *Vault* | |
| | | ⊙ *Commander* | |
| *Tiger* | *Ox* | *Rat* | *Pig* |

Chapter 6.7 - The Self as Vault in the 12 Chambers 151

# VAULT in Self in the Ox or Goat Chamber

### The Self—Vault

Vault is a major prosperity star from the conservative faction, attracting and storing wealth. It is a characteristic that it will never lack for earthly possessions. This star, at its Brilliant state, would shine on careers having to do with Administration and Management. Professionally, these are perfectionists with very high expectations for themselves and those working for them.

If attached by Fame✿ here, many will hear of their wizardry in managing finance. On the reverse, albeit off-chance, of things going awry, watch out for the Killing Stars. Their influence might make an infamous mockery of his name.

### Career—Mirror

With Mirror in Career, therefore, the pair will provide balanced guidance all around. The Vault-Mirror combination is a suitable candidate for Government Service or Administration in large organizations where their diplomatic skills can be put to good use. Working amongst people is its forte. Therefore, Human Resources, Personnel, Customer Care, or After Sales Service would be suitable.

### Prosperity—Emperor & Opportunity Opposite

With no major stars here, we will look at its opposite chamber where Emperor (which guards finance) and Opportunity (investments, gaming and gambling) reside. Coupled with Vault in Self, we have someone who is cautiously risk-tolerant.

With Fame✿attached, many will hear about him; however, if hemmed in or opposed by the killing stars, The Emperor with Fame, may gain notoriety through misguided channels. This individual must be wary of the Killing Stars (e.g. Ram and Top) or the Obstruction ▪ Catalyst entering the triangle of influence. These will be times of losses so it's important to refrain from any business endeavor in the face of Obstruction in the same house or opposite.

The times to take advantage of the Emperor-Opportunity savvy would be when the strong, supportive stars are around (in the same house, opposite, or at 120°).

# Self: Vault

Career: Mirror    Prosperity: (Emperor & Opportunity)

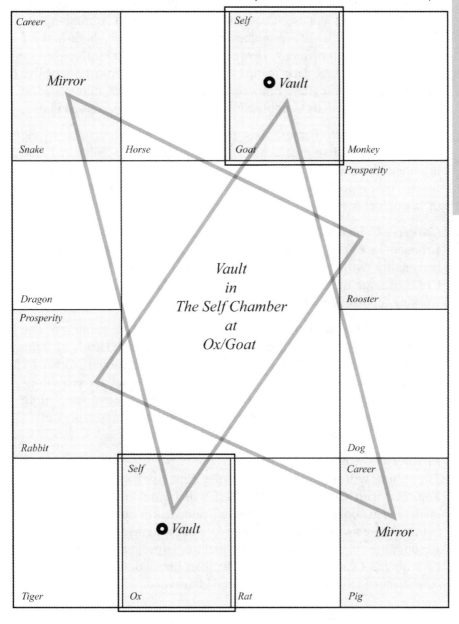

| Career | | Self | |
|---|---|---|---|
| *Mirror* | | ● *Vault* | |
| Snake | Horse | Goat | Monkey |
| | | | Prosperity |
| Dragon | | *Vault in The Self Chamber at Ox/Goat* | Rooster |
| Prosperity | | | |
| Rabbit | | | Dog |
| | Self | | Career |
| | ● *Vault* | | *Mirror* |
| Tiger | Ox | Rat | Pig |

Chapter 6.7 - The Self as Vault in the 12 Chambers 153

# VAULT in Self in the Tiger or Monkey Chamber

**The Self—Vault & Emperor**
We have the two rulers—Emperor from the North and Vault, king of the South—meeting up in Self. This is indicative of respect and admiration. Vault shines on careers having to do with Administration and Management. It produces outstanding and high-ranking administrators and officials. However, at twinkling and influenced by the Killing Stars, its dark features may surface. Otherwise, they live by honesty and integrity. Emperor, if enhanced by the ministers and the lucky stars such as Completion will be propelled to great heights.

An Emperor with Fame✪ has most of the qualities of a strong monarch. With Fame attached, these qualities are enhanced and highlighted. However, if hemmed in or opposed by in Auspicious Stars, The Emperor with Fame may gain notoriety through misguided or fraudulent means.

**Career—Crimson & Mirror**
Crimson in Career is people-oriented. The Vault-Emperor-Crimson personality will, therefore, strengthen the positions of leaders or CEOs of large multinational organizations, who need to be constantly working alongside their sizeable workforce.

Blessed with great tenacity, the Mirror in Career points to one unswerving career throughout the whole working life. Heads of large organizations will not fail to benefit by having the loyal Mirror by their side. Ministers, Secretaries, or anyone who is second-in-command will have this star in their career chart. If free of the Killing Stars, the Vault-Emperor-Crimson-Mirror combination will do well in any exclusive high-end business.

**Prosperity—Commander**
The Vault will restrain some of the Emperor's willfulness here. Together with Commander, the Self will be dealing with financial matters. This does not necessarily indicate wealth because it can also indicate careers in financial control, money management, etc. The surrounding stars will give a fuller picture. However, should he meet up with the Obstruction Catalyst ■, then that would be the time to steer clear of any business or financial endeavors.

# SELF: VAULT & EMPEROR
## CAREER: CRIMSON & MIRROR    PROSPERITY: COMMANDER

| Career | | Self |
|---|---|---|
| *Crimson Mirror* | | ▲ *Vault* ⊙ *Emperor* |
| Snake | Horse | Goat | Monkey |

*Prosperity*

*Commander*

*Dragon*

*Vault in The Self Chamber at Tiger/Monkey*

*Rooster*

*Prosperity*

*Commander*

*Rabbit*

*Dog*

*Self*

○ *Vault*
○ *Emperor*

*Crimson Mirror*

*Tiger*

*Ox*

*Rat*

*Pig*

# VAULT in Self in the Rabbit or Rooster Chamber

**The Self—Vault**
Vault is a major prosperity star from the conservative faction that attracts and stores wealth. It is a characteristic that it will never lack for earthly possessions. Professionally, these are perfectionists with very high expectations for themselves and those working under them.

With Fame ✪ attached, many will hear of his wizardry in managing finance. On the reverse, albeit off-chance, of things going awry, he must watch out for the detrimental stars. Their influence might make an infamous mockery of his name.

The Vault in the Self sector will produce outstanding, high-ranking administrators and officials. However, if hemmed in by the killing stars, its dark nature may surface, and they would become miserly or suspicious. If free of these, they will live by honesty and integrity.

Coupled with General-Commander opposite, this pair of action leaders will factor in creativity and innovation.

**Career—Mirror**
Blessed with great tenacity, the Mirror in Career points to one unswerving career (or employer) throughout the working life. He will rise above the rest. Heads of large organizations will not fail to benefit by having the loyal Mirror by their side. Ministers, Secretaries, and anyone who is second-in- command will have this star in their career chart.

The Vault-Mirror combination denotes well-balanced leadership. A career in Human Resources, Personnel or Customer-Care in large, multi- national businesses or charitable organizations is suitable.

**Prosperity—Crimson & Opportunity Opposite**
Devoid of stars here, we shall look into the opposite chamber where the Crimson-Opportunity pair resides. Vault at Self, however, takes precedence and leads with a cautious approach to investing.

Crimson and Opportunity will introduce medium risk and diversification. If well supported by the Brilliant and Auspicious Stars, e.g., Completion, higher risk-tolerance may be acceptable. In the face of the Killing Stars, the Vault's cautious, well-tried strategies must be followed.

# SELF: VAULT

## CAREER: MIRROR    PROSPERITY: (CRIMSON & OPPORTUNITY)

| Prosperity | | Career | |
|---|---|---|---|
| | | *Mirror* | |
| Snake | Horse | Goat | Monkey |
| | | | Self |
| | | | **✗** *Vault* |
| Dragon | | *Vault*<br>*in*<br>*The Self Chamber*<br>*at*<br>*Rabbit/Rooster* | Rooster |
| Self | | | |
| **▲** *Vault* | | | |
| Rabbit | | | Dog |
| | Career | | Prosperity |
| | *Mirror* | | |
| Tiger | Ox | Rat | Pig |

Chapter 6.7 - The Self as Vault in the 12 Chambers 157

# VAULT in Self in the Dragon or Dog Chamber

## The Self—Vault and Crimson

The conservative Vault gets a dose of dare-devil adventure by the outgoing Crimson. These two apparently opposites are far from being at odds with each other. Vault takes pride in its work. Crimson cares about performance. Both, therefore, will aim towards the same commitment. If helped by the Auspicious Stars, we can expect outstanding achievements.

The Vault will be careful and detailed. It is a characteristic that this person will never lack for earthly possessions.

Crimson is an artist by nature and loves being surrounded by art, music, and theatre. She can deftly weave her influence and reach her goals with dexterity. Also, having to do with blood, with $ attached, the wealthy Crimson is indicative of blood relations coming in with wealth or propitious situations. This sociable star blesses with her prosperity.

## Career—Commander & Mirror

With Commander here, The Self will likely hold down a job that enjoys autonomy and has a say in the running of the business. Mirror duplicates; this indicates working in the printing or mass manufacturing industries. With Commander and Mirror, which stand for action and responsibility, combined with the above, we see a people-oriented career—one in the public sector and service industries, e.g., hotels. If enhanced by Fame✪, The Commander will bring in wealth. With wealth in place, fame follows.

## Prosperity—Emperor

Presided by The Emperor here, The Self will deal with or possess financial prowess. The Emperor is involved with the exclusive niche markets. If well-supported by Pioneer, General and Commander, the four Ministers and Stardust and Delight, a brilliant outcome would be in place. The Vault/Emperor combination in finance will incline toward the conservative. Finance and investing, therefore, will be carefully monitored and include a variety of long- and short-term products and risks.

The traditional values of Vault and Emperor will also be spiced up by Crimson's daring personality. With the right stars in harmony, we will see a shrewd and successful investor.

# SELF: VAULT & CRIMSON
## CAREER: COMMANDER & MIRROR    PROSPERITY: EMPEROR

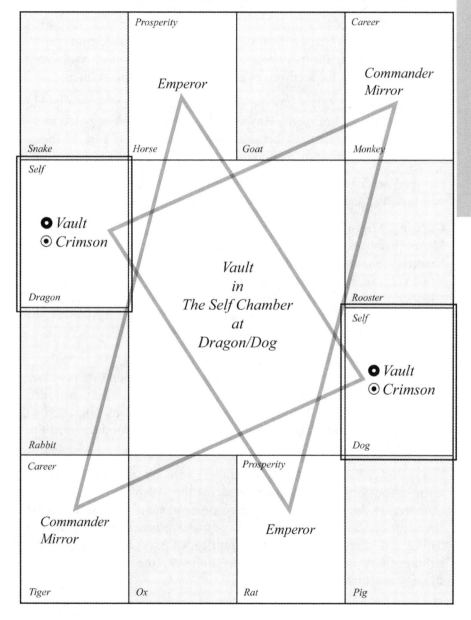

# VAULT in Self in the Snake or Pig Chamber

**The Self—Vault**
Vault is a major prosperity star from the conservative faction, attracting and storing wealth. It is a characteristic that it will never lack for earthly possessions. This star at Brilliant and well supported by the Auspicious Stars will shine on high achievers in administration and management. Professionally, these are perfectionists with very high expectations for themselves and those working under them.

The Vault in the Self sector produces outstanding and high-ranking administrators and officials. However, at twinkling and hemmed in by the Killing Stars, its dark personality may surface. If free of these, they will live by honesty and integrity.

Coupled with Emperor-General opposite, this pair of action leaders will push the usually retiring Vault into the limelight.

**Career—Mirror**
Mirror balances all with its influence in Career, which adds well-balanced support and diplomacy to the working environment. However, this is not one to count the rewards. The larger picture of whether it had makes a difference is more important. A career in human resources, personnel, customer care in large businesses, or charitable organizations is, therefore, suitable.

**Prosperity—Commander & Opportunity Opposite**
Devoid of any major star here, we shall look into its opposite chamber where the Commander-Opportunity pair resides. Vault at Self, however, takes precedence and leads with a cautious approach to investing. The Commander-Opportunity pair will introduce medium risk and diversification.

With Power↗ to boost, Commander will be rewarded for his relentless efforts. If well supported by the Auspicious Stars, e.g., Completion, higher risk-taking may be acceptable. An obstructed■ Opportunity, however, may see it going overboard with being too daring and, therefore, will incur significant losses. In the face of the Killing Stars or the Obstruction Catalyst■, the Vault's cautious strategy must take precedence.

# SELF: VAULT

## CAREER: MIRROR     PROSPERITY: (COMMANDER & OPPORTUNITY)

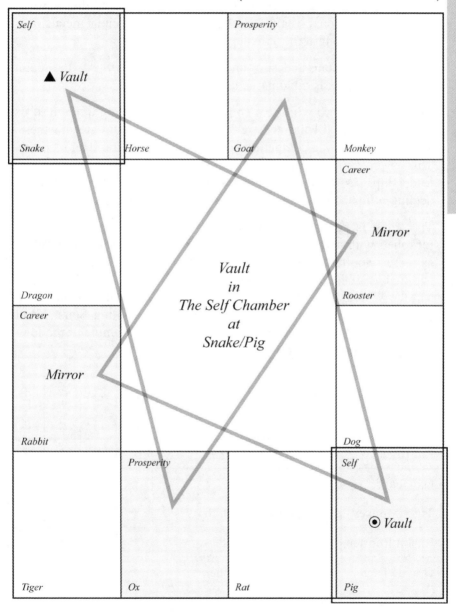

| Self | | Prosperity | |
|------|------|------|------|
| ▲ *Vault* | | | |
| Snake | Horse | Goat | Monkey |

*Vault*
*in*
*The Self Chamber*
*at*
*Snake/Pig*

Career — Mirror (Rooster)

Career (Dragon) — Mirror (Rabbit)

Self (Dog) — ⊙ *Vault* (Pig)

Prosperity (Ox) — Tiger — Rat

# VAULT in the Self House Investment Strategy

**A Serious Investor**

On a par with Emperor, as its name implies, the Vault brings in possessions and wealth. Grounding in every sense of the word, it represents traditional wealth—real estate and the precious metals. It is the epitome of long-term, safe deposits.

At its Brilliant state and surrounded by Auspicious Stars, the Vault leads by example, is diplomatic, and even-tempered.

Because of this, we will see a conviction and following through of its chosen life-path till the end. It stands for loyalty and steadfastness. Vault is above being competitive or striving to be better than its peers. This is professionalism at its peak and many will opt to follow its leadership. As with Emperor, Vault is suitable to be in business dealing in finance or high-end exclusive products and services.

The Vault is not one to show off. However, his following is to be reckoned with as many will seek out this groundedness and wisdom as more important than star quality high profile. A career in Finance is suitable. If helped by nearby Auspicious Stars, e.g. Completion, and the Wealth $ or Power↗ catalyst, it would benefit by being a tad more adventurous. However, in the face of the Killing Stars, Vault should never go against its instincts to be a prime example of the low-risk, long-term, serious investor.

| HOURS | SELF HOUSE | PROSPERITY | LONG | SHORT | DIVERSE | FOCUS |
|---|---|---|---|---|---|---|
| Rat/Horse | Vault/Comdr | Crmsn | ✦ | ✦ | ✦ | ✦ |
| Ox/Goat | Vault | | ✦ | | ✦ | |
| Tiger/Monkey | Vault/Emper | Comdr | ✦ | ✦ | ✦ | ✦ |
| Rabbit/Rooster | Vault | | ✦ | | ✦ | |
| Dragon/Dog | Vault/Crmsn | Emper | ✦ | ✦ | ✦ | ✦ |
| Snake/Pig | Vault | | ✦ | | ✦ | |

# The Self as Moon in the 12 Chambers

| Snake | Horse | Goat | Monkey |
|---|---|---|---|
| Dragon | DEEPAK CHOPRA — ✦ — *In the midst of movement and chaos, keep stillness inside of you* | | Rooster |
| Rabbit | | | Dog |
| Tiger | Ox | Rat | Pig |

## MOON in Self in the Rat or Horse Chamber

**The Self—Moon & Waif**

The helpful Moon shares house with the easy-going Waif. The Wealth part of the Chinese character for Opulence, a Brilliant Moon in The Self sector makes for a wealthy soul. However, in her dark hours, the Moon will take on the benevolence of the Sun. She would then be more concerned with helping humanity (Bill Gates' Life Chart).

Moon-Waif is about being helpful. These rather similar sisters would, therefore, be in supportive roles and would not mind at all if they were doing these for very little and let the others enjoy the accolades.

**Career—Intelligence & Scholar**

At its best, Intelligence shines on steady employees, not entrepreneurs or business owners. As a employee, Intelligence can look to apply all his positive traits to good use.

With Moon-Waif in the Self backed up by Intelligence and Scholar here, this constellation is highly geared toward working tirelessly for social causes without the need or desire for monetary gains. Indeed, their success lies in the selfless support for/within religious groups and charities.

**Prosperity—Sun & Messenger Opposite**

The above constellation shines on the social causes. It is also for this reason that Prosperity is devoid of stars. Borrowing light from the Sun and Messenger opposite, we may see them reigning in public support for these plights. Moon's patience and support remain strong here in Prosperity. These stars are not interested in any money-spinning activities at all. A long-term, safe approach to investments is, therefore, necessary. Moreover, if Sun becomes obstructed■, a betrayal may undermine, resulting in loss. Otherwise, because of money or money invested, there may be a serious blow to the reputation. Be wary of males.

Moon is about the gradual accumulation of wealth. The Auspicious Stars or the Power↗ or Wealth $ catalyst would also improve Moon's wealth. With charity and the social causes being highlighted, any business venture or investment undertaking that would involve risk is strictly not advisable. This would be especially so if Obstruction■ is in tow.

## Self: Moon & Waif

### Career: Intelligence & Scholar

### Prosperity: (Sun & Messenger opposite)

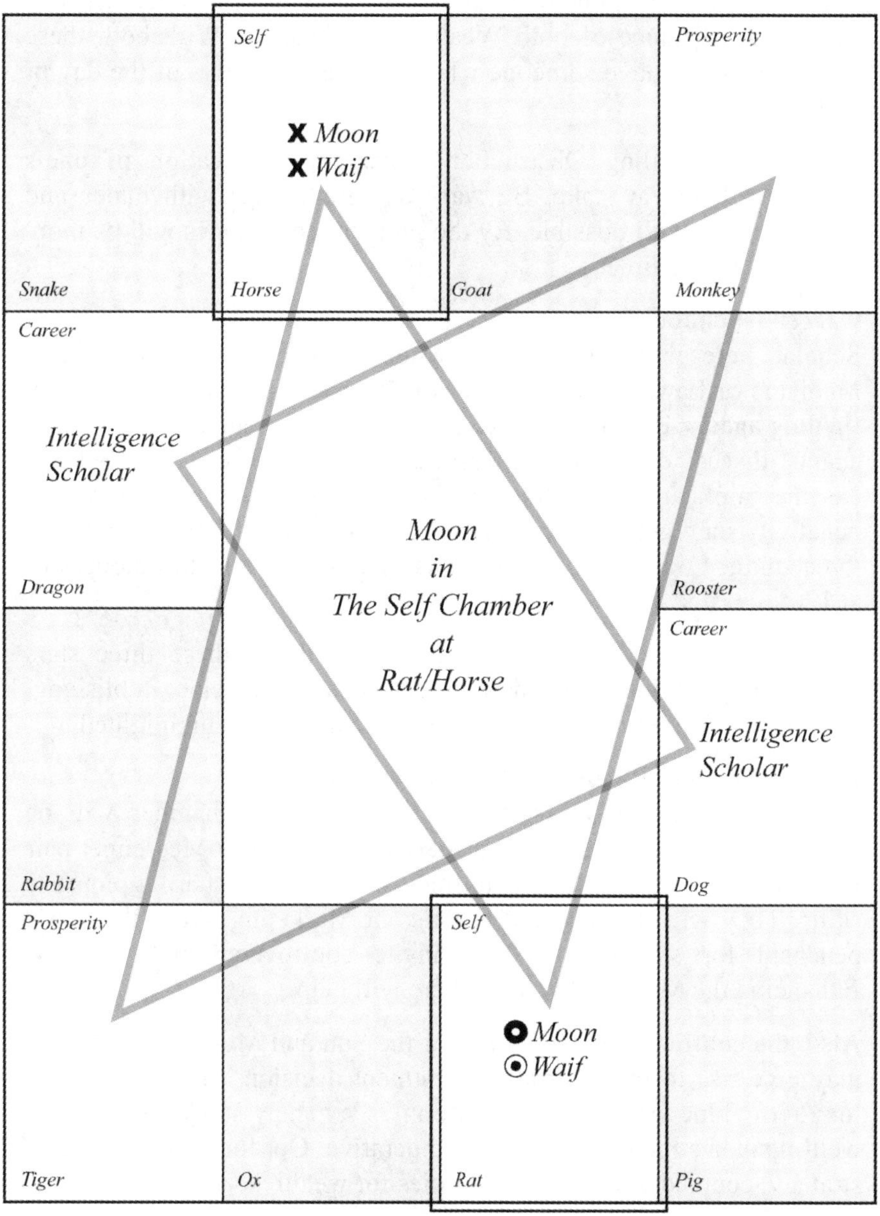
Self
Moon
Waif
Prosperity
Snake
Horse
Goat
Monkey
Career
Intelligence
Scholar
Moon
in
The Self Chamber
at
Rat/Horse
Dragon
Rooster
Career
Intelligence
Scholar
Rabbit
Dog
Prosperity
Self
Moon
Waif
Tiger
Ox
Rat
Pig

## MOON in Self in the Ox or Goat Chamber

**The Self—Moon & Sun**
The wealthy Moon here will be joined by the Sun's elegance. At Ox, the Brilliant Moon and the dark Sun are interrelated and point to the accumulation of wealth. At twinkling in the Goat Chamber, we will be seeing a balance of both Wealth and Elegance. With both these stars at Self, we have someone who will work all hours of the day or night.

The Sun, if trailing Obstruction■, has the implication of one's reputation being at stake. Be wary of partnerships with males and avoid these if at all possible. By the same token, females will be more beneficial at this time.

**Career—Scholar**
Scholar here will pursue lofty career goals, e.g., in fields like Medicine or Law. Scholar with Power↗ especially will be positively fighting against dark forces, e.g., medical workers engaged in fighting against disease or a lawyer litigating injustice. Power to the Scholar has the implication of adding weight to Scholar's traits. However, negativity may get enhanced. Take these in stride. They are not life-threatening. Look for redeeming qualities in the reflecting houses or at 120°.

With the Sun and Moon in Self, we would see these three stars cooperating in Education and the Social causes, Medicine, Publishing, or Broadcasting. Management and Administration are highlighted.

**Prosperity—Intelligence & Messenger Opposite**
With the Moon/Sun in Ox/Goat, the Prosperity Chamber will be devoid of any major star. At opposite, the Intelligence-Messenger pair indicates outstanding rhetoric abilities, coupled with sharp diplomatic skills. They will find success in Sales or Marketing. Alas, the pair's penchant for showing off will invite controversy and jealousy. Enhancing the Moon's discretion here will help.

Also, the conflicting personalities of the Sun and Moon, both in Self, may give rise to rather erratic investment decisions. The Sun favors long-term blue chips whereas Moon is a penny-stock investor. A well-planned strategy is therefore imperative. Opt for Sun's long-term strategy, coupled with Moon's abilities for wealth accumulation.

# Self: Moon & Sun
## Career: Scholar
## Prosperity: (Intelligence & Messenger opposite)

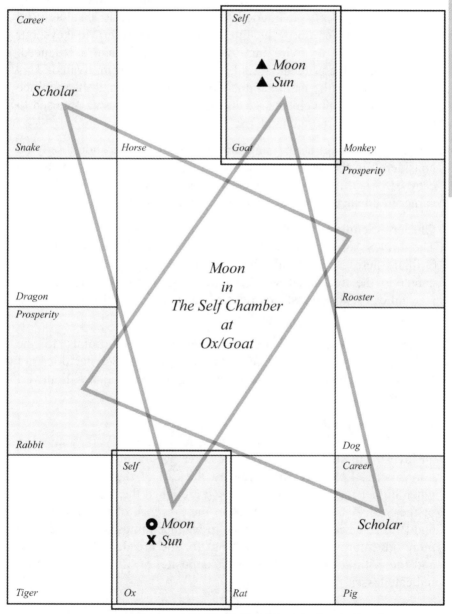

Career

Self

▲ *Moon*
▲ *Sun*

*Scholar*

Snake | Horse | Goat | Monkey

Prosperity

*Moon*
*in*
*The Self Chamber*
*at*
*Ox/Goat*

Dragon | Rooster

Prosperity

Rabbit | Dog

Self | Career

O *Moon*
X *Sun*

*Scholar*

Tiger | Ox | Rat | Pig

Chapter 6.8 - The Self as Moon in the 12 Chambers 167

# MOON in Self in the Tiger or Monkey Chamber

## The Self—Moon & Intelligence
A twinkling moon at these hours stands for care and support. The Moon-Intelligence combination will make for an unsullied servitude towards her fellowmen. However, the pair may make us overly careful, even miserly. It is good to remember there is absolutely no harm in a balanced portfolio. Intelligence at the Tiger/Monkey hour would be Bright or twinkling. As such, he will have a balanced, strong mind which breeds a kind leader who is also motivated. This star is a strategist by nature and is mechanically inclined. Its presence indicates lateral movements—a change of job or duties as opposed to moving up the corporate ladder.

Investments should be medium/low risk. Higher risks should only be considered in the presence of the Auspicious Stars and the Wealth $ catalyst. Also, if the Power↗ catalyst becomes attached to Moon, a career in Finance, Equity, or Money Management may be considered.

## Career—Scholar
The lofty Scholar is a friendly, auspicious star on the whole and is at Brilliant here. Being highly disciplined, the Self may be drawn to a career in the traditional services—Medicine, Law or Science. This star indicates slow but steady development, which is also what Moon is about.

Therefore, Patience will be the keyword, which points to the Judiciary, Religious, or Social services. However, Scholar does not like being in business or money-making ventures and will thwart these projects.

## Prosperity—Waif
Contented by nature, The Waif is at twinkling here. Waif is suited to an investment strategy which reflects her personality: long term and not volatile. Low risk strategies are the call of the day. The times when higher risk-taking can be placed are when the Auspicious Stars or the $ or ↗ Catalysts come in. In the presence of a positive Waif and Bright, positive stars, it is time to balance things out and be a tad more adventurous. Always watch out for the dreaded Obstruction ■ and the Killing Stars in Prosperity, opposite, or 120°. These would indicate losses.

# SELF: MOON & INTELLIGENCE
## CAREER: CRIMSON & MIRROR     PROSPERITY: COMMANDER

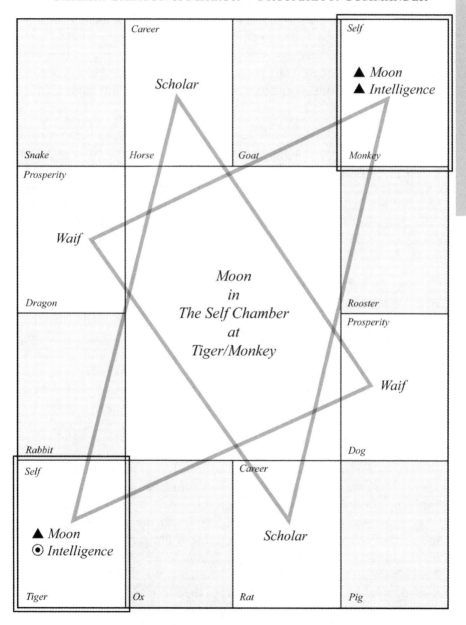

| | Career | | Self |
|---|---|---|---|
| | *Scholar* | | ▲ *Moon* ▲ *Intelligence* |
| Snake | Horse | Goat | Monkey |
| Prosperity | | | |
| *Waif* | | *Moon in The Self Chamber at Tiger/Monkey* | |
| Dragon | | | Rooster / Prosperity |
| | | | *Waif* |
| Rabbit | | | Dog |
| Self | | Career | |
| ▲ *Moon* ◉ *Intelligence* | | *Scholar* | |
| Tiger | Ox | Rat | Pig |

# MOON in Self in the Rabbit or Rooster Chamber

**The Self—Moon**
The Moon in Self will be cooperative, helpful, and supportive of others. However, if Moon becomes obstructed■, do not be involved with investments (other than managing other people's money) at this time. With the Moon veiled in dark energy, it would be a good idea to go over unanswered questions once more because they may hide a yet unnoticed critical error. Litigation will be high on the agenda for this period. Avoid business associations with females, who may be the instigators.

With the Waif opposite, we'll see enjoyment here and not too much striving towards goal achievement. Surprisingly, the Killing Stars would prod her on. Their fiery nature will put some pizzazz into her complacency and prod her towards achievement and success! The Moon-Waif pair, being similar, would, therefore, be engaging themselves in supportive roles and would not mind at all if they were doing these for very little. They'd also let the others enjoy the limelight or accolades.

**Career—Scholar**
With Waif-Moon in the Self, backed up by Scholar here, this constellation would be geared towards working tirelessly for the social causes without the need or desire for monetary gains. Indeed, their success would lie in the selfless dedication within religious groups and charities. It should be remembered that Scholar does not bode well for businesses or money-making ventures and will thwart these projects. If attached by Power↗, Scholar's traits would be enhanced.

**Prosperity—Sun**
Sun stands for benevolence and the betterment of humankind without desire for reward. It is also not one to count the small change. The Sun's position in investments, therefore, will be far-reaching and long-range, and this will take precedence over the Moon's hesitancy and penny- counting. This is all very fine if the surrounding stars are auspicious and supportive, including the presence of the Wealth $ and Power↗ Catalysts and Completion. Alternatively, the Killing Stars, if around, would be indication to revert to the Moon's cautious policies.

# SELF: MOON
## CAREER: SCHOLAR    PROSPERITY: SUN

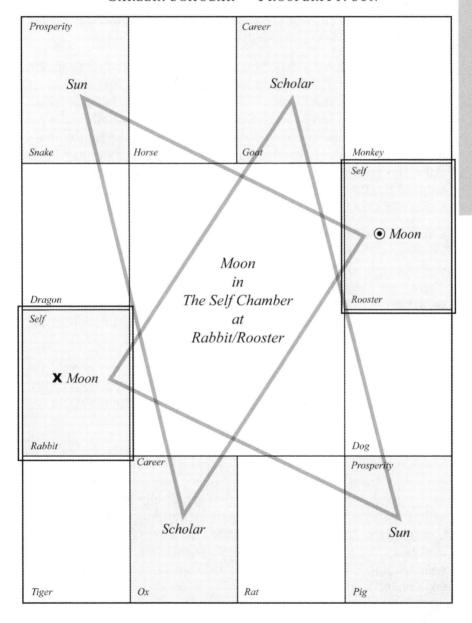

| Prosperity<br><br>*Sun*<br><br>Snake | Horse | Career<br><br>*Scholar*<br><br>Goat | Monkey |
|---|---|---|---|
| Dragon | | Moon<br>*in*<br>*The Self Chamber*<br>*at*<br>*Rabbit/Rooster* | Self<br><br>⊙ *Moon*<br><br>Rooster |
| Self<br><br>✗ *Moon*<br><br>Rabbit | Career<br><br>*Scholar*<br><br>Ox | Rat | Dog |
| Tiger | | | Prosperity<br><br>*Sun*<br><br>Pig |

# MOON in Self in the Dragon or Dog Chamber

**The Self—Moon**

A lone Moon at this chamber will be retiring and shy away from the limelight. They'd prefer to be quietly working in the background caring for others. Therefore, many will find this an admirable quality and will not hesitate to assist with support and praise.

At opposite, we have a dark Sun, which would invite in recognition for any good work it does—and more often than not, this would come in the form of wealth. A dark Sun would have the ability to amass great wealth. The Sun-Moon pair can, therefore, also find wealth for themselves in their social causes. The Sun also stands for one's reputation. If trailing Obstruction ■, one's good name may be at stake. Be especially wary of partnerships with males. Avoid these if at all possible. By the same token, females would be more beneficial to you at this time.

**Career—Waif & Scholar**

Together with the Waif and Scholar here, the trio will form a strong constellation, which will shine brilliantly on their benevolent projects. These people will best perform in large, well-established organizations managing projects having to do with scientific or medical advancements. Alternatively, the promotion of such in the publishing or broadcasting fields will also be suitable.

It should be remembered that Scholar does not bode well for businesses or money-making ventures and will thwart these projects. If attached by the Power↗ catalyst, Scholar's traits would be enhanced.

**Prosperity—Intelligence**

The Moon will always be careful, choosing to go the "safe" way in any investments. However, because of the presence of Intelligence here, we will see the Moon-self becoming radically more adventurous and speculative. This would be well if the Auspicious Stars and Catalysts are around, e.g., Completion or Power↗ and Wealth $. However, the Killing stars will always strike at the riskier undertakings. They are, therefore, indicative for safe ventures or taking No Position for the moment.

# SELF: MOON

## CAREER: WAIF & SCHOLAR    PROSPERITY: INTELLIGENCE

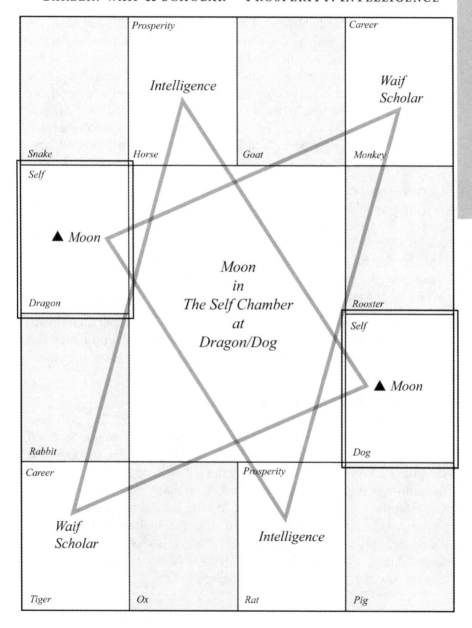

MOON IN SELF

Chapter 6.8 - The Self as Moon in the 12 Chambers 173

# MOON in Self in the Snake or Pig Chamber

## The Self—Moon
A lone Moon at this chamber will be retiring, and shying away from the limelight. They'd prefer to be quietly working away in the background helping others. Therefore, many will find this an admirable quality and will not hesitate to provide support and praise for Moon's many social causes. At opposite, Intelligence lends strength by providing drive and a fair amount of creativity. The Moon-Intelligence combination will make for an unsullied servitude towards her fellowmen. When it comes to investing, however, the pair may become overly careful, even miserly. It is well to remember that there is absolutely no harm in a balanced portfolio with sound risk-management in place.

## Career—Sun & Scholar
The Sun-Scholar pair indicates benevolence and justice, pointing to careers in Law and Judicial system, Law-making, Religious, and Social Orders. It should be remembered that Scholar does not bode well for businesses and any moneymaking venture and will thwart these projects. If attached by the Power↗ catalyst, Scholar's traits would be enhanced.

If trailing Obstruction, the Sun∎ indicates one's reputation—your good name may be at stake. Be wary of partnerships with males and avoid these if at all possible. By the same token, females will be more beneficial to you at these times.

## Prosperity—Waif & Messenger Opposite
In investments, Moon's basic careful and wise personality will take precedence here, as this chamber is devoid of any major star. Of interest, is the Waif-Messenger pair at opposite. In its financial dealings, therefore, this star combination will opt for the low- to medium-risk investments. With the Auspicious Stars around, plus Completion and the Power↗ or the Wealth $ catalyst, it may be well to be a tad more adventurous and aim for higher, faster returns. However, the Killing Stars will always strike at the riskier undertakings. They are, therefore, indicative for taking No Position or very low risks until the moment passes.

# SELF: MOON
## CAREER: SUN & SCHOLAR
### PROSPERITY: (WAIF & MESSENGER OPPOSITE)

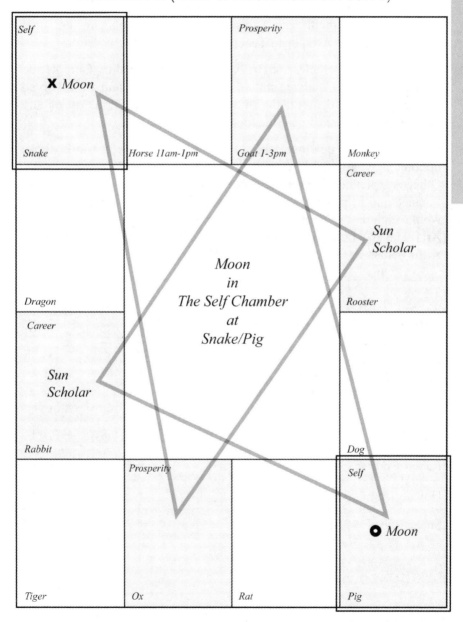

| | | | |
|---|---|---|---|
| *Self*<br><br>**X** *Moon*<br><br>*Snake* | *Horse 11am-1pm* | *Prosperity*<br><br><br>*Goat 1-3pm* | *Monkey* |
| *Dragon*<br>*Career* | *Moon*<br>*in*<br>*The Self Chamber*<br>*at*<br>*Snake/Pig* | | *Career*<br><br>*Sun*<br>*Scholar*<br><br>*Rooster* |
| *Career*<br><br>*Sun*<br>*Scholar*<br><br>*Rabbit* | | | *Dog* |
| *Tiger* | *Prosperity*<br><br><br>*Ox* | *Rat* | *Self*<br><br>**O** *Moon*<br><br>*Pig* |

Chapter 6.8 - The Self as Moon in the 12 Chambers 175

# MOON in the Self House Investment Strategy

**Steady Accumulation of Wealth**

Being Yin, Moon signifies stillness and is strongest during the dark hours the night. It will be providing support quietly in the background and doesn't mind repetitive, insignificant tasks at all. We will, therefore, find them as Administrative Assistants or Personal Secretaries, in the Arts, or in Teaching and Nursing.

A wealth star nonetheless, a Brilliant Moon, if helped by Completion or the Wealth $ Catalyst, should go into business and be involved with anything to do with the "Earth" element, i.e., Property or any kind of farming (getting abundance from the land).

In her financial dealings, the Moon would incline towards those options that would allow her to "steadily accumulate her wealth. Other Auspicious Stars around her would always fan her interest in Finance and help her make riskier, more lucrative investments. These would include the Fame ✿ and Power ↗ Catalysts, the Literary and Arts, and the Left and Right Ministers. This would bode well if the Killing Stars or Obstruction Catalyst ■ were not in sight.

| HOURS | SELF HOUSE | PROSPERITY | LONG | SHORT | DIVERSE | FOCUS |
|---|---|---|---|---|---|---|
| Rat/Horse | Moon/Waif | | ✦ | | ✦ | |
| Ox/Goat | Moon/Sun | | ✦ | | ✦ | |
| Tiger/Monkey | Moon/Intel | Waif | ✦ | ✦ | ✦ | ✦ |
| Rabbit/Rooster | Moon | Sun | ✦ | | ✦ | |
| Dragon/Dog | Moon | Intel | ✦ | ✦ | ✦ | ✦ |
| Snake/Pig | Moon | | ✦ | | ✦ | |

# The Self as Opportunity in the 12 Chambers

| | | | |
|---|---|---|---|
| | | | |
| Snake | Horse | Goat | Monkey |
| Dragon | W. SOMERSET MAUGHAM ✦ The ladder of | | Rooster |
| Rabbit | SUCCESS is best climbed by stepping on the rungs of Opportunity | | Dog |
| Tiger | Ox | Rat | Pig |

OPPORTUNITY IN SELF

# OPPORTUNITY in Self in the Rat or Horse Chamber

## The Self—Opportunity

"Life's made to be enjoyed" is Opportunity's motto, for Opportunity is concerned with physical pleasures. He is, therefore, multi-talented and often pulled in all directions by his many interests. This sensuality will draw him to be involved with fine dining, wines, and the nightlife. Entertainment, the performing arts, travel, anything that's pleasurable will be twirled by Opportunity.

Opportunity here will benefit with having Emperor at its opposite, giving up some of its flamboyance for the Emperor's stability and wisdom. Then it will become responsible and wise in its decision-making. Added to Opportunity's flair and creativity, if aided by the Auspicious Stars, we will be seeing exciting and new leadership.

## Career—General

In cooperation with General here in Career, its actions are goal-oriented instead of ego-oriented. The General brushes away obstacles and will strive towards its goals with dexterity. Such strong leadership points to successes in a wide range of glamorous businesses having to do with fine dining, lifestyle, hotel, or travel.

## Prosperity—Pioneer

With the action-packed Pioneer here, together with the gambling-prone Opportunity in Self, chances for speculations may become excessively high. The presence of the Killing Stars (Spinning Top, Ram, Void and Punishment) may, therefore, bring in the win-all-lose-all sequence of events. This calls for extra caution or taking no positions at all until such times pass.

Backed by Emperor, the Opportunity-General-Pioneer formation is a tremendously powerful triangle of stars. This investor will go far and will not be taking a back seat when it comes to wealth management. If helped by the Auspicious Stars (such as Completion) and the Power↗ and Wealth $ Catalysts, Emperor reflecting the Self, will see to it that any highly diversified and complicated trades will be done with level-headed professionalism.

# SELF: OPPORTUNITY

## CAREER: GENERAL    PROSPERITY: PIONEER

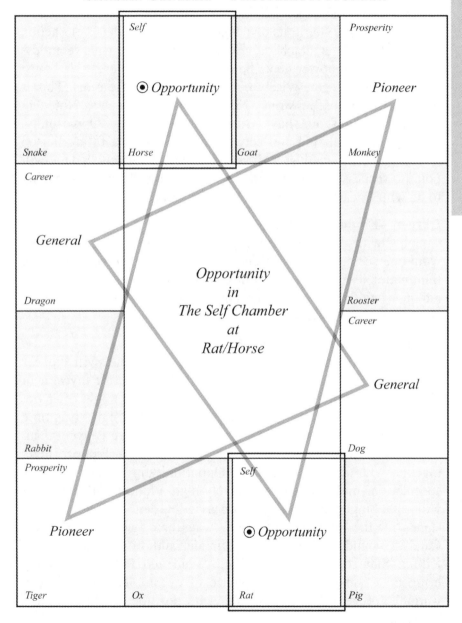

Chapter 6.9 - The Self as Opportunity in the 12 Chambers 179

# OPPORTUNITY in Self in the Ox or Goat Chamber

**The Self—Opportunity & Commander**

The Opportunist here joins forces with the action-packed Commander whose desires for fame and success are, therefore, realized through skill, socializing, and hard work.

A prosperous star in its own right, the Commander is our action hero. If Power↗ is attached, he will be rewarded for his relentless efforts. Self-empowerment here is the key word. He must remember to delegate wisely but never let go of the reins. This is the sign for success in Money Management and Finance. Note that Commander must not have Obstruction ■ trailing. Opportunity, the star for socializing and networking, will form a fitting liaison with the Wealth catalyst $ should this become attached. This will point to successes in a wide range of glamorous businesses, having to do with fine dining, lifestyle, hotel, or travel.

**Career—Emperor & General**

Coupled with the Emperor-General pair in the Career house, we would be seeing decisive leadership or management skills in large multinational financial institutions. The Auspicious Stars would aid in a swift rise up the corporate ladder or help us become successful business leaders.

**Prosperity—Crimson & Pioneer**

The delightfully diversified Crimson is joined by the swift Pioneer here. Together these two may be just too daring on the investment front. In their enthusiasm to jump right in, the pair might often get their fingers burnt for lack of preparation and foresight. It is time to put the brakes on at this point and opt for a more conventional, safer investment mode. With the action-packed Pioneer here, together with the gambling-prone Opportunity in Self, chances for speculations may become excessively high. Pioneer with Power ↗ will see a bigger role to play or a heavier burden. The Pioneer also stands for the introduction of new ways or concepts. The Power Catalyst would, therefore, give him the authority to do so. The Killing Stars (Spinning Top, Ram, Void and Punishment) may bring in a win-all-lose-all sequence of events. This would be a warning for very low risk or taking no position at all until such times pass.

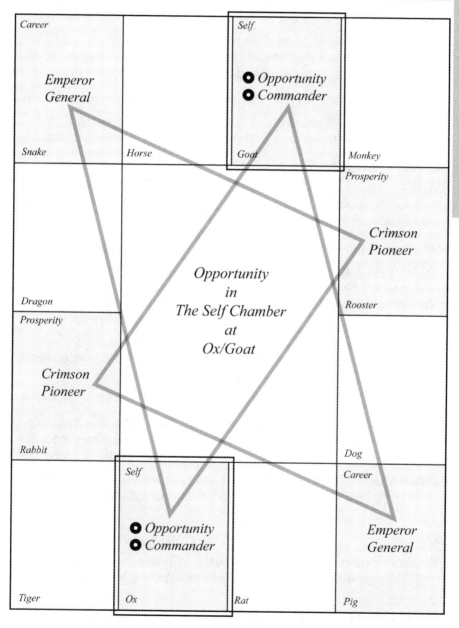

# SELF: OPPORTUNITY & COMMANDER
## CAREER: EMPEROR & GENERAL   PROSPERITY: CRIMSON & PIONEER

| | | | |
|---|---|---|---|
| *Career*<br><br>*Emperor<br>General*<br><br>Snake | *Horse* | *Self*<br><br>○ *Opportunity*<br>○ *Commander*<br><br>Goat | Monkey |
| *Dragon* | | *Opportunity<br>in<br>The Self Chamber<br>at<br>Ox/Goat* | *Prosperity*<br><br>*Crimson<br>Pioneer*<br><br>Rooster |
| *Prosperity*<br><br>*Crimson<br>Pioneer*<br><br>Rabbit | | | Dog |
| *Tiger* | *Self*<br><br>○ *Opportunity*<br>○ *Commander*<br><br>Ox | Rat | *Career*<br><br>*Emperor<br>General*<br><br>Pig |

Chapter 6.9 - The Self as Opportunity in the 12 Chambers 181

# OPPORTUNITY in Self in the Tiger or Monkey Chamber

**The Self—Opportunity**

"Life's made to be enjoyed" is Opportunity's motto; thus, Opportunity is concerned with Physical pleasures. He is multi-talented and often pulled in all directions by his many interests. This sensuality will draw him to be involved with fine dining, wines, and the nightlife. entertainment, the performing arts, travel, and anything that's pleasurable will be twirled by Opportunity.

At its opposite is Crimson. Driven by performance, Crimson will add pizzazz with confidence and a dynamic approach to life to the liaison and push the pair to become high flyers in its chosen field.

**Career—General**

With the right stars (e.g. Completion and the Power↗, Fame✿and Wealth $ Catalysts) the Opportunity-Crimson pair will do famously well in the entertainment or Acting arena.

Whether male or female, the General in Career sector is a sure indicator of a brilliant career. This is a person with great tenacity who will set goals and overcome any obstacle in order to get there. Not unlike Pioneer, General will have his share of turbulence (to a slightly lesser degree), for both immediately respond to the beckoning of adventure, even danger. This star in the Career sector will leave a mark of outstanding achievements in core management in large multinational corporations.

**Prosperity—Pioneer**

With the action-packed Pioneer here, together with the gambling-prone Opportunity in Self, chances for speculations may become excessively high. The Killing Stars (Spinning Top, Ram, Void and Punishment) may, therefore, bring in the win-all-lose-all sequence of events. This would call for extra caution or taking no position at all until such times pass.

Reflected by the Emperor-Mirror pair, the Opportunity-General-Pioneer formation is a tremendously powerful triangle of stars. This investor will go far and will not be taking a back seat when it comes to wealth management. In any investment situation, follow the level-headed professionalism of Emperor and Mirror.

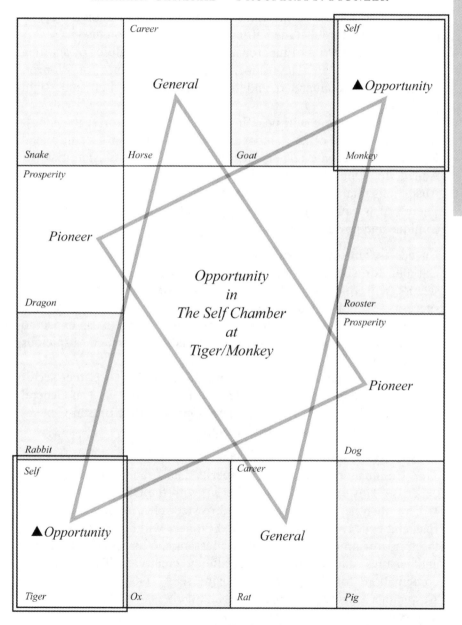

## OPPORTUNITY in Self in the Rabbit or Rooster Chamber

**The Self—Opportunity & Emperor**

Opportunity relishes every bit the interest he creates in the seemingly never-ending rounds of meetings. However, with brightness only at twinkling, take care that the Killing Stars do not turn on his vices.

Also here, a Bright Emperor has most of the qualities of a strong monarch. In aid of The Emperor, are the presence of Pioneer, General, and Commander, and preferably also his Left and Right Ministers.

Opportunity here will benefit with having Emperor at its side. It will eschew some of its flamboyance for the Emperor's stability and wisdom, and become responsible and wise in its decision-making. Added to Opportunity's flair and creativity, if aided by the Auspicious Stars, we will be seeing exciting and new leadership. There's also support from Pioneer, General and Commander, forming a unique and powerful triangle.

**Career—Crimson & General**

Cut out for social activities, those with Crimson in their Career sectors will find themselves basking in attention and, ultimately, success. Look for situations that require constant communication/dealings with the opposite sex. Crimson can expect to shine if found in the Career sector, especially with other Auspicious Stars around.

Whether male or female, the General in the Self or Career sector is an indicator of a powerful leader and brilliant career. The General empowers the Career Sector. The Opportunity-Crimson-General liaison denotes high-profile leadership.

**Prosperity—Commander & Pioneer**

The Commander, being a prosperity star, commands financial expertise. However, should he meet up with the Obstruction Catalyst ■ here, then he must be forewarned to steer clear of any business or financial endeavors. Opportunity and Pioneer will benefit with having the Emperor around. This regal star lessens the throes of speculation and ensures stability without sacrificing creativity. This is a star-combination for high profile businesses. The presence of the Auspicious Stars (e.g., Completion) and the $ or ↗ Catalysts will also lend strength.

# SELF: OPPORTUNITY & EMPEROR
## CAREER: CRIMSON & GENERAL
### PROSPERITY: COMMANDER & PIONEER

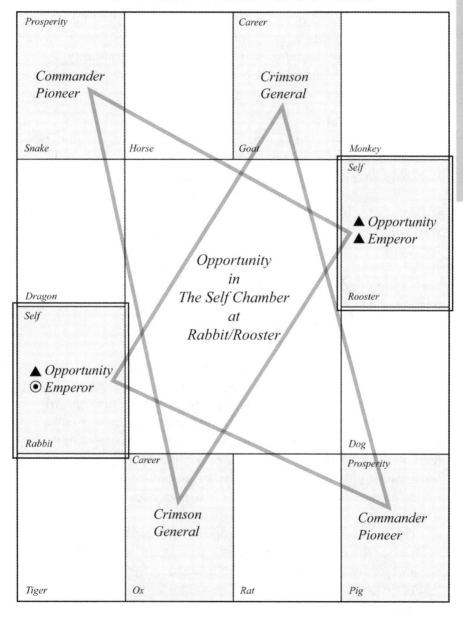

# OPPORTUNITY in Self in the Dragon or Dog Chamber

**The Self—Opportunity**

"Life's made to be enjoyed" is Opportunity's motto, so Opportunity is concerned with Physical pleasures. He is multi-talented and often pulled in all directions by his many interests. This sensuality will draw him to be involved with fine dining, wines, and the nightlife. entertainment, the performing arts, travel, anything that's pleasurable will be twirled by Opportunity. At its opposite is Commander. This pair of dynamic wealth stars will be cut out for business leadership.

**Career—General**

With the right stars (e.g. Completion and the Power↗, Fame✪and Wealth $ Catalysts), the Opportunity-Crimson pair will do famously well in the entertainment or Acting arena.

Whether male or female, the General in Career sector is a sure indicator of a brilliant career. This is a person with great tenacity, who will set goals and overcome any obstacle in order to get there. Not unlike Pioneer, General will have his share of turbulence (to a slightly lesser degree), for both immediately respond to the beckoning of adventure, even danger. This star in the Career sector will leave a mark of outstanding achievements in core management in large multinational corporations.

**Prosperity—Pioneer**

Supporting and protecting the Emperor, this star fighter is constantly in the thick of battle. He charges forward with total disregard for his own safety, fighting for, and protecting his turf.

The Pioneer, one of the tri-star formation (the other two being Opportunity and General), stands for great changes, uprooting, and tearing down. The period that Pioneer appears will be a time for the greatest upheavals with life-shattering consequences. This will be an exceedingly creative leader when it comes to finding his fortunes.

The Killing Stars (Spinning Top, Ram, Void and Punishment) or the Obstruction ■ Catalyst may bring in a win-all-lose-all sequence of events. This would be a warning for very low risk or taking no position at all until such times pass.

# SELF: OPPORTUNITY
## CAREER: GENERAL    PROSPERITY: PIONEER

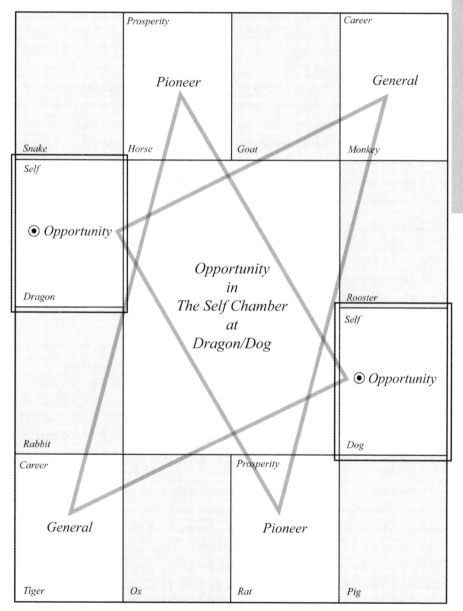

# OPPORTUNITY in Self in the Snake or Pig Chamber

**The Self—Opportunity and Crimson**

Opportunity is joined by Crimson with Wealth. With both these popular and people-oriented stars in Self, we are seeing tremendous attraction surrounding them. If anyone, they would have the power to pull in the crowd. Very often, movie stars, actors, and entertainers, as well as politicians will have this star combination. Adding to this, with Opportunity at play here, we will see them milling about in rather complicated circumstance.

Crimson is an artist by nature and loves being surrounded by art, music, and theatre. She can deftly weave her influence and reach her goals with dexterity. Also, having to do with blood, Crimson with $ attached indicates close relations bringing in wealth or propitious situations. This sociable star blesses with her prosperity.

**Career—Commander and General**

The Commander brings in wealth. With wealth in place, Fame✧will follow. Commander is joined by General here. These are hardworking, pioneering people who will forge ahead of the pack with strategy and courage. This star combination indicates lucrative career success.

**Prosperity—Emperor and Pioneer**

Here we have Emperor and Pioneer. The Crimson-Opportunity star combination brings out the gambler in us. In investing, therefore, we will see them as high risk-takers. Should these come face to face with the killing stars (Ram or Top) or the Obstruction Catalyst■, the roller-coaster ride is just not worth it! It is fortunate, therefore, that we see the Brilliant Emperor, aided by Pioneer in Prosperity.

Pioneer will be juggling different roles. If aided by Power↗, we are seeing a bigger role to play or a heavier burden in the House this star rests in. The Pioneer also stands for the introduction of new ways or concepts. The Power Catalyst here will give him the authority to do so. The level-headed Emperor quells Opportunity's tendency to gamble and ensures shrewdness in their investment strategy. Adopting a conservative strategy in investments would work for Crimson-Opportunity in Self.

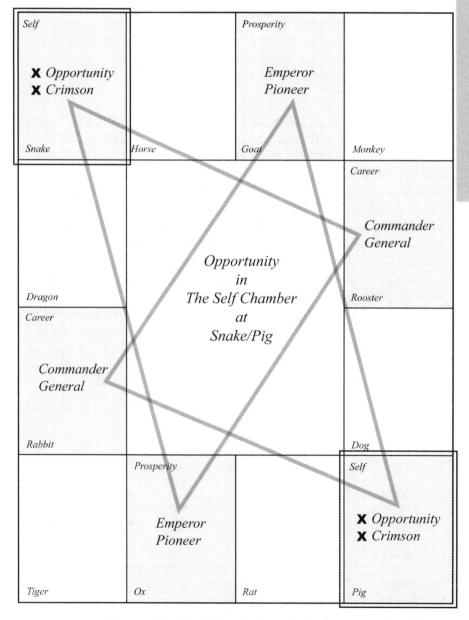

# SELF: OPPORTUNITY & CRIMSON
## CAREER: COMMANDER & GENERAL
## PROSPERITY: EMPEROR & PIONEER

# OPPORTUNITY in the Self House Investment Strategy

## The Need to Avoid Speculation

Being multi-talented, Opportunity is often pulled in all directions. Fine dining, wines, the nightlife, entertainment, the performing arts, travel, anything that's pleasurable will be twirled by Opportunity. His chameleon-like ability to flow with the circumstance is legendary and is happiest working his playground that's forever evolving. He does not like to operate alone and will look for support from multi-talented staffers. He is, therefore, made out to be a business leader in any of the above fields.

At the outset, it should be noted that Opportunity is not a wealth star. For Opportunity, therefore, the Wealth $ catalyst alone does not mean huge winnings—only that huge amounts of money will be changing hands. In their financial dealings, The Gambler would be Opportunity's middle name. We would see them playing the high-risk-high-return markets and at the same time instigating borrowings or margins to up the stakes. This is a speculative investor who can tolerate tremendous risk and volatility. If the Auspicious Stars are gathered (in the same house, opposite, or at 120°) plus Completion and Wealth $, we may see them strike huge winnings. Conversely, the Killing Stars will deal the reverse. It is, therefore, of utmost importance for Opportunity to learn and practice risk management and Opportunity individuals must quell their appetite for speculation.

| HOURS | SELF HOUSE | PROSPERITY | LONG | SHORT | DIVERSE | FOCUS |
|---|---|---|---|---|---|---|
| Rat/Horse | Oppor | Pneer | ✦ | | ✦ | |
| Ox/Goat | Oppor/Comdr | Pneer/Crmsn | ✦ | ✦ | ✦ | ✦ |
| Tiger/Monkey | Oppor | Pneer | ✦ | | ✦ | |
| Rabbit/Rooster | Oppor/Emper | Pneer/Comdr | ✦ | ✦ | ✦ | ✦ |
| Dragon/Dog | Oppor | Pneer | ✦ | | ✦ | |
| Snake/Pig | Oppor/Crmsn | Pneer/Emper | ✦ | ✦ | ✦ | ✦ |

CHAPTER 6.10

# The Self as Messenger in the 12 Chambers

| | | | |
|---|---|---|---|
| Snake | Horse | Goat | Monkey |
| Dragon | CHRISTOPHER MORLEY ✦ There's no secret about SUCCESS. Did you ever know a successful man who didn't tell you about it? | | Rooster |
| Rabbit | | | Dog |
| Tiger | Ox | Rat | Pig |

191

# MESSENGER in Self in the Rat or Horse Chamber

## The Self—Messenger

The most articulate of the stars, Messenger dominates the Self here. True to its name, at its strongest and most positive it will eloquently deliver its ideas with a passion and conviction able to move mountains.

Addressing an audience with or without preparation is second-nature. The Messenger uses its voice in any capacity to get its message across. At Brilliant and surrounded by Auspicious Stars or the Power↗, Wealth $, or Fame✿ Catalysts, we will see them attaining mega-star status and success through using the voice.

## Career—Sun

With Sun in Career, this indicates a career associated with light, lighting, the transmission and communication fields, as well as the transportation business.

The Messenger-Sun partnership would, therefore, see the pair tirelessly campaigning for social issues. These are beacons of light, shining towards a brighter, happier tomorrow. We will see the pair engaging in education, The Arts, social work, development training, etc.

## Prosperity—Waif & Scholar Opposite

Being devoid of any major star in this chamber, Messenger's overall financial savvy will dominate here. Playing the markets is one of its many interests. Messenger will be entering its many trades into its diversified portfolio. Its views on finance are like those of professional traders—quick and precise.

However, the Waif-Scholar pair is housed opposite, which will add caution. In its financial dealings, therefore, this star combination will opt for the low to medium risk investments.

With the Auspicious Stars around (Completion and the Power↗ and Wealth $ Catalysts), it may be well to be a tad more adventurous and aim for higher, faster returns.

However, the Killing Stars will always strike at the riskier undertakings. They are, therefore, indicative that the individual should take very low risks or no position at all for the moment.

# SELF: MESSENGER
## CAREER: SUN
### PROSPERITY: (WAIF & SCHOLAR OPPOSITE)

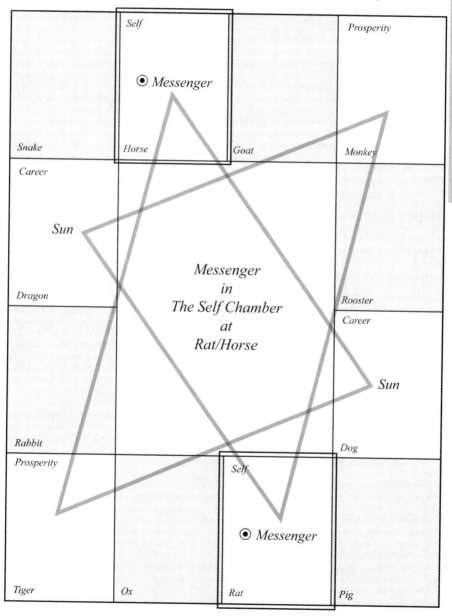

6.10 The Self as Messenger in the 12 Chambers 193

# MESSENGER in Self in the Ox or Goat Chamber

## The Self—Messenger & Waif
In a sector that is also filled with several Auspicious Stars, the Messenger, if attached with Wealth $, will make its fortunes via the voice. However, any surrounding Killing star will strip away any splendor and The Messenger with ■will subsequently strike a loss through slander or litigation.

With enjoyment being the order of the day for Waif when teamed up with Messenger, the propagator of news or knowledge, we have the pair in Promotion or Marketing. The wide range of products would fall under the umbrella of lifestyle and fine dining.

## Career—Intelligence
Intelligence stands for wide-ranging interests. In alignment with Messenger and Waif, we would see these promoting international products and services in the art of fine living. Careers would include Education, Social Work, The Arts & entertainment, Public Relations, or Marketing the latest technologies of such. Employment in any large concerns, including government bodies, would be suitable.

## Prosperity—Sun & Scholar Opposite
With Messenger in Self, we would see more thoughts and questions that need to be answered before taking any positions in trading matters. Instead of the happy-go-lucky Waif Self, we would see the Messenger's slightly more serious, thoughtful side emerging. This would be the dominant personality, especially since the Prosperity Chamber is devoid of stars. With Sun and Scholar reflecting Prosperity, these two benevolent stars would rather see us engaging in the social issues. Therefore, this constellation will not shine on business deals or money-making ventures.

If anything, long-term savings plans would be the order of the day. However, should there be an Obstructed ■ Sun in Prosperity, a betrayal will undermine financial investments, resulting in loss. Because of the loss of money/money invested, there will be a serious blow to the reputation, especially if the individual is male. During these times, be wary of males. Avoid doing business with them if at all possible. By the same token, working with females would be more beneficial.

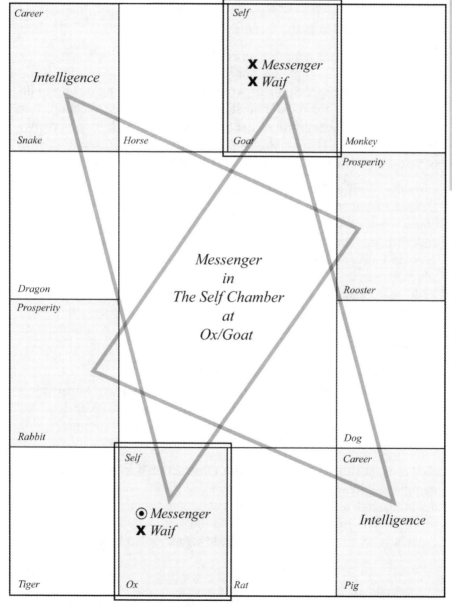

## SELF: MESSENGER & WAIF
### CAREER: INTELLIGENCE
### PROSPERITY: (SUN & SCHOLAR OPPOSITE)

| Career | | Self | |
|---|---|---|---|
| *Intelligence* | | **✗** *Messenger*  **✗** *Waif* | |
| Snake | Horse | Goat | Monkey |
| | | | Prosperity |
| Dragon | *Messenger in The Self Chamber at Ox/Goat* | | Rooster |
| Prosperity | | | |
| Rabbit | | | Dog |
| | Self | | Career |
| | **◉** *Messenger*  **✗** *Waif* | | *Intelligence* |
| Tiger | Ox | Rat | Pig |

6.10 The Self as Messenger in the 12 Chambers 195

# MESSENGER in Self in the Tiger or Monkey Chamber

**The Self—Messenger & Sun**
Messenger in the Self indicates a person who is careful and detailed. However, it also stands for events developing under the surface like an undercurrent; thus, things may not be what they seem. Depending on adjacent stars, The Messenger may eradicate bad influences or bring dissatisfaction to the surface.

The Brilliant Messenger is joined by Sun here, which stands for broadcasting, light, lighting, or transmission and communication fields. The Messenger-Sun pair would shine on anything having to do with teaching, the dissemination of knowledge, acting, or entertainment. The warmth of the Sun benefits all with its generosity. We are, therefore, also looking at public service, management training or self-development would be suitable for the Sun-Messenger pair.

**Career—Waif & Moon Opposite**
Devoid of any major stars in Career, we shall look to its opposite house where Waif and Moon are present. In the Self or Career houses and with the absence of the killing stars to prod her on, Waif may become too complacent. It is apparent this star does little for career advancement.
Redeeming qualities may be found in a Brilliant Moon where this pair may be working late into the night. They may be in entertainment, travel, or international corporations engaging in promotions or marketing.

**Prosperity—Intelligence & Scholar Opposite**
The Tiger-Monkey hours are just at sunrise or sunset. Joined by a Brilliant Messenger and devoid of the major stars in Prosperity, we are seeing the Messenger-Sun investment personality dominating. At Tiger, the Bright Sun would make level-headed, wise decisions.

However, at sunset, especially with Obstruction■ in tow in Monkey, its rays will be about casting shadows and giving way to Messenger's doubting and negligence. Investments soon become speculative. In this light and especially if the Killing Stars are around, it's wise to be especially cautious and adopt a safe, low-risk, or No Position strategy.

# Self: Messenger & Sun
## Career: (Waif & Moon Opposite)
## Prosperity: (Intelligence & Scholar Opposite)

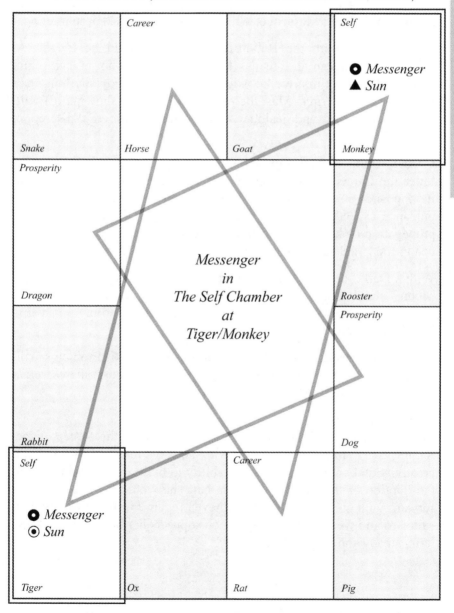

6.10 The Self as Messenger in the 12 Chambers 197

# MESSENGER in Self in the Rabbit or Rooster Chamber

## The Self—Messenger & Intelligence

Messenger in the Self sector indicates outstanding rhetoric abilities. Coupled with sharp diplomatic skills that are associated with the star, this is surely an obvious prompt for any career path! As an eloquent speaker, a Brilliant Messenger will find success in sales or marketing.

Intelligence at both the Rabbit/Rooster hour would be Bright. A balanced, strong mind breeds this kind leader who is calm but motivated with a thirst for knowledge and intrigued by anything that is new and pioneering. Alas, the pair's penchant for showing off will invite controversy and jealousy. Enhancing the Moon's discretion here will help.

## Career—Sun & Moon Opposite

Since the Career sector is devoid of major stars, we read those from its opposite. Sun and Moon in Career strengthen the leadership and guidance aspects of Intelligence and Messenger. Here we have the propagation of knowledge in lifestyle, entertainment, gourmet and/or health food, and supporting roles in the service industries.

With a Dark Sun, the Self usually takes on the qualities of a Brilliant Moon—slowly but surely accumulating wealth. Both the Sun and Moon in Career would entail doing shift duties or working unusually long hours often spilling deep into the night.

Beware the Obstruction Catalyst attached to Moon■. Problems will come from disputes regarding money—commissions, shares, etc., with a female colleague or friend.

## Prosperity—Waif

This is a lucky, Brilliant star which can withstand the forces of the Killing Stars. In their presence, Waif actually moves forward with creativity and aplomb! She has the ability to build from nothing. With the ignition of the (dormant) fire in her, she would be able to move forward with great tenacity and will even regain fortunes lost. Waif is suited to an investment strategy which supports her personality—long term, steady and with little volatility.

# SELF: MESSENGER & INTELLIGENCE
## CAREER: (SUN & MOON OPPOSITE)    PROSPERITY: WAIF

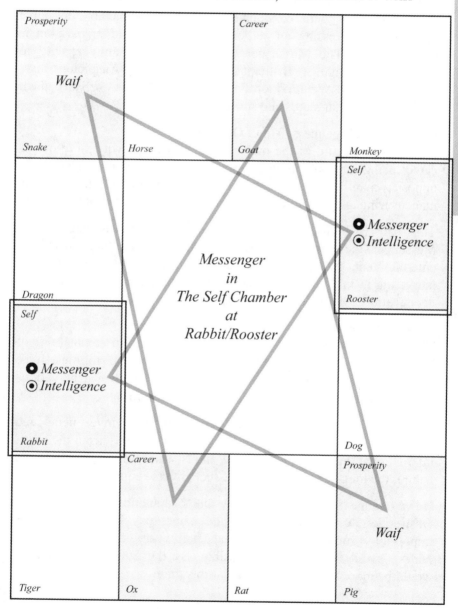

6.10 The Self as Messenger in the 12 Chambers 199

# MESSENGER in Self in the Dragon or Dog Chamber

## The Self—Messenger
The most articulate of the stars, Messenger dominates the Self here. True to its name, at its strongest and most positive, it will eloquently deliver its ideas with passionate conviction and is able to move mountains. Addressing an audience with or without preparation is second-nature. The Messenger uses its voice in any capacity to portray its message. At Brilliant and surrounded by Auspicious Stars or the Power↗, Wealth↗ or Fame✿ Catalysts, we will see them attaining mega-star status and success.

## Career—Intelligence & Moon Opposite
With Career devoid of the major stars, Messenger will carve out its career using its most obvious asset–the voice. In compliance, at the opposite chamber, we have Intelligence, which represents strategic maneuvering and Moon, which stands for support and cooperation.

This pair is highly geared towards service. In association with Messenger, therefore, the careers we will likely see them in will be entertainment, travel, or the service industries, public relations or marketing in international concerns. We will also see them engaging in education, The Arts, social work, or development and training.

## Prosperity—Sun
The Sun, representing broadcasting and the dissemination of knowledge, is matched by the Messenger's rhetoric abilities. It is, therefore, expected to find him addressing an audience at various venues. It is here that he will find success and reward.

With Sun in Prosperity, its preferences towards investments and finance will be in the holding of blue chips, especially from the large, international medical and service industries. In line with Sun's nature, the long-term acquisition of such diverse equities is preferred.

However, the Sun also stands for one's reputation. If carrying the Obstruction ■ Catalyst, one's good name may be at stake. It is important in such situations to be especially wary of partnerships with males. Avoid these if at all possible. By the same token, females would be more sympathetic to you at this time.

# SELF: MESSENGER
## CAREER: (INTELLIGENCE & MOON OPPOSITE)
## PROSPERITY: SUN

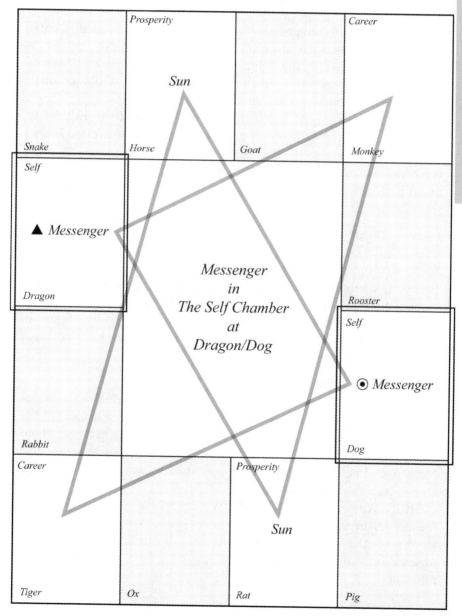

6.10 The Self as Messenger in the 12 Chambers 201

# MESSENGER in Self in the Snake or Pig Chamber

## The Self—Messenger

Messenger, the most articulate of the stars, dominates the Self here. True to its name, at its strongest and most positive it will eloquently deliver its ideas with a passion and conviction that is able to move mountains.

Addressing an audience with or without preparation is second-nature. The Messenger uses its voice in any capacity to get its message across. At Brilliant and surrounded by Auspicious Stars or the Power↗, Wealth$, or Fame✿ Catalysts, we will see them attaining mega-star status and success.

Opposite Messinger, Sun dispenses warmth and light. Both stars, therefore, are about campaigning for social issues. However, having an Obstruction Catalyst ■ present is a sign to be wary of one's reputation or good name being at stake. In addition, it's important to avoid partnerships with males. By the same token, females would be more helpful at this time.

## Career—Waif

The Waif in Career will not be seeking any acknowledgement because this person prefers to provide support from behind the wings. We will, therefore, see them in social work or large community organizations attending to special needs in education or training.

This lucky star can withstand the forces of the Killing Stars. In their presence, Waif actually moves forward has the ability to build from nothing and will even regain fortunes lost.

## Prosperity—Intelligence

Messenger enjoys playing the markets and carefully entering its many trades into its diversified portfolio. Its views on finance are similar to professional traders—quick and precise. Intelligence is about diversification and would bring in some measure of speculation. The Messenger-Intelligence pair will, therefore, become a dynamic duo able to take calculated risks.

If the Auspicious Stars and the Wealth $ catalyst are in place, the Messenger-Intelligence pair will meet with spectacular success. However, the Killing Stars will always strike at the riskier undertakings. It is then time to take low risks or No Position for the moment.

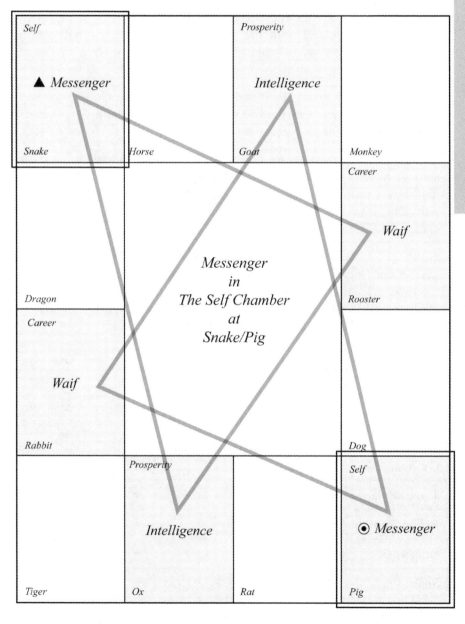

# SELF: MESSENGER

## CAREER: WAIF    PROSPERITY: INTELLIGENCE

| Self | | Prosperity | |
|---|---|---|---|
| ▲ *Messenger* | | *Intelligence* | |
| Snake | Horse | Goat | Monkey |

| | | | Career |
|---|---|---|---|
| | | | *Waif* |
| Dragon | | | Rooster |
| Career | *Messenger in The Self Chamber at Snake/Pig* | | |
| *Waif* | | | |
| Rabbit | | | Dog |

| | Prosperity | | Self |
|---|---|---|---|
| | *Intelligence* | | ⊙ *Messenger* |
| Tiger | Ox | Rat | Pig |

6.10 The Self as Messenger in the 12 Chambers 203

# MESSENGER in the Self House Investment Strategy

## Long Term Low to Medium Investments

Messenger is the most eloquent of speakers and will be found at the pinnacle of success in sales and marketing. From insurance to multi-level marketing or Masters of Ceremony, they will be a pleasure to hear. At Brilliant and with the right stars around, they will attain international stardom on stage or as world leaders. It is in these contexts, therefore, that Messenger will attain Success.

In the Self sector that is also filled with several Auspicious Stars and few or none of the bad ones, Messengers with Wealth $ will earn fortunes by using their voice.

On the contrary, Messenger is also likened to a shadow. In its dark state or trailing the Obstruction ■ Catalyst, it will cast its shadow of doubt over propitious or happy events, turning praises into blame and publicity into gossip. Messenger with Obstruction attached will subsequently strike a loss through slander or litigation.

Although careful by nature, when it comes to its own finances, Messenger lacks the know-how of Emperor and the savvy of Crimson. Because of this, it should go by the long-term, low to medium risk strategies. Riskier investments should only be taken if aided by the Wealth Catalyst and the Auspicious Stars.

| HOURS | SELF HOUSE | PROSPERITY | LONG | SHORT | DIVERSE | FOCUS |
|---|---|---|---|---|---|---|
| Rat/Horse | Mesgr | | + | | + | |
| Ox/Goat | Mesgr/Waif | | + | | + | |
| Tiger/Monkey | Mesgr/Sun | | + | | + | |
| Rabbit/Rooster | Mesgr/Intel | Waif | + | | + | |
| Dragon/Dog | Mesgr | Sun | + | | + | |
| Snake/Pig | Mesgr | Intel | + | | + | |

CHAPTER 6.11

# The Self as Mirror in the 12 Chambers

| | | | |
|---|---|---|---|
| | | | |
| Snake | Horse | Goat | Monkey |

| | | |
|---|---|---|
| Dragon | **WARREN BUFFETT** | Rooster |
| | ✦ | |
| Rabbit | *In the business world, the rearview Mirror is always clearer than the windshield* | Dog |

| | | | |
|---|---|---|---|
| | | | |
| Tiger | Ox | Rat | Pig |

# MIRROR in Self in the Rat or Horse Chamber

### The Self—Mirror & Crimson
The outstanding feature for the Mirror is Responsibility. Here is a responsible person—both to himself and those close to him. Mirror is joined by the vivacious Crimson. Mirror's reliability and carefulness is matched by Crimson's outgoing personality—the perfect combination for success. Moreover, Crimson will be given recognition by Mirror's caution and stability. In any situation, you will see this person moving forward with hard work, determination, and integrity.

### Career—Commander
Commander, also a hard worker, will not be daunted by setbacks. We will see these individuals at the forefront of the Armed Forces. Together with Crimson and Mirror, this personality would perform best in planning, leadership, and people-oriented roles. If strengthened by the Auspicious Stars and Catalysts, we will see them rising to top ranking positions. With Fame✿ attached, many will hear about this person's successes. Commander, being a Wealth$ star, would also be adept at working in Finance.

### Prosperity—Emperor & Vault
Working among the people is Mirror-Crimson's forté. It would suit this personality to get his information from real-life situations, such as technical analysis, market surveys, the media, and talking with like-minded friends. Crimson's adventurous personality would indicate high risk tolerance. However, this is balanced by Mirror's prudence.

Emperor, if joined with Fame✿, indicates strength, wisdom, and courage being enhanced and highlighted. However, if hemmed in or opposed ■ by the Killing Stars, The Emperor with Fame✿ may gain notoriety through misguided or fraudulent channels.

Vault is another major wealth and investment star here in Prosperity. Stable and conservative, we are seeing investments in long-term, significant projects. With the major wealth$ stars making up this constellation, this person's financial status would be quite awesome.

# SELF: MIRROR & CRIMSON
## CAREER: COMMANDER    PROSPERITY: EMPEROR & VAULT

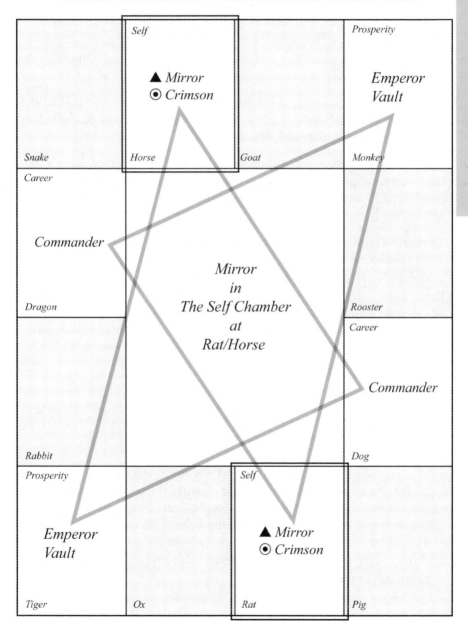

| | Self | | Prosperity |
|---|---|---|---|
| | ▲ Mirror<br>☉ Crimson | | *Emperor*<br>*Vault* |
| Snake | Horse | Goat | Monkey |

Career

Commander

*Dragon*

Mirror
in
*The Self Chamber*
at
*Rat/Horse*

Rooster

Career

Commander

Rabbit

Dog

Prosperity

*Emperor*
*Vault*

Self

▲ Mirror
☉ Crimson

Tiger

Ox

Rat

Pig

6.11 The Self as Mirror in the 12 Chambers 207

# MIRROR in Self in the Ox or Goat Chamber

**The Self—Mirror**
The outstanding feature of Mirror is Responsibility. Here is a responsible person both to himself and those close to him. Being just and impartial, he sees himself as totally answerable to everything that he puts his seal on. He will be recognized by the care and detail he applies to his dress, home, and office. Mirror in the Self indicates a careful individual.

Upright and blessed with a big heart, he fits into everyone's ideal of the Big Brother. If necessary, he will go out of his way to fight for what he believes in (Bruce Lee's Lift Chart).

Emperor and Pioneer are stationed at its opposite chamber. This adds the pioneering and leadership qualities to its personality. With Pioneer here, our Emperor is well supported. They lend support to each other and ensure a smooth, dynamic transition.

**Career—Crimson & Opportunity Opposite**
With Career devoid of stars, we shall look into its opposite. With the vivacious Crimson-Opportunity pair reflecting Career, we will see them taking an active interest in the Performing Arts, entertainment, or management of large multinational corporations. These two sociable stars will be outstanding in positions that require constant change and contact with the opposite sex. Look for where you can bask in attention, for there lies success.

This attractive pair, given the excellent back-up of Mirror, Emperor, and Pioneer, will be in the forefront of international lifestyles, fashion, or the entertainment businesses.

**Prosperity—Vault**
Vault is a major prosperity star from the conservative faction. As The Emperor rules the North, so the Vault rules the South. The conservative Vault likes to quietly build wealth and guard it well. This star would shine on careers having to do with administration and management. The Vault in Prosperity would focus on being highly cautious when it comes to investments, preferring to deal in low to medium long range risk products.

# SELF: MIRROR

## CAREER: (CRIMSON & OPPORTUNITY OPPOSITE)  PROSPERITY: VAULT

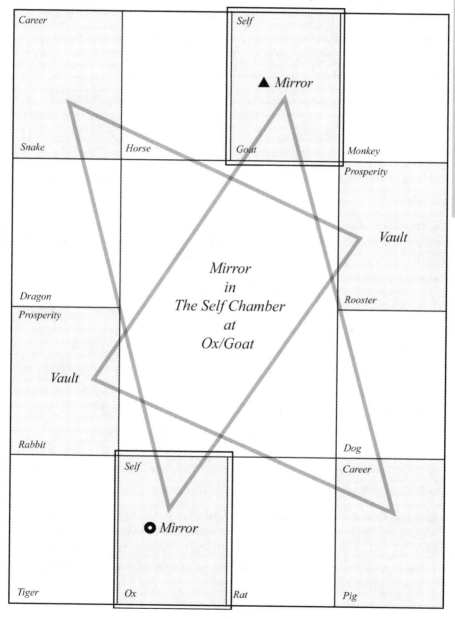

6.11 The Self as Mirror in the 12 Chambers 209

# MIRROR in Self in the Tiger or Monkey Chamber

## The Self—Mirror & Commander
The action-packed, Brilliant Commander joins forces with a Brilliant Mirror here, which is the stabilizing force. This partnership ensures a smooth running of their business with just the right balance of forethought, force, and action. These people will forge ahead with honesty and integrity. However, because of what Mirror is, he may tend to repeat past lessons (Donald Trump's Life Chart).

The Commander, also here, is likened to a "wealth mine." Fame ✿and Wealth$ ensure more Fame. However, should Commander meet up with the Obstruction Catalyst ■ here, then he must steer clear of all business or financial transactions at that time.

Mirror will always reflect The Pioneer in its opposite (Prosperity) sector, which brings great changes.

## Career—Emperor
The Emperor in career would command respect as the CEO of large multinational concerns. These would deal in high-end products, precious metals, jewelry or the financial institutions, including insurance. The Emperor would be involved in the exclusive niche markets. If well-supported by the Left & Right Ministers and Stardust & Delight, a brilliant career would be in place.

## Prosperity—Crimson & Vault
Crimson in Prosperity denotes highly diversified and high-risk undertakings. We will see Crimson among the crowd, happily enjoying all the attention and at the same time creating wealth.

If attached by Wealth $ here, Crimson would indicate emotional wealth, that is, happiness. Close relations or siblings will bring wealth or will introduce propitious situations. This sociable star blesses you with her prosperity. Put into the crowd she has everything to gain!

In their financial transactions, the Commander's adventurous instinct would be balanced by Mirror's presence. The Vault here is also lending the same weight to the excitable Crimson. We can, therefore, expect to see a successful, balanced portfolio of high, medium, and low risk products.

# SELF: MIRROR & COMMANDER
## CAREER: EMPEROR   PROSPERITY: CRIMSON & VAULT

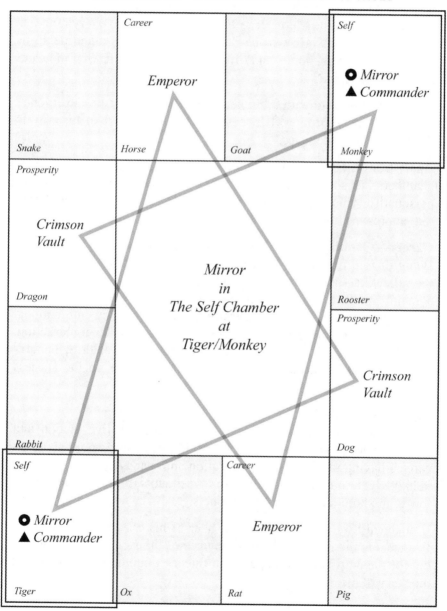

6.11 The Self as Mirror in the 12 Chambers 211

# MIRROR in Self in the Rabbit or Rooster Chamber

## The Self—Mirror

The outstanding feature of Mirror is Responsibility. Here is a responsible person both to himself and those close to him. Being just and impartial, he sees himself as totally answerable to everything that he puts his seal on. He will be recognized by the care and detail he applies to his dress, home, and office. The Mirror in the Self indicates a careful individual.

Upright and blessed with a big heart, he just fits right into everyone's ideal of the Big Brother. If necessary, he will go out of his way to fight for what he believes.

Apart from this, Crimson and Pioneer are stationed at its opposite chamber. This adds the vivacious, pioneering qualities to its personality. This makes for someone who will always be well turned out, interesting, and delightfully original.

## Career—Commander & Opportunity Opposite

Being devoid of stars in Career, this chamber will be influenced by the reflecting stars Commander and Opportunity. Commander, being a major wealth star, is spiced by Opportunity's daring, high risk-taking personality. We will, therefore, see the pair in multinational businesses or finance, including insurance and multi-level marketing. The Auspicious Stars (e.g., Completion) and the Wealth $, Fame ✿ and Power ↗ Catalysts will aid in their swift rise up the success ladder.

## Prosperity—Vault

Vault is a major prosperity star from the conservative faction and likes to quietly build and guard its wealth. This star would shine on careers having to do with administration and management. Vault here is highly cautious when it comes to investments, preferring to deal in low to medium long range risk products.

If attached by Fame ✿, many will hear of his wizardry in managing finance. On the reverse, albeit off-chance of things going awry, watch out for the detrimental stars. Their influence might make an infamous mockery of his name.

# SELF: MIRROR
## CAREER: (COMMANDER & OPPORTUNITY OPPOSITE)
### PROSPERITY: VAULT

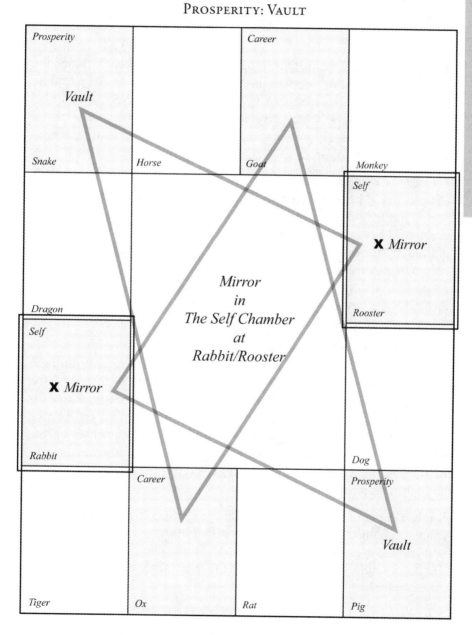

| Prosperity | | Career | |
|---|---|---|---|
| *Vault* | | | |
| Snake | Horse | Goat | Monkey |

*Self*

**X** *Mirror*

*Mirror in The Self Chamber at Rabbit/Rooster*

| Dragon | | | Rooster |
|---|---|---|---|
| *Self* | | | |
| **X** *Mirror* | | | |
| Rabbit | | | Dog |

| | Career | | Prosperity |
|---|---|---|---|
| | | | *Vault* |
| Tiger | Ox | Rat | Pig |

6.11 The Self as Mirror in the 12 Chambers 213

# MIRROR in Self in the Dragon or Dog Chamber

### The Self—Mirror & Emperor

The outstanding feature of Mirror is Responsibility to himself and those close to him. He will be recognized by the care and detail he applies to his dress, home, and office. The Mirror in the Self indicates a careful individual.

Together with Mirror in the Self House is The Emperor. If dark, he will very often fall prey to his emotions and pride. The public adoration that he is capable of inviting, if used unwisely, might also result in liaisons he would live to regret. He must be wary of the negative, detrimental qualities of this star—pride, frustration, anger, etc., for these are destructive to business and investment conduct.

### Career—Crimson

Crimson is a natural socialite. Those with Crimson in their Career sector will find themselves basking in attention and ultimately success. They will soar above the rest whether they are in PR or politics. Crimson will do famously well in situations which require constant communication/ dealings with the opposite sex—a man in cosmetics, a woman in finance. Crimson can expect to shine if found in the Career sector, and if there are other Auspicious Stars around, this career can expect a lift-off!

### Prosperity—Commander & Vault

Commander is a major star that dispenses direct prosperity through sheer, hard work. To have this prosperity star coming to rest in the Prosperity Chamber of our chart is undoubtedly the best scenario for taking higher risks for higher returns. This is unless, of course, the dreaded Obstruction Catalyst (■) should become attached or the appearance of Void or Punishment. Should this happen in any moment in time, including the lifetime, it is important not engage in any business or investment venture.

Vault is a major prosperity star from the conservative faction. As the Emperor pioneers, so the Vault guards. Safely trekking paths hewn and hacked by others before him, the Vault quietly builds fortunes. This star would shine on careers having to do with administration and management.

# SELF: MIRROR & EMPEROR
## CAREER: CRIMSON   PROSPERITY: COMMANDER & VAULT

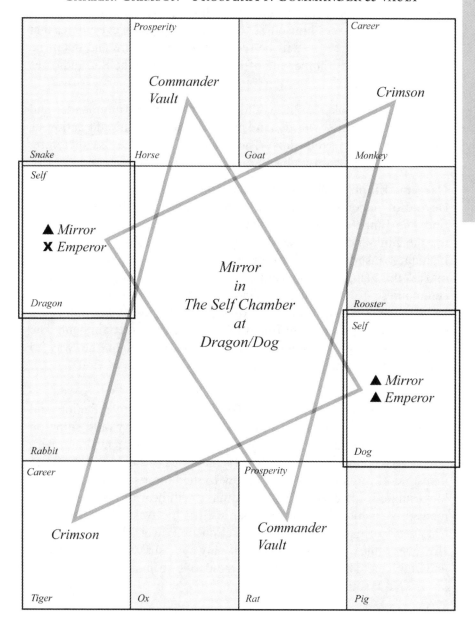

6.11 The Self as Mirror in the 12 Chambers 215

# MIRROR in Self in the Snake or Pig Chamber

**The Self—Mirror**

The outstanding feature of Mirror is Responsibility. Here, if ever, is a responsible person both to himself or those close to him. Being just and impartial, he sees himself as totally answerable to everything that he puts his seal on. He will be recognized by the care and detail he applies to his dress, home, and office. The Mirror in the Self indicates a careful individual.

The Mirror at Snake or Pig would be influenced by Commander and Pioneer at opposite. The dynamism of the pair would add action as well as creativity and flair. The resulting outcome is, therefore, success-oriented against a background of honesty and integrity.

**Career—Emperor & Opportunity Opposite**

Devoid of major stars, we shall look at Career's opposite where we find The Emperor and Opportunity. The Emperor indicates working for the high-end businesses having to do with lifestyle or finance, including insurance and multi-level marketing. Opportunity also makes its glamorous appearance here and provides the opening ceremonies to anything having to do with entertainment—investments, banks, jewelry, movies, or casinos. Opportunity in Career indicates a constant round of partying and entertainment. The addition of a few Auspicious Stars would then light the way to entrepreneurial success.

**Prosperity—Vault**

Vault is a major prosperity star from the conservative faction and likes to quietly build and guard its wealth. This star would shine on careers having to do with administration and management. Vault here would have us becoming highly cautious when it comes to investments, preferring to deal in low to medium risk products on the long range. If attached by Fame ✿, many will hear of his wizardry in managing finance. This would bode well if the Auspicious Stars and Catalysts are gathered, e.g., Completion or Power ↗ and Wealth $. However, the Killing Stars will always strike at the riskier undertakings. They are, therefore, indicative to pursue safe ventures or take No Position for the moment.

# SELF: MIRROR
## CAREER: (EMPEROR & OPPORTUNITY opposite)
### PROSPERITY: VAULT

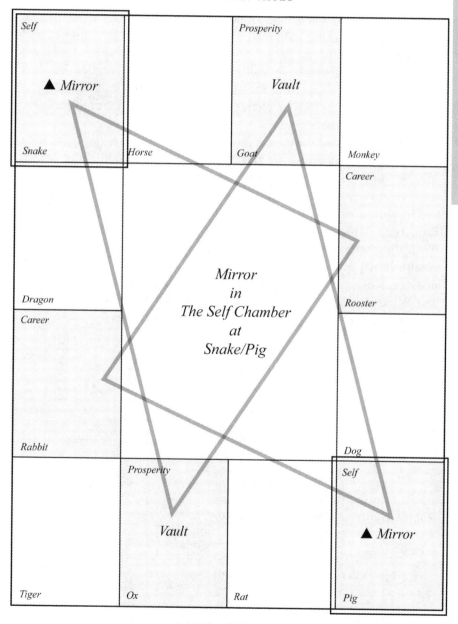

6.11 The Self as Mirror in the 12 Chambers 217

Text within the image:

Self | Prosperity
▲ Mirror | Vault
Snake | Horse | Goat | Monkey
Career
Dragon | Mirror in The Self Chamber at Snake/Pig | Rooster
Career
Rabbit | Dog
Prosperity | Self
Vault | ▲ Mirror
Tiger | Ox | Rat | Pig

MIRROR IN SELF

# MIRROR in the Self House Investment Strategy

## Investing in the Physical Metal Industries

Since its element is Water, Mirror would benefit by investing in anything having to do with the physical metal industries from copper and steel to gold and silver since these enhance Water. Moreover, with honesty and decisiveness being second-nature, Mirror is also well suited to working with jewelry or the finance sectors (money and finance which are Metal).

Mirror in Self will have Vault in the Prosperity Chamber. Vault is a major prosperity star from the conservative faction and thus attracts and stores wealth. It is a characteristic that it will never lack for earthly possessions.

With Vault and Emperor both in Prosperity, we have the two major rulers—Emperor from the North and Vault, ruler of the South, joining together. Investments would, therefore, center around exclusive, large-scale projects or long-term holdings and blue-chips.

If paired with Commander, Vault will restrain some of the Emperor's willfulness here. Together with Commander, the Self will be dealing with financial matters. This does not necessarily indicate wealth itself, for it could also be careers in financial control, money management, etc. If helped by the Auspicious Stars (e.g., Completion and Winged Horse), we can expect to receive significant rewards. If Fame↗ is attached, our success would bring eminence.

| HOURS | SELF HOUSE | PROSPERITY | LONG | SHORT | DIVERSE | FOCUS |
|-------|-----------|------------|------|-------|---------|-------|
| Rat/Horse | Miror/Crmsn | Vault/Emper | ✦ | ✦ | ✦ | ✦ |
| Ox/Goat | Miror | Vault | ✦ | | ✦ | |
| Tiger/Monkey | Miror/Cmdr | Vault/Crmsn | ✦ | ✦ | ✦ | ✦ |
| Rabbit/Rooster | Miror | Vault | ✦ | | ✦ | |
| Dragon/Dog | Miror/Emper | Vault/Comdr | ✦ | ✦ | ✦ | ✦ |
| Snake/Pig | Miror | Vault | ✦ | | ✦ | |

CHAPTER 6.12

# The Self as Scholar in the 12 Chambers

| | | | |
|---|---|---|---|
| Snake | Horse | Goat | Monkey |
| Dragon | | | Rooster |
| Rabbit | | | Dog |
| Tiger | Ox | Rat | Pig |

ARTHUR
SCHOPENHAUER

———— ✦ ————

*Great men
are like eagles,
and build their nest
on some
lofty solitude*

# SCHOLAR in Self in the Rat or Horse Chamber

## The Self—Scholar

At Brilliant at both Rat and Horse Houses, the Scholar will exert its most positive influence here. At best, this is a compassionate, generous, and elegant star. It shines on professionals, i.e., medical doctors, lawyers, professors, scientists, etc. Intellectually gifted, it is proud of its academic achievements and cannot be bothered with business ventures, moneymaking, plus all such other things that these activities encompass. Although behind the Sun in elegance and compassion, on the whole it is friendly and kind.

Reflected by the elegant Sun, its lofty pursuits for the relief of humanity's ills and suffering will be heightened. Therefore, we will see compassion and honor at its highest. If trailing the Wealth $ Catalyst, Sun will be professionally successful.

## Career—Waif

With Waif in career, we will not be seeing much incentive towards achievements. It is apparent that this star does little for career advancement. On the contrary, the Killing Stars would have the abilities to ignite the fire in her and so propel her to develop tenacity, and she might even regain fortunes lost. So look for these in the same house, opposite, or at 120°. The Scholar-Waif pair will be applying themselves towards the social causes, and religious and community services.

## Prosperity—Intelligence & Moon

The Moon is a Wealth$ star. Residing in Prosperity, she will see to it that there should be no problems when it comes to drawing in wealth. It should be remembered that the Moon's wealth is always gradually accumulated. In this respect, savings or very low-risk investments, such as annuities, fixed deposits, or mutual funds, should be the target.

Intelligence, very much the active trader, is also here. In the presence of the Auspicious Stars, this would draw in some lucrative rewards.

However, the Killing Stars will always strike at the riskier undertakings. They are, therefore, reminders to pursue safe ventures or take No Position for the moment.

# SELF: SCHOLAR
## CAREER: WAIF    PROSPERITY: INTELLIGENCE & MOON

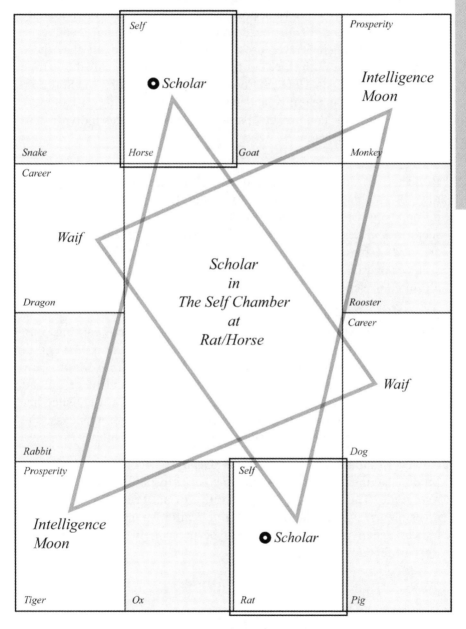

6.12 The Self as Scholar in the 12 Chambers 221

# SCHOLAR in Self in the Ox or Goat Chamber

### The Self—Scholar

Scholar exerts most of its positive influence here as a friendly, kind, compassionate, generous and elegant star that shines on professionals, i.e., medical doctors, lawyers, professors, scientists, etc. Intellectually gifted, it is proud of its academic achievements and cannot be bothered with business ventures, moneymaking, and all that these activities entail. With the conflicting personalities of the active Intelligence (opposite) and cautious Scholar at play here, the Self may veer between changeability and complacency. Working in calmness and solitude may counteract distractions and help the individual to come to logical decisions.

### Career—Sun

Reflected by Intelligence, Scholar will become even more geared towards teaching or management training. Coupled with the Sun and its opposite, Messenger, here in Career would emphasize the Self's rhetoric abilities. We would, therefore, see them teaching, lecturing, and addressing audiences. Higher educational institutions, including colleges and universities, business and management schools, etc., are all suited to Scholar with Sun in Career.

### Prosperity—Moon

Moon in Prosperity will have us putting the bulk of our earnings into savings. The Self will be able to accumulate savings or a nest egg in the long run. Note this is the general source of wealth for Moon. Low risk investments would be recommended, like retirement or mutual funds. The Auspicious Stars around Moon would always enhance her moneymaking abilities; after all, she is a wealth star. In this case, she could always upgrade to medium risk investments for higher earnings.

However, should the Obstruction■ Catalyst become attached, The Moon, having to do with income or prosperity, would be in retrograde. There will be the possibility of suffering losses through investments or speculations. The implication of having been lured into bogus investments would also be present. It's also wise to be wary of females in this situation.

# Self: Scholar
## Career: Sun   Prosperity: Waif

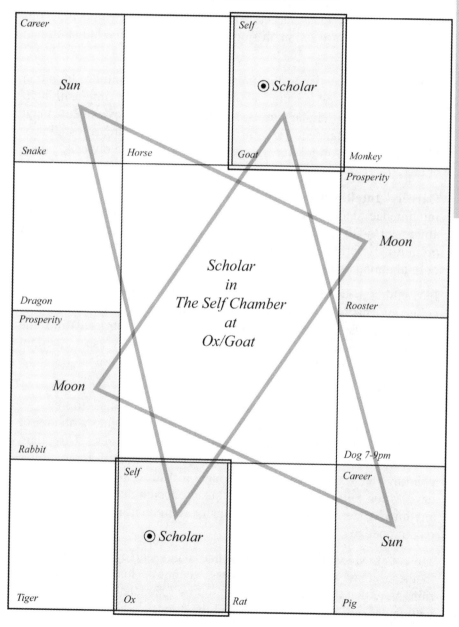

| Career | | Self | |
|---|---|---|---|
| *Sun* | | ☉ *Scholar* | |
| Snake | Horse | Goat | Monkey |

Prosperity

*Moon*

*Scholar
in
The Self Chamber
at
Ox/Goat*

| Dragon | | | Rooster |
| Prosperity | | | |
| *Moon* | | | |
| Rabbit | | | Dog 7-9pm |
| Self | | Career | |
| ☉ *Scholar* | | *Sun* | |
| Tiger | Ox | Rat | Pig |

6.12 The Self as Scholar in the 12 Chambers 223

# SCHOLAR in Self in the Tiger or Monkey Chamber

## The Self—Scholar & Waif

The righteous and protective Scholar is met up by the retiring, albeit auspicious, Waif here. Scholar also shines on the professions, i.e., medicine, law or the sciences. This star, therefore, would prod our leisurely Waif into action, lifting her up to his lofty humanitarian pursuits.

Note that Scholar stands for support, protection, solitude, litigation and injury. Power➚ to the Scholar would have the implication of adding weight to Scholar's traits. Negativity against investments may, therefore, be enhanced. Take these in stride. They are, after all, not life threatening, so look for redeeming qualities in the opposite house or at 120°.

## Career—Intelligence

Intelligence stands for wide-ranging interests and changeability. In alignment with Waif and Messenger, we would see these three promoting international products and services in the art of fine living or in planning and marketing the latest technologies of such.

If Wealth $ is attached, it would have this Strategist maneuvering and collecting his due. However, if hemmed in by the Killing or Obstructed stars, especially The Moon being Obstructed■ in the Prosperity sector, Intelligence with Wealth may spell certain misfortunes, e.g., robbery.

## Prosperity—Moon

The Waif does not care much for investments. This sentiment is exacerbated with the addition of Scholar, who absolutely abhors or has issues with money and moneymaking ventures. This pair, therefore, does not bode well for financial or business transactions, pointing the way to depressive thoughts. Adding to the picture, we have Moon here in Prosperity, the steady accumulation of wealth. If anything, a steady, non-risky savings or retirement plan is, therefore, recommended.

Moreover, Moon also stands for dimness and secrecy. Obstructions ■ in these areas would include illness, economic loss, conspiracy, or ruin. Note that these will be brought on by a female, so joining forces with males will be more beneficial at this time.

# SELF: SCHOLAR & WAIF
## CAREER: INTELLIGENCE    PROSPERITY: MOON

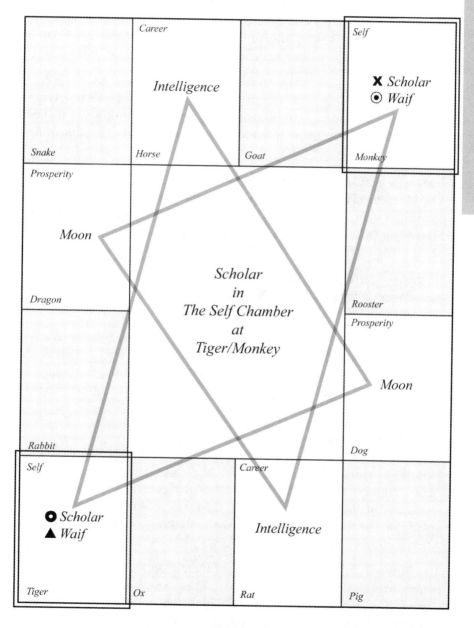

6.12 The Self as Scholar in the 12 Chambers 225

# SCHOLAR in Self in the Rabbit or Rooster Chamber

### The Self—Scholar & Sun
The protective Scholar here joins the elegant, benevolent Sun. Being of similar nature, these two stars stand for broadcasting and teaching. However, note the different Catalysts attached to Sun: Obstruction■ to Sun warns of libelous situations. If one is male, your good name may be at stake. Whether male or female, be wary of partnerships with males.

The Sun with the Power ↗ Catalyst carries the obvious trait of having the majority or male supporters on your side. Power to the Sun makes for a highly independent mind which gives rise to the pioneering spirit.

### Career—Waif & Messenger Opposite
The Messenger is all about making the voice heard. In a sector that is also filled with several auspicious stars and none of the bad ones, the Messenger with the Wealth $ catalyst attached, points to fortunes being made by the voice.

However, the Killing Stars will strip away any splendor and The Messenger with Obstruction■ attached will suffer a loss through slander or litigation.

With Waif having to do with enjoyment, the Sun-Scholar-Waif-- Messenger constellation will shine on social work, teaching, preaching, and counseling. This star combination stands for being in service to mankind in religious or social undertakings (Princess Diana's Lift Chart).

### Prosperity—Moon
With Sun already a benevolent star being joined by Scholar, brimming with analytical sense, the pair can come up with just the right amount of detachment for investment success. However, there is weakness in the setting sun at the Monkey chamber. It should be noted that the rising sun in Tiger has a more positive sense for success when it comes to investments.

The Moon in Prosperity is always an indication for savings with any gains being slowly accumulated. The Auspicious Stars (e.g., Completion) would also enhance Scholar-Sun. In this case, a higher-risk strategy may be tolerated in return for higher earnings.

# SELF: SCHOLAR & SUN
## CAREER: (WAIF & MESSENGER OPPOSITE)   PROSPERITY: MOON

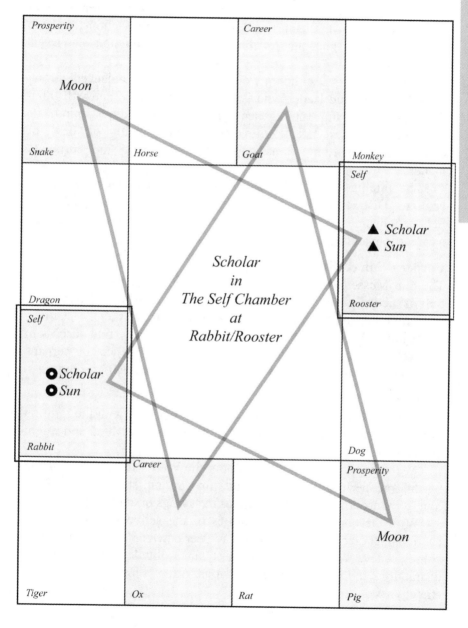

| Prosperity | | Career | |
|---|---|---|---|
| *Moon* | | | |
| Snake | Horse | Goat | Monkey |

Self

▲ *Scholar*
▲ *Sun*

*Scholar
in
The Self Chamber
at
Rabbit/Rooster*

Dragon | Rooster

Self

**○** *Scholar*
**○** *Sun*

Rabbit | Dog

Career | Prosperity

*Moon*

Tiger | Ox | Rat | Pig

6.12 The Self as Scholar in the 12 Chambers   227

# SCHOLAR in Self in the Dragon or Dog Chamber

## The Self—Scholar & Intelligence

Scholar will be Bright at Dragon/Dog. Possessing its own brand of pride, Scholar would positively not be suited to any entrepreneurial pursuits of his own. Business entails monetary transactions, and the pursuit of money goes against much of Scholar's opinion of what is lofty and right.

Intelligence at these hours would be Brilliant. A balanced, strong mind breeds a kind leader who is calm but motivated and will thirst for knowledge, and Intelligence here ensures a quick mind. Its presence indicates lateral movements—the pursuit of new or challenging opportunities as opposed to climbing the corporate ladder.

The Intelligence-Scholar combination here indicates a need for caution. Distraction being Intelligence's weakness, coupled with Scholar's disinterest in wealth indicates that it would be good to seek a career in planning, management, or teaching.

## Career—Sun & Messenger Opposite

The Sun-Messenger combination here points to a career whereby the Self is actively communicating his thoughts and knowledge, e.g., education, theatre, broadcasting, the Arts, culinary arts, etc.

If joined by the positive stars, this individual may find success in marketing or sales, i.e., the financial sectors, insurance, or perhaps what is considered the platform of the century—Internet Marketing.

## Prosperity—Waif & Moon

A Bright Waif has the ability to build from nothing; with the ignition of the (dormant) fire in her, she would become motivated and might even regain fortunes lost.

Accompanied by a Brilliant Moon, the Waif will be helped along by this prosperity star. Moon stands for caution, steadiness, and the long-term accumulation of wealth, as in savings or annuity plans.

With the conflicting personalities of the active Intelligence and cautious Scholar at play, the Self may veer between changeability and complacency. Working in calmness and solitude may counteract distractions and lead to logical decisions. Adopt a low to medium risk strategy.

# SELF: SCHOLAR & INTELLIGENCE
## CAREER: (SUN & MESSENGER OPPOSITE)
### PROSPERITY: WAIF & MOON

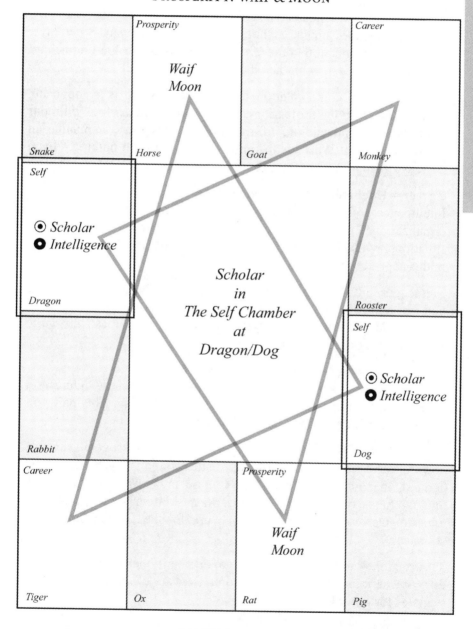

6.12 The Self as Scholar in the 12 Chambers 229

# SCHOLAR in Self in the Snake or Pig Chamber

## The Self—Scholar
At best, Scholar is a compassionate, generous, and elegant star. It shines on professionals, i.e., medical doctors, lawyers, professors, scientists, etc. Intellectually gifted and proud of its academic achievements, the Scholar cannot be bothered with business ventures, moneymaking, and all that these activities encompass. Trailing behind the Sun's elegance, it is on the whole friendly and kind.

Waif, in idyllic contemplation about social issues, is at opposite. Scholar shines on the professions, so this star will, therefore, prod our leisurely Waif into action, lifting her up to its lofty, humanitarian ideals. A Brilliant Waif has the abilities to build from nothing. Given tenacity, it would regain lost ground or fortunes.

## Career—Intelligence & Messenger Opposite
Intelligence signifies diversified servicing in multinational organizations regarding global issues or humanitarian or aid situations. It also likes the planning and administration fields, and it is in this capacity that it will shine.

Messenger in Career always points to the use of the voice, i.e., selling and marketing. These two stars together with Scholar and Waif in the Self could propagate lifestyle or leisure activities in large multinational organizations.

## Prosperity—Sun & Moon
The Sun-Moon pair occupying Prosperity would ignite interest in investing which has been lacking in Scholar all along. This pair will be looking into long-range, low-risk undertakings.

The Moon's wealth would also figure into Scholar's overall attitude towards investing. Because of this, if there aren't any Killing Stars around, it may be worthwhile to venture into low to medium risk mutual funds or other investments. In any circumstance, high risk investments or ventures would not work for the Scholar-Sun-Moon alliance.

Obstruction ■ to the Sun or Moon would signify betrayal, resulting in loss or a serious blow to the reputation. Be wary of males for Sun■ or females for Moon■.

# SELF: SCHOLAR
## CAREER: (INTELLIGENCE & MESSENGER
### PROSPERITY: SUN & MOON

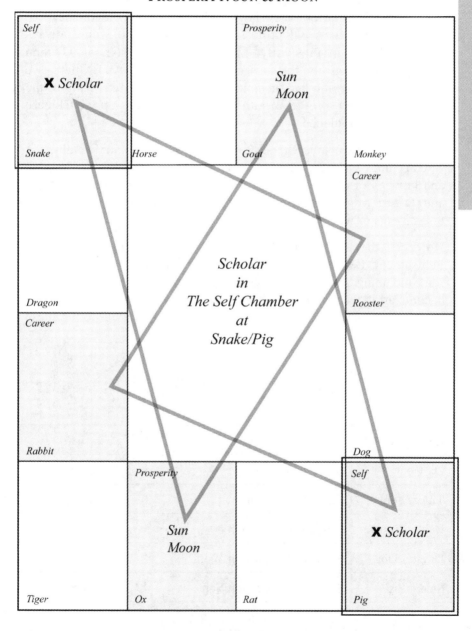

6.12 The Self as Scholar in the 12 Chambers 231

# SCHOLAR in the Self House Investment Strategy

**Long Term Diverse Investor**

Note that Scholar does not bode well for business or moneymaking ventures of any sort. Brimming with lofty intellectual ideals, this star shines on the professions—law, judicial system, medicine, the sciences, or teachers and professors. Scholar in Self would always have the Moon in Prosperity. Moon is a wealth star, slowly and quietly shoring up her fortunes over the long run. At Brilliant, we would see her flexing her financial prowess and deftly ringing in the cash. She is, after all, the Wealth part of what makes up the Chinese characters for Opulence.

With other Auspicious Stars supporting (Stardust and Delight, the Literary and Arts Ministers, Completion and the Wealth $, Fame ✪ and Power ↗ Catalysts), her road to wealth would be even smoother and faster. Moon is, therefore, predisposed to be in finance and investments or wealth and money management.

However, the Obstruction■ Catalyst and the Killing Stars (Void, Punishment, Bell and Ram) will strike the deathblow to any wealth star, including Moon. With these surrounding, Moon will tend to become erratic and engage in high-risk speculations. There should not be any investment or business activity taking place at all during these times.

| HOURS | SELF HOUSE | PROSPERITY | LONG | SHORT | DIVERSE | FOCUS |
|-------|-----------|-----------|------|-------|---------|-------|
| Rat/Horse | Schol | Moon/Intel | ✦ | | ✦ | |
| Ox/Goat | Schol | Moon | ✦ | | ✦ | |
| Tiger/Monkey | Schol/Waif | Moon | ✦ | | ✦ | |
| Rabbit/Rooster | Schol/Sun | Moon | ✦ | | ✦ | |
| Dragon/Dog | Schol/Intel | Moon/Waif | ✦ | | ✦ | |
| Snake/Pig | Schol | Moon/Sun | ✦ | | ✦ | |

# The Self as General in the 12 Chambers

| | | | |
|---|---|---|---|
| Snake | Horse | Goat | Monkey |

## SUN TZU

✦

*The General who advances*
*without coveting fame and*
*retreats without fearing disgrace,*
*whose only thought*
*is to protect his country and do*
*good service for his sovereign,*
*is the Jewel of the Kingdom.*

| | | | |
|---|---|---|---|
| Dragon | | | Rooster |
| Rabbit | | | Dog |
| Tiger | Ox | Rat | Pig |

# GENERAL in Self in the Rat or Horse Chamber

**The Self—General**
Whether male or female, the General in Self or Career sector is a sure indicator of a brilliant career. This is a person with great tenacity, who will set goals and overcome any obstacle in order to achieve them. Like Pioneer, General will have his share of turbulence  but to a slightly lesser degree, for both immediately respond to the beckoning of adventure, even danger. The Survivor being its middle name, it can withstand any work environment, learning and sharpening its skills as it carves its way to success.

**Career—Pioneer**
With Pioneer here in Career, it would not be surprising to see this star fighter creating a new post, department, or working system for itself. With its innovative style and ideas, it will lead its team to places never seen, known, or experienced before. It is often seen tearing through extreme difficulties with a conviction that only true pioneers have and then emerging victorious.

At its best, a Brilliant Pioneer would be an inspired, strong leader that should be put in positions in places like large multinational organizations and opening up new markets and frontiers while guiding its band of brothers to success. Alternatively, a Brilliant Pioneer with Power↗ would top the ranks in any of the Armed Forces. The Pioneer juggles different roles. With the Power Catalyst↗, we see a heavier burden in the House this star rests in. The Pioneer also stands for the introduction of new ways or concepts. The Power Catalyst here brings authority.

**Prosperity—Opportunity**
With the intensely risk-oriented Opportunity here, plus the swiftness of both the General and Pioneer, we have a formation that is radically inclined towards speculation and gambling. This would be good and could even reap big winnings under the light of the Auspicious Stars (Stardust & Delight, Completion). However, the Killing Stars (Ram, Spinning Top, Void and Punishment) and the Obstruction■ Catalyst will always ignite that tendency to gamble and so will pave the way to ruin.

# SELF: GENERAL

## CAREER: PIONEER    PROSPERITY: OPPORTUNITY

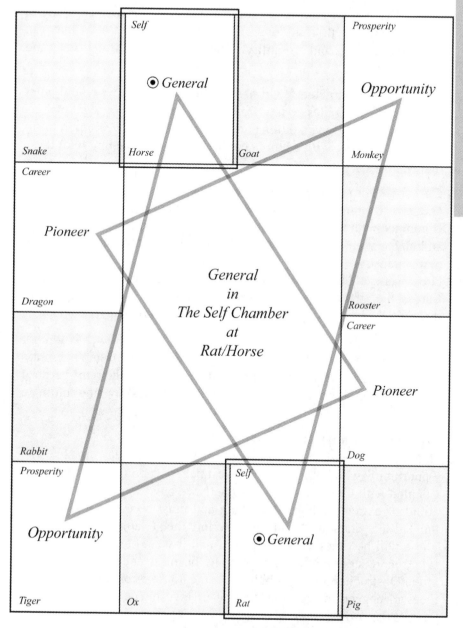

Self

⊙ General

Prosperity

*Opportunity*

Snake | Horse | Goat | Monkey

Career

*Pioneer*

General
in
*The Self Chamber*
at
Rat/Horse

Dragon | Rooster

Career

*Pioneer*

Rabbit | Dog

Prosperity

*Opportunity*

Self

⊙ General

Tiger | Ox | Rat | Pig

6.13 The Self as General in the 12 Chambers 235

# GENERAL in Self in the Ox or Goat Chamber

### The Self—General & Crimson

General in the Ox or Goat chamber would share house with Crimson, which prides itself in putting on the best performance. The action-oriented General would lend power to the outgoing Crimson. These two, therefore, will join forces to create a dynamic duo that can withstand action and volatility. They would thrive on risk and adventure.

However, an obstructed ■ Crimson in the Self Chamber would point to conflicts or disputes arising from interrelationships or legal matters with or involving one's siblings or blood relations. It is important to be prepared to act with caution and humility when dealing with these matters.

### Career—Commander & Pioneer

We have Commander and Pioneer here, which indicates hard work. Combined with the above, we are witnessing changeability, creativity, and physical challenges. You will be out there at the forefront of any new industry, perhaps wearing different hats as befitting the circumstance. The Armed Forces would suit Commander-Pioneer in Career,, i.e., the police, army, peace-keeping, etc. Auspicious stars in the same house, opposite, or at 120° would aid career advancement.

A prosperous star in its own right, Commander with Power ⏶ to boot can expect to be rewarded for its relentless efforts. Self-empowerment is the key word. Delegate wisely, but never let go of the reins because only you can hold the power to your own destiny and ultimate success.

### Prosperity—Emperor & Opportunity

Holding court are the far-sighted Emperor that rules finance and Opportunity which focuses on investments, gaming and gambling. Coupled with Crimson-General in Self, we have someone who is not afraid of extremely high risk-taking and must be especially wary of the Killing Stars or Catalysts entering the Triangle of Influence. These will be times of major losses, and it would be well to adopt a safe, secure strategy. Refrain from any business endeavor in the face of the Obstruction Catalyst ■ in the same house or opposite. The only times to engage in high-risk trading or investments would be when you see the strong, supportive stars.

# SELF: GENERAL & CRIMSON
## CAREER: COMMANDER & PIONEER
### PROSPERITY: EMPEROR & OPPORTUNITY

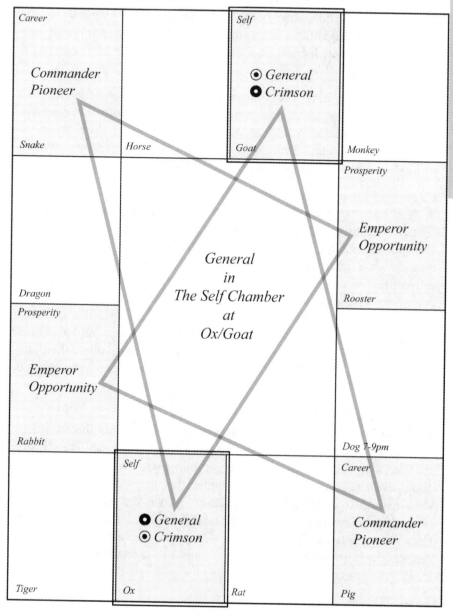

6.13 The Self as General in the 12 Chambers 237

# GENERAL in Self in the Tiger or Monkey Chamber

**The Self—General**

Whether male or female, the General in the Self or Career sector is a sure indicator of a brilliant career. Blessed with great tenacity, it will set goals and overcome anything. Like Pioneer, General will have his share of turbulence, for both will immediately respond to the beckoning of adventure, even danger. General can withstand any work environment, learning and sharpening its skills as it carves its way to success.

At opposite, we have the Emperor-Vault pair, giving the Self the distinctions of the traditional long-term investor. Both the Emperor and Vault are major wealth stars. At Brilliant and helped by other positives, the General-Emperor-Vault constellation would make for a shrewd, coolheaded investor who could play the markets well.

**Career—Pioneer**

With Pioneer in Career, it would not be surprising to see this star fighter creating a new post, department, or working system for itself. With its innovative style and ideas, it will lead its team to places no one has ever been before. It is often seen tearing through extreme difficulties with a conviction that only true Pioneers have and emerging victorious. At its best, a Brilliant Pioneer will be an inspired, strong leader who should be put in positions in large multinational organizations, opening up new markets and frontiers and guiding its band of brothers to success. Alternatively, a Brilliant Pioneer with Power⬈ would top the ranks in any of the Armed Forces.

**Prosperity—Opportunity**

With the intensely risk-oriented Opportunity here, plus the swiftness of both the General and Pioneer, we have a formation that is radically inclined towards speculation, even gambling. This would be good and could even reap in big winnings under the auspices of the positive stars (Stardust & Delight, Completion); however, the Killing Stars (Ram, Spinning Top, Void and Punishment) and the Obstruction■ Catalyst will always ignite their tendency to gamble and so will pave the way to ruin. In the face of these, only the safest trades should be executed or none at all.

# SELF: GENERAL
## CAREER: PIONEER    PROSPERITY: OPPORTUNITY

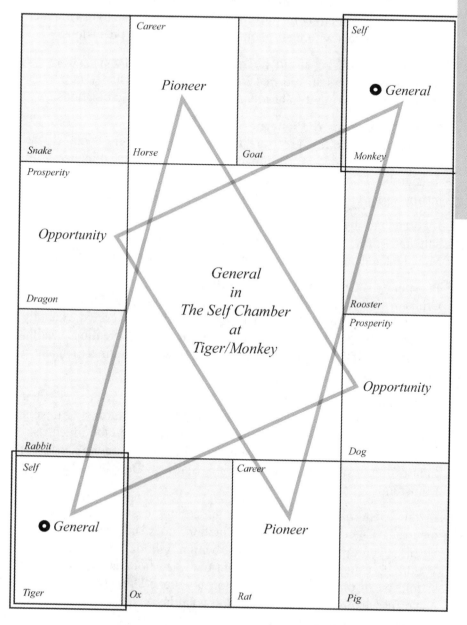

6.13 The Self as General in the 12 Chambers 239

# GENERAL in Self in the Rabbit or Rooster Chamber

## The Self—Commander & General

With Commander, the action-oriented wealth star here, we are seeing a decisive leader who will lead his army to their goals under any circumstance. Joined by the unstoppable General, these two will reach their mutual goals with well-planned actions and swift decisions.

This pair will forge ahead no matter the circumstance. These are qualities of leaders in the making, and they will usually not waste much time in making it to head large multinational organizations.

## Career—Emperor & Pioneer

Joining them here in Career are Emperor and Pioneer. Together, the 4-star constellation of Commander-General-Emperor-Pioneer is a force to be reckoned with. CEOs of major organizations and financial institutions would have this combination of stars.

If attached by Power↗, the Emperor—already a hot-headed autocrat—may become overburdened. Look for calmness from his Ministers and advisors (the Auspicious Stars) to assist him to success.

## Prosperity—Crimson & Opportunity

Crimson in Prosperity denotes highly diversified and high-risk undertakings. We will see Crimson among the crowd, happily enjoying all the attention and at the same time creating wealth. Opportunity if joined by Fire and/or Bell will combine to make a dynamic duo.

Commander and General would be swift risk-takers in their investment strategy. Joined by the highly adventurous Crimson-Opportunity pair here in Prosperity, there may just be too much risk-taking. Therefore, any speculation should only be undertaken in the light of the positive stars (Completion, Stardust, Delight and the four Ministers).

In the event of the Killing Stars appearing, heavy losses may be incurred. Then this 4-star combination does not bode well for business ventures at all. Even in the benign light of Completion or the Wealth $ Catalyst, a well thought-out plan for risk management should be in place before any action is taken. This array of several powerful wealth stars may just be too volatile. At these times, keep to a well-balanced financial plan.

# SELF: GENERAL & COMMANDER
## CAREER: EMPEROR & PIONEER
## PROSPERITY: CRIMSON & OPPORTUNITY

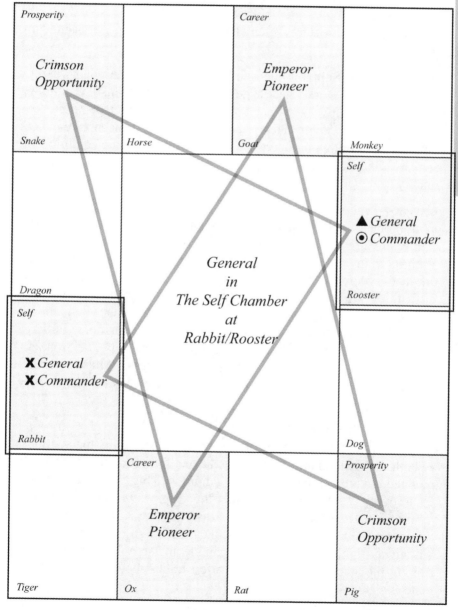

6.13 The Self as General in the 12 Chambers 241

# GENERAL in Self in the Dragon or Dog Chamber

**The Self—General**
Whether male or female, the General in the Self or Career sector is a sure indicator of a brilliant career. Blessed with great tenacity, it will set goals and overcome anything. Like Pioneer, General will have his share of turbulence, for both will immediately respond to the beckoning of adventure, even danger. General can withstand any work environment.

At opposite, the Self is influenced by the Crimson-Vault pair whereby the conservative Vault gets a dose of adventure from the outgoing Crimson. These two apparent opposites are far from being at odds with each other. Vault takes pride in its work. Crimson cares about performance. Both, therefore, will aim towards the same commitment. Led by General, we can expect this constellation to produce star quality achievers.

**Career—Pioneer**
With Pioneer here in Career, it would not be surprising to see this star fighter creating a new post, department, or working system for itself. With its innovative style and ideas, it will lead its team to places no one had ever been before. It is often seen tearing through extreme difficulties with a conviction that only true pioneers have and emerging victorious. At its best, a Brilliant Pioneer would be an inspired, strong leader who should be put in positions in large multinational organizations, opening up new markets and frontiers, and/or guiding its band of brothers to success. Alternatively, a Brilliant Pioneer with Power ↗ would top the ranks in any of the armed forces.

**Prosperity—Opportunity**
With the intensely risk-oriented Opportunity here, plus the swiftness of both the General and Pioneer, we have a formation that is radically inclined towards speculation, even gambling. This would be good and could even reap big winnings under the auspices of the positive stars (Stardust & Delight, Completion). However, the Killing Stars (Ram, Spinning Top, Void and Punishment) and the Obstruction■ Catalyst will always ignite the tendency to gamble and so will pave the way to ruin. In the face of these, only the safest trades should be executed or none at all.

# SELF: GENERAL

## CAREER: PIONEER     PROSPERITY: OPPORTUNITY

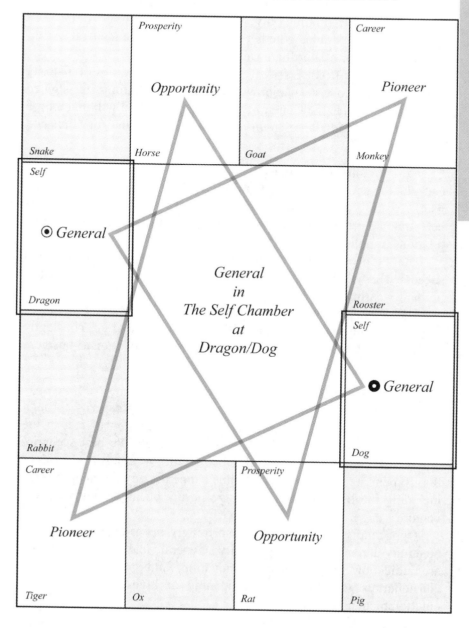

6.13 The Self as General in the 12 Chambers 243

# GENERAL in Self in the Snake or Pig Chamber

### The Self—General & Emperor
General will set goals and overcome any obstacle in order to succeed. Like The Pioneer, General will have its share of turbulence but to a lesser degree. At twinkling only, be wary of surrounding Killing Stars turning on its dark side. Whether male or female, the General in Self is a sure indicator of a brilliant career.

Also here, a Bright Emperor has most of the qualities of a strong monarch. Emperor is a major wealth star. With strong, far-sighted leadership in place, the General-Emperor combination will make for a dynamic CEO in large multinational corporations or financial institutions.

### Career—Crimson & Pioneer
Cut out for social activities, Crimson in the Career sector will find itself basking in attention and ultimately success. Crimson is performance-driven and will soar above the rest whether it is in public relations or politics.

The Pioneer, also here in Career, indicates inventiveness and success. He will be out there at the forefront of any new industry, perhaps wearing different hats as befitting the circumstance.

The General-Emperor-Crimson-Pioneer constellation will be about emerging markets or international concerns that are constantly evolving. With the Auspicious Stars, this is a constellation of business leaders.

### Prosperity—Commander & Opportunity
Commander is a major star that dispenses direct prosperity through sheer hard work. To have the prosperity star coming to rest in the Prosperity Chamber of one's chart is undoubtedly the best scenario, unless, of course, the dreaded Obstruction ■ Catalyst, Void, or Punishment are there, too. Should this happen in any moment in time, including the lifetime, do not engage in any business or investment venture.

Opportunity here relishes the seemingly never-ending rounds of meetings and partying. Opportunity, General, and Pioneer together are indication for turbulence, innovation, and great change. This constellation will shine on the opening of high-end markets like entertainment and lifestyle.

# SELF: GENERAL & EMPEROR
## CAREER: CRIMSON & PIONEER
## PROSPERITY: COMMANDER & OPPORTUNITY

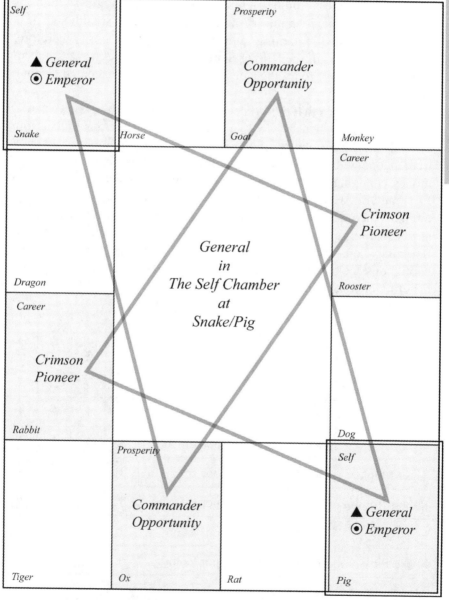

| Self | | Prosperity | |
|---|---|---|---|
| ▲ *General* ⊙ *Emperor* | | *Commander Opportunity* | |
| Snake | Horse | Goat | Monkey |

| | Career |
|---|---|
| *General in The Self Chamber at Snake/Pig* | *Crimson Pioneer* |
| Dragon | Rooster |

Career

*Crimson Pioneer*

Rabbit

| Prosperity | | Self |
|---|---|---|
| *Commander Opportunity* | | ▲ *General* ⊙ *Emperor* |
| Ox | Rat | Pig |

Tiger

Dog

6.13 The Self as General in the 12 Chambers 245

# GENERAL in the Self House Investment Strategy

**Completion or Auspicious Stars Needed**
General in Self will have Opportunity in the Prosperity. It will have many life lessons hurled from all directions. Coupled with Opportunity, the pair will have more than its fair share of investment/business foibles. Opportunity is very aggressive in its strategy. However, it should be noted that it is not a wealth star. It is about making deals, gaming, and entertainment. It must, therefore, heed the warnings of the Killing Stars and the Obstruction ■ Catalyst. In the face of these, only the safest trades should be executed or none at all.

The only times that the Wheel of Fortune will turn in its favor will be when it is assisted by Completion and the Auspicious Stars. Note that the Wealth $ Catalyst, if attached to Opportunity does not equal a tremendous winning streak. This only means a tremendous amount of money changing hands! It would form a positive liaison if found with Fire and/or Bell. This dynamic formation would create the circumstance whereby Opportunity could hit the Jackpot. However, if at the same time, it should meet up with Obstruction, Ram, or Spinning Top, any such winnings would soon be lost again. The contiguous locking-in of earnings (e.g., in gold or real estate) would benefit General-Opportunity in the long run.

| HOURS | SELF HOUSE | PROSPERITY | LONG | SHORT | DIVERSE | FOCUS |
|---|---|---|---|---|---|---|
| Rat/Horse | Genrl | Oppor | + | + | + | + |
| Ox/Goat | Genrl/Crmsn | Oppor/Emper | + | + | + | + |
| Tiger/Monkey | Genrl | Oppor | + | + | + | + |
| Rabbit/Rooster | Genrl/Comdr | Oppor/Crmsn | + | + | + | + |
| Dragon/Dog | Genrl | Oppor | + | + | + | + |
| Snake/Pig | Genrl/Emper | Oppor/Comdr | + | + | + | + |

# The Self as Pioneer in the 12 Chambers

| | | | |
|---|---|---|---|
| | | | |
| *Snake* | *Horse* | *Goat* | *Monkey* |
| | | | |
| *Dragon* | | | *Rooster* |
| *Rabbit* | | | *Dog* |
| | | | |
| *Tiger* | *Ox* | *Rat* | *Pig* |

CHARLES MARION

RUSSELL

———— ✦ ————

*A Pioneer*

*destroys things*

*and*

*calls it civilization*

# PIONEER in Self in the Rat or Horse Chamber

## The Self—Pioneer
Pioneer is about challenges, bravery, and adventure and will be at the forefront, opening new doors. At the Rat or Horse, the Brilliant Pioneers will throw themselves into their careers and have little time for anything else.

Pioneer, Opportunity, and General make up the perfect action-oriented triangle. Individuals with this constellation in Self will realize exceptional achievements at the helm of large multinational corporations. If free of the Killing Stars or the Obstruction■ Catalyst in this triangle of influence, their achievements will be awesome.

## Career—Opportunity
Opportunity in Career carries the implication of a highly competitive work atmosphere in the arenas of entertainment and luxury items/experiences like cars, couture, fine wines and dining.

With Pioneer at play in the Self, we would see them dealing in high-end security products, e.g., weapons, armaments or counter-terrorism, security, cinema and entertainment. The Auspicious Stars would also shine the way towards success in these areas.

## Prosperity—General
It is Pioneer's personality to be the typical emotional investor. This will be especially so when the Self moves into the Prosperity Chamber.

The General will set goals and overcome any obstacle. However, General here in Prosperity would lack forethought and planning. His investment strategy is just to jump in!

Like The Pioneer, The General will have his share of turbulence (to a lesser degree). Therefore, in finance, the Pioneer-General pair is set for great turmoil.

Even in the benign light of the Auspicious Stars, this constellation should call for tight risk management strategies before any action is taken. Stricken by the Killing Stars or Obstruction■ in any moment in time, including the lifetime, this individual must not engage in any business or investment venture at all.

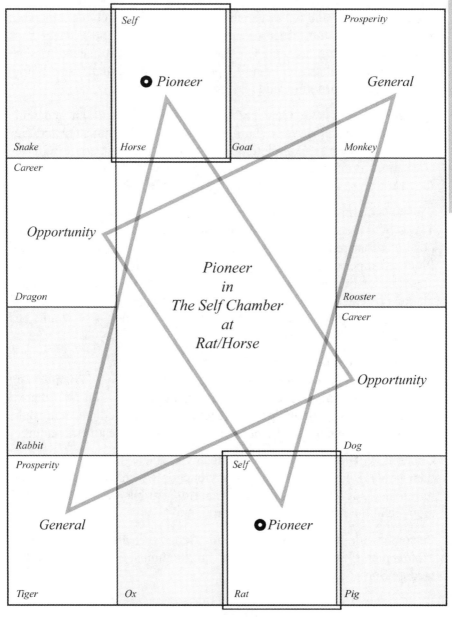

# SELF: PIONEER
## CAREER: OPPORTUNITY   PROSPERITY: GENERAL

Self

○ Pioneer

Prosperity

General

Snake

Horse

Goat

Monkey

Career

Opportunity

Dragon

Rooster

Pioneer
in
The Self Chamber
at
Rat/Horse

Career

Opportunity

Rabbit

Dog

Prosperity

General

Self

○ Pioneer

Tiger

Ox

Rat

Pig

6.14 The Self as Pioneer in the 12 Chambers 249

# PIONEER in Self in the Ox or Goat Chamber

## The Self—Pioneer & Emperor

With a Brilliant or Bright Pioneer here, our Emperor is well-supported. The Pioneer benefits with having the Emperor around–the highest authority and only one who would be able to subdue him. The Emperor lessens the throes of upheaval caused by The Pioneer and ensures a smooth transition. The Pioneer of the action-packed tri-star formation (the other two being Opportunity and General), stands for great changes, uprooting, and tearing down.

Whether at the Ox or Goat hour, our Emperor is Brilliant and will display all of his positive strengths. Enhanced by the ministers and the lucky stars, such as Completion and Winged Horse, his rise will be even more dramatic. At its zenith, it enriches and banishes evil. In fact, he is so strong that he accommodates more than eradicates.

## Career—Crimson & Opportunity

These two sociable and accommodating stars will be outstanding in positions that require constant exchanges with the opposite sex. The Pioneer-Emperor-Crimson-Opportunity formation would do well in any field or business venture that would involve the high-end niche markets of entertainment, fine-dining, fast cars, jewelry or the design or creation of such. With the Auspicious Stars, their rise would be phenomenal.

## Prosperity—Commander & General

Commander and General here make up the perfect Triangle of Success. However, if stricken by the dreaded Obstruction (■) in any moment in time, including the lifetime, it's expedient that this individual not engage in any business or high-risk investment venture.

Generals will set goals and overcome any obstacle in order to achieve their goals. Like The Pioneers, The Generals will have their share of turbulence but to a lesser degree. Therefore, in business and finance, they are at the forefront of great turmoil and change.

Persons with this constellation in Self will attain exceptional achievements at the helm of large multinational corporations, e.g., George Soros.

# Self: Pioneer
## Career: Crimson & Opportunity
## Prosperity: Commander & General

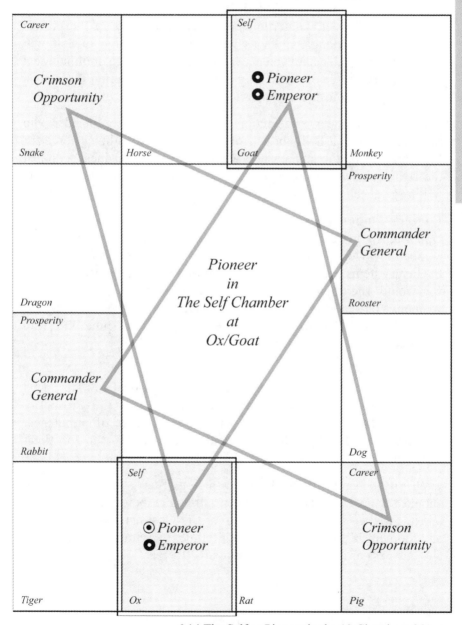

6.14 The Self as Pioneer in the 12 Chambers 251

# PIONEER in Self in the Tiger or Monkey Chamber

## The Self—Pioneer

Pioneers will be at the forefront, opening new doors. They are about challenges, bravery, and adventure. However, at Tiger or Monkey, they must beware of the Killing Stars activating their dark negative personality. Pioneer, Opportunity and General make up the perfect action-oriented triangle. Persons with this constellation in Self will attain exceptional achievements at the helm of large multinational corporations. If free of the Killing Stars or the Obstruction ■ Catalyst in this triangle of influence, their achievements will be great.

Opposite the Pioneer is the action-packed, Brilliant Commander who joins forces with a Brilliant Mirror, which is the stabilizing force for Pioneer. This partnership ensures a smooth-running business with just the right balance of forethought, strength, and action. These people will forge ahead with honesty and integrity.

## Career—Opportunity

Opportunity in Career carries the implication of a complicated, competitive work atmosphere, having to do with entertainment and the luxury items, e.g., jewelry, wines. With Pioneer at play in the Self, we would see them dealing in high-end security products, e.g., weapons or counter-terrorism, security, fast cars, cinema and entertainment. The Auspicious Stars would also shine the way towards success in these areas.

## Prosperity—General

It is Pioneer's personality to be the typical emotional investor. This will be especially so when the Self moves into the Prosperity Chamber. Like Pioneer, General will have his share of turbulence. Therefore, in finance, the Pioneer-General pair is set for great turbulence.

Even in the benign light of the Auspicious Stars, this constellation should set up tight risk management strategies before any action is taken. Stricken by the Killing Stars or the Obstruction■ Catalyst in any moment in time, including the lifetime, they must not engage in any business or investment venture at all.

# SELF: PIONEER

## CAREER: OPPORTUNITY    PROSPERITY: GENERAL

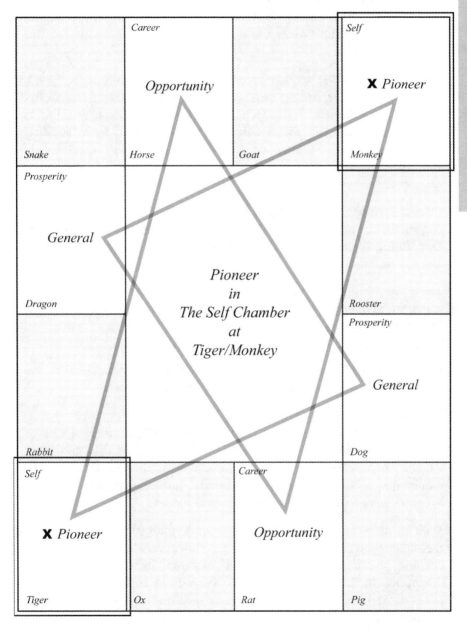

| Career | | | Self |
|---|---|---|---|
| *Opportunity* | | | **X** *Pioneer* |
| Snake | Horse | Goat | Monkey |

Prosperity — *General* — Dragon

*Pioneer in The Self Chamber at Tiger/Monkey*

Rooster — Prosperity — *General* — Dog

| Self | Career | | |
|---|---|---|---|
| **X** *Pioneer* | *Opportunity* | | |
| Tiger | Ox | Rat | Pig |

6.14 The Self as Pioneer in the 12 Chambers 253

# PIONEER in Self in the Rabbit or Rooster Chamber

### The Self—Pioneer & Crimson

Pioneers are about challenges, bravery, and adventure, so they will be at the forefront, opening new doors to explore what is there. If attached with the Power ↗ Catalyst, we are seeing even bigger responsibilities. The Power Catalyst here will offer authority to this busy leader.

Crimson is an artist by nature and loves being surrounded by art, music, and theatre. Being performance-driven, Crimson can deftly weave her influence and reach her goals with dexterity. She is splendidly munificent. Since Crimson also has to do with blood, if Crimson has Wealth $ attached, we would have powerful innovation combined with brilliant performance. The outcome should bring success and wealth.

### Career—Commander and Opportunity

A Brilliant Commander with Fame✿ shares house with the Brilliant Opportunity here. The Commander brings in wealth. With wealth in place, Fame follows.

These four major stars of power↗, action and performance are well-suited to be placed in a career of politics, acting or entertainment. An individual with this combination will be right at home if placed on stage facing an audience. Success would be found here.

If joined by Completion (or better still, Completion and Horse), we will see this individual rising to great heights in this arena.

### Prosperity—Emperor & General

Presided by The Emperor and General here, The Self will deal with or have financial prowess. However, this does not necessarily indicate a wealthy person but may indicate a career in financial control or money management. If surrounded by the Auspicious Stars, these two Wealth$ stars will then attract wealth and success.

With Crimson and Pioneer in Self, we are looking at a highly versatile risk-taker when it comes to investing. However, should Opportunity become obstructed ■ at 120°, it is essential be wary of financial downfalls. In this instance, it would be wise to curb risk-taking and adopt a safer and more secure strategy until the moment passes, and the stars turn positive again.

6.14 The Self as Pioneer in the 12 Chambers 255

# PIONEER in Self in the Dragon or Dog Chamber

## The Self—Pioneer

Pioneer is about challenges, bravery, and adventure. At the Rat or Horse Chamber, the Brilliant Pioneers will throw themselves into their careers and have little time for anything else. Pioneer, Opportunity and General make up the perfect action-oriented triangle. Persons with this constellation in Self will achieve exceptional results at the helm of large multinational corporations if free of the Killing Stars or the Obstruction■ Catalyst. Opposite the Pioneer-Self is Emperor. The Pioneer benefits with having the Emperor around who will lessen the throes of upheaval caused by Pioneer and ensure a smooth transition. A leader in every sense of the word, the Emperor will transfer this trait to the volatile Pioneer, raising its vibrations positively to new heights.

## Career—Opportunity

Opportunity in Career carries the implication of a complicated, competitive work environment and has to do with entertainment and the luxury items, e.g., jewelry, wines. Pioneer-Emperor at play in the Self, plus Opportunity would be seen in any field or business venture that would involve the high-end niche markets of entertainment, fine dining, fast cars, or financial planning, design or the creation of such. If Auspicious Stars are nearby, their rise would be phenomenal.

## Prosperity—General

It is Pioneer's personality to be the typical emotional investor. This will be especially so when the Self moves into the Prosperity Chamber. At this time, many Killing Stars will gather around. The General will set goals and overcome any obstacle in order to achieve his goals. However, General here in Prosperity will lack forethought and planning. His investment strategy is just to jump right in!

Therefore, in finance, the Pioneer-General pair is set for great turbulence. Even in the benign light of the Auspicious Stars, this constellation should call for tight risk management before any action is taken. If stricken by the Killing Stars or Obstruction ■ in any moment in time, especially throughout the lifetime, they must not engage in any business or investment venture at all.

# SELF: PIONEER

## CAREER: OPPORTUNITY    PROSPERITY: GENERAL

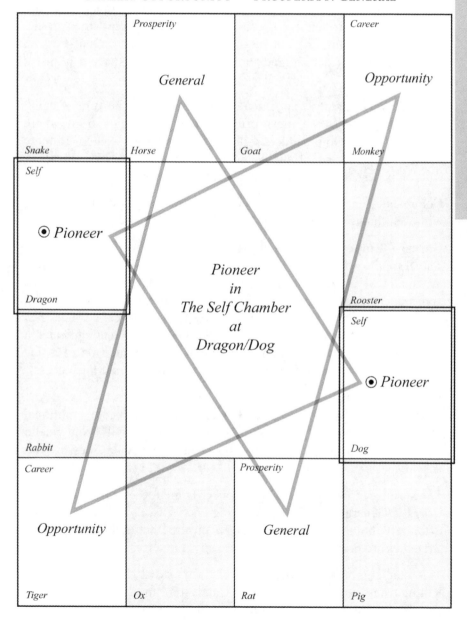

| | Prosperity | Career | |
|---|---|---|---|
| | *General* | *Opportunity* | |
| *Snake* | *Horse* | *Goat* | *Monkey* |
| Self | | | |
| ⊙ *Pioneer* | *Pioneer in The Self Chamber at Dragon/Dog* | | |
| *Dragon* | | *Rooster* | |
| | | Self ⊙ *Pioneer* | |
| *Rabbit* | | *Dog* | |
| Career | Prosperity | | |
| *Opportunity* | *General* | | |
| *Tiger* | *Ox* | *Rat* | *Pig* |

6.14 The Self as Pioneer in the 12 Chambers 257

# PIONEER in Self in the Snake or Pig Chamber

## The Self—Pioneer & Commander

Joining Pioneer in the same house is Commander, our action hero. These two sensational stars will combine power, creativity, and adventure in their run for success. We are seeing craftsmen of the highest order, who will not be daunted by any obstruction. For the goal-oriented and determined Pioneer-Commander, success is just a matter of time.

If the Power➚ Catalyst is present, Commanders can be sure of being rewarded for their relentless efforts. Taking the reins from where Pioneers began, Commanders will see them through to their ultimate destiny and success. Heading new ventures and seeing these to fruition is best suited to the Pioneer-Commander pair.

Commanders are wealthy in their own right. If joined by Fame✿, with wealth already in place, Fame will follow.

## Career—Emperor & Opportunity

The Emperor here will guide towards the high-end, exclusive multinational organizations. Opportunity also makes his glamorous appearance here and provides the opening ceremonies for anything having to do with entertainment and lifestyle—movies, casinos, fast cars, or couture and jewelry, etc. Opportunity in Career indicates a constant round of partying and entertainment. The addition of a few Auspicious Stars would then light the way to entrepreneurial success.

## Prosperity—Crimson & General

If attached by Wealth $ here, Crimson would indicate emotional wealth, that is, happiness. Close relations or siblings will bring wealth or will introduce propitious situations. This sociable star blesses with her prosperity.

The surging of Commander and Pioneer is met up by the enthusiastic Crimson/General pair. The risk-taking energy is, therefore, becoming extremely high, so it's essential to ensure that risk management strategies are properly in place before anything else.

This star combination would become very weak if faced with the Killing Stars and/or Obstruction Catalyst■. In this instance, any entrepreneurial or trading pursuits should be shelved.

# SELF: PIONEER & COMMANDER
## CAREER: EMPEROR & OPPORTUNITY
## PROSPERITY: CRIMSON & GENERAL

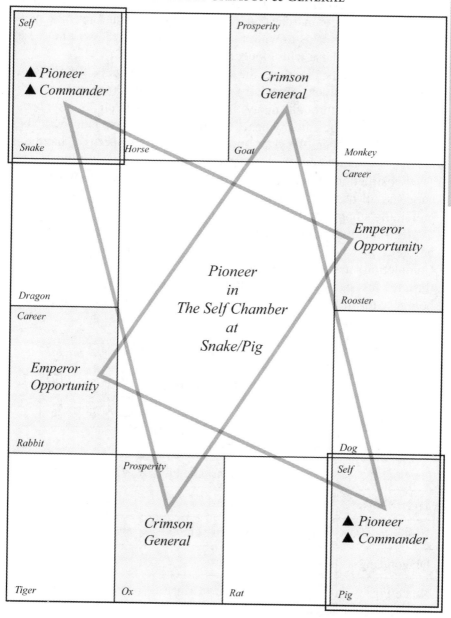

| Self | | Prosperity | |
|---|---|---|---|
| ▲ Pioneer<br>▲ Commander | | Crimson<br>General | |
| Snake | Horse | Goat | Monkey |
| | | | Career |
| | | | Emperor<br>Opportunity |
| Dragon | | | Rooster |
| Career | Pioneer<br>in<br>The Self Chamber<br>at<br>Snake/Pig | | |
| Emperor<br>Opportunity | | | |
| Rabbit | | | Dog |
| | Prosperity | | Self |
| | Crimson<br>General | | ▲ Pioneer<br>▲ Commander |
| Tiger | Ox | Rat | Pig |

6.14 The Self as Pioneer in the 12 Chambers 259

# PIONEER in the Self House Investment Strategy

## An Emotional Investor

Pioneer is one of the major stars which supports and is benefitted by the Emperor. Its nature involves tearing down and rebuilding which brings in far greater consequences than General. Leaving destruction in its wake, Pioneer marches on, hacking new paths, and opening new doors for the rest of us to walk through. The road ahead will not be a bed of roses for those with Pioneer in Self.

In investments, therefore, the same lessons will apply—it will win some but lose much, especially with General in Prosperity, which fights its way through many hardships as well. It is Pioneer's personality to be the typical emotional investor. This will be especially so when this star moves into the Prosperity Chamber, making any entrepreneurial or trading pursuit extremely vulnerable. The Obstruction ■ Catalyst will also add to its woes. When this happens, all business or entrepreneurial plans should be low risk or preferably stopped and shelved until the stars turn.

Its time will come when the Wealth $ or Power ↗ Catalyst becomes attached, and the other Auspicious Stars (e.g. Emperor, Completion) appear in the same house, opposite, or at 120°; then fortunes lost can be retrieved. Pioneer's investment approach should be one with full risk management strategies in place and a low-risk, longer-term portfolio.

| HOURS | SELF HOUSE | PROSPERITY | LONG | SHORT | DIVERSE | FOCUS |
|---|---|---|---|---|---|---|
| Rat/Horse | Pneer | Genrl | ✦ | | ✦ | |
| Ox/Goat | Pneer/Emper | Genrl/Comdr | ✦ | | ✦ | |
| Tiger/Monkey | Pneer | Genrl | ✦ | | ✦ | |
| Rabbit/Rooster | Pneer/Crmsn | Genrl/Emper | ✦ | | ✦ | |
| Dragon/Dog | Pneer | Genrl | ✦ | | ✦ | |
| Snake/Pig | Pneer/Comdr | Genrl/Crmsn | ✦ | | ✦ | |

# EARTH

SUSTAINS 地利

# JACK WALCH

*Control your*

*DESTINY*

*or*

*someone else will.*

# Chapter 7

# *Interpretation*

## *The Life, 10-Year, & Current Year Charts*

The Chinese word for destiny is made up of two characters 命 *ming*, "the life," and 運 *yun*, "that which surrounds." By learning to read the meaning of the stars in our charts, we would be able to understand and come to terms with our specific destiny and be able to work with the different energy that comes in and surrounds us at any given time zone to determine the best strategy towards our destiny and success. Here is where we learn when to ebb and when to flow by following the stars and listening to what they are telling us in the twelve important sectors of our life.

This is all that Stargate is about—the study of the energy that would surround us at any given time—the lifetime, 10-year cycles, specific years, months, weeks, even days or hours.

As you'll discover, this book mirrors real-life circumstances as much as possible. If it is considered that certain sections of the book depart from what would be considered a real-life situation, these were created to illustrate how to attain success or to read the stars and charts at each specific time span, be it the whole life, specific years, or 10-year phases.

The following pages are examples to help you begin to use the Stargate program quickly so you can begin to read the charts with confidence. As we are dealing with the topic of success here, all the charts shown have lines connecting the Self Chamber with its opposite (Career) and 120° (Prosperity) so you can easily identify the Success Triangle.

## Mr. Right = Mr. Wrong (Flower's Story)

**Born January 31, 1969 @ 8:00 a.m., Xiao Hua (Flower)** was newly arrived in Hong Kong from China. At the time, slender, young and beautiful at thirty-five, she, nevertheless, thought she was "over the hill" and believed her biological clock was quickly ticking away. She was not going to waste any more time.

Slightly desperate, her concern was beginning to show as she scoured the dating scene, looking for her Mr. Right. Through friends of friends, she met a young man who claimed to be an ABC (American-Born Chinese) jewelry merchant, having just arrived in the city for business purposes. Immediately, it seemed that ABC was besotted with her.

Needless to say, Flower was overjoyed and couldn't believe her luck in "catching" him. She started planning the wedding and their life together. She had no idea! In the end, in little over a few months, Flower was swindled out of over HK $1 million (US $130,000).

She was heart-broken and became depressed that she had been fooled so completely. Eventually, ABC was arrested and charged with fraud and felony. However, that offered little comfort to Flower as nothing was left of her entire savings.

*In her Life Chart, Flower has a twinkling Crimson plus a dark Pioneer in Self, which makes for an attractive, sought-after person who is also headstrong. Coupled with Pond (C32) which brings carnal misadventure, the groundwork was already laid for someone who could easily be taken advantage of. Like Encounter, Pond is flirtatious but delivers much more vice. With none of Encounter's artistic leanings, its low vibrations are only about sexual gratification and lust. If paired with a Killing Star in Self, it is a sure sign of scandals and destruction. Its pull becomes even more detrimental if paired with another flirtatious star, a Killing Star or the Obstacle■ Catalyst. In Career, we have Opportunity with Wealth $ attached. This is indicative of working in entertainment, clubs, casinos, etc. She also has the pair of romance stars C7 (Happiness) and C31 (Lover—which is always opposite). These occupying Career and Spouse indicate that the career-romantic circles are intertwined with many helpful individuals, i.e., clients. Flower's profession can more or less be deduced.*

*Flower's 10-Year Chart 2001-2010 (Age 33-42)*

| SELF | OPPOSITE | PROSPERITY | KARMIC |
|---|---|---|---|
| RAM/FIRE | WAIF | SUN | ARTS |
| LIT. MINISTER | MOON | MESSENGER | |

| PEERS | 2011-2020 丁<br>PROSP/L 巳 | THE SELF | 2001-2010 戊<br>MINORS 午 | ELDERS | 1991-2000 己<br>SPOUSE 未 | KARMIC | 1981-1990 庚<br>PEERS 申 |
|---|---|---|---|---|---|---|---|
| ⊛ EMPER | | | | | | | |
| ▲ GENRL | | | | | | | |
| COMP | | RAM FIRE | | DELI VOID | | | |
| 8 | | 9 4 | | 6 | | 7 3 | |
| | | *LITE* | | | | | ARTS |
| T  T | | T  J  E  F | | C  **G** | | T  T | |
| D  C | | c  S  G  g | | 31 S | | X  g | |
| B   BS   **JS**   TD | | A   GF   **ZS**   DK | | DW  **FB**  **TS**  BF | | LG  **DH**  SJ  ZB | |

| SPOUSE | 2021-2030 丙<br>HEALTH 辰 | | | | | PROPERT | 1971-1980 辛<br>THE SELF 酉 |
|---|---|---|---|---|---|---|---|
| ○ INTEL ■ ■ | | | **Ten Year Chart** | | | ▲ CRMSN | |
| ⊛ SCHOL | | | **A 10 year analysis** | | | ✕ PNEER | |
| SPIN | | | | | | | |
| 10 | | | **2001-2010** | | | 1 | |
| | | | **(33-42)** | | | | |
| S  Y  F  H  t | | | | | | T  P  C | |
| T  S  L  G  s | | 1971-1980<br>(3-12) | 1981-1990<br>(13-22) | 1991-2000<br>(23-32) | | K  S  32 | |
| S   LS   HG   BH | | | | | | GD  **BF**  **HQ** D46 | |

| MINORS | 2031-2040 乙<br>TRAVEL 卯 | 2001-2010<br>(33-42) | 2011-2020<br>(43-52) | 2021-2030<br>(53-62) | | CAREER | 2081-2090 壬<br>ELDERS 戌 |
|---|---|---|---|---|---|---|---|
| ✕ MIROR | | 2031-2040<br>(63-72) | 2041-2050<br>(73-82) | 2051-2060<br>(83-92) | | | |
| LEFT PUNI | | | | | | | |
| 2 | | 2061-2070<br>(93-102) | 2071-2080<br>(103-112) | 2081-2090<br>(113-122) | | | |
| T  T | | | | | | B  T  T | |
| f  G | | | Back | | | Z  k  F | |
| M   QL   Xs   LD | | | | | | MY  XS  **SM** Ys | |

| PROSPER | 2041-2050 甲<br>STAFF 寅 | HEALTH | 2051-2060 乙<br>CAREER 丑 | TRAVEL | 2061-2070 甲<br>PROPERT 子 | STAFF | 2071-2080 癸<br>KARMIC 亥 |
|---|---|---|---|---|---|---|---|
| ⊛ SUN  ○ ○ | | ○ COMDR | | ⊛ WAIF | | ⊛ VAULT | |
| ○ MESGR | | ○ OPPOR $ $ | | ○ MOON ↗ ↗ | | | |
| HORS BELL | | STAR | | | | RIGT | |
| | | 5 | | | | | |
| T  T  F  T | | K  C  Y  T | | J  C  L | | T  G | |
| Y  x  G  s | | W  7  D  S | | L  20 C | | W  C | |
| J   XH  SY  SP | | T   JJ   PA  **XH** | | Y   Zs   JX  **Gf** | | CS  FL  **GS**  WS | |
| Y  x  G  s | | W  7  D  S | | L  20 C | | W  C | |
| J   XH  SY  SP | | T   JJ   PA  **XH** | | Y   Zs   JX  **Gf** | | CS  FL  **GS**  WS | |

However, a *Killing Star, Void, is also in Spouse in the Life Chart, which brings broken romances and/or failed marriages. This star also works against anything having to do with Prosperity and wealth. Its characteristic is that any wealth gained will eventually be lost. With it being found in Spouse, it indicates these grievances are being caused by her significant other. Unfortunately, this is a lifetime phenomenon. A second or late marriage should counteract this.* All this happened during 2004, in her 4th 10-year period of 2001-2010 (33-42).

Note that the Self has a gathering of the Killing Stars Ram and Fire (Bright). *The Ram in the Self sector indicates a serious accident in the early part of this cycle, the effects of which will be lifelong. Fire is also present. As its name suggests, Fire would be able to quash Ram (its element being metal). However, it can be imagined that with these two ferocious Killing Stars both in Self and in conflict with each other, these ten years will not be a time of peace and tranquility.*

The dark Arts Minister (4) is also in Self. *If either of the Ministers is found in the Self sector, it makes for very interesting company. In their Brilliant hours, aided by other Brilliants, these individuals are heartbreakingly attractive to the opposite sex. Unfortunately, this one is too flighty for her own good, and any romantic pursuit will bring about much chagrin and unhappiness.*

Also in Self are Nemesis *(An Enemy will appear with regard to financial matters)*, Subpoena *(Possibility of legal disputes)*, and Literary Minister—all dark, all indicating disputes or hurt as their negative traits would be turned on in full force.

It is also obvious that the Spouse sector is obstructed with the fickle and extremely unreliable Intelligence■■ in double dosage. *Any long-term plan launched at the time that Obstruction prevails will fail to seed. As we are also dealing with (lateral) movements here, watch out for losses and delays or destruction of deliveries, communication, and travel plans. If allowed to escalate, the outcome would be feelings of despair and being out of control.* Can she blame herself for making all the wrong decisions during this time?

The good news is that opposite the Self she had the Waif. *Prodded by Fire and Ram, the normally indifferent Waif would have the ability to regain fortunes lost. The Brilliant and very powerful Moon↗↗ would also reap income and reestablish her savings plans.* Further, her marriage prospects should improve with her next ten year cycle (from age 43 to 52).

*Flower's 10-Year Chart 2001-2010 (Age 33-42)*

| SELF | OPPOSITE | PROSPERITY | KARMIC |
|---|---|---|---|
| RAM/FIRE | WAIF | SUN | ARTS |
| LIT. MINISTER | MOON | MESSENGER | |

| PEERS 2011-2020 丁 PROSP/L 巳 | THE SELF 2001-2010 戊 MINORS 午 | ELDERS 1991-2000 己 SPOUSE 未 | KARMIC 1981-1990 庚 PEERS 申 |
|---|---|---|---|
| ◉ EMPER | | | |
| ▲ GENRL | | | |
| COMP | RAM FIRE | DELI VOID | |
| 8 | 9 4 | 6 | 7 3 |
| | LITE | | ARTS |
| T T | T J E F | C G | T T |
| D C | c S G g | 31 S | X g |
| B BS JS TD | A GF ZS DK | DW FB TS BF | LG DH SJ ZB |

| SPOUSE 2021-2030 丙 HEALTH 辰 | Ten Year Chart | PROPERT 1971-1980 辛 THE SELF 酉 |
|---|---|---|
| ◯ INTEL ■ ■ | A 10 year analysis | ▲ CRMSN |
| ◉ SCHOL | | ✕ PNEER |
| SPIN | 2001-2010 | |
| 10 | (33-42) | 1 |

| | 1971-1980 (3-12) | 1981-1990 (13-22) | 1991-2000 (23-32) | |
|---|---|---|---|---|
| S Y F H t | 2001-2010 (33-42) | 2011-2020 (43-52) | 2021-2030 (53-62) | T P C |
| T S L G s | | | | K S 32 |
| S LS HG BH | 2031-2040 (63-72) | 2041-2050 (73-82) | 2051-2060 (83-92) | GD BF HQ D46 |

| MINORS 2031-2040 乙 TRAVEL 卯 | 2061-2070 (93-102) | 2071-2080 (103-112) | 2081-2090 (113-122) | CAREER 2081-2090 壬 ELDERS 戌 |
|---|---|---|---|---|
| ✕ MIROR | | | | |
| LEFT PUNI | | Back | | |
| 2 | | | | |
| T T | | | | B T T |
| f G | | | | Z k F |
| M QL Xs LD | | | | MY XS SM Ys |

| PROSPER 2041-2050 甲 STAFF 寅 | HEALTH 2051-2060 乙 CAREER 丑 | TRAVEL 2061-2070 甲 PROPERT 子 | STAFF 2071-2080 癸 KARMIC 亥 |
|---|---|---|---|
| ◉ SUN ◯◯ | ◯ COMDR | ◉ WAIF | ◉ VAULT |
| ◯ MESGR | ◯ OPPOR $ $ | ◯ MOON ↗↗ | |
| HORS BELL | STAR | | RIGT |
| | 5 | | |
| T T F T | K C Y T | J C L | T G |
| Y x G s | W 7 D S | L 20 C | W C |
| J XH SY SP | T JJ PA XH | Y Zs JX Gf | CS FL GS WS |

# CONFUCIUS

—✦—

*If you think in terms of a year,*

*plant a seed—*

*if in terms of ten years,*

*plant trees—*

*if in terms of 100 years,*

*teach the people.*

# The 10-Year Chart

When interpreting these charts, the most important chart to bear in mind at any given time would be the current 10-year chart. This is the first rule in chart reading.

For example, the current year chart may give a person all the green lights to go ahead; however, if the 10-year chart says that it's time out, and the best thing we could do for ourselves is to take a break, it's important to heed the advice of the 10-year chart.

It is no accident that the 10-year chart in Chinese is referred to as the 10-Year Overall Energy. It is essential to remember this rule. **Apply the 10-year chart (the stars and sub-headings colored blue) to all the subsequent yearly, monthly, weekly, and daily charts.**

Pay special attention to the blue-colored Catalysts ($☼↗■). They hold the key as to where we stand in any 10-year phase. The Obstruction Catalyst■ is the post powerful because it will destroy Wealth $ and turn Fame☼ into notoriety. Only Power↗ can withstand Obstruction■ and not be poisoned by its presence.

Given that every ten years the Self moves one slot (chamber) in the 10-year chart, we can all expect to have more or less eight different 10-year charts in this lifetime never to be repeated. (With twelve chambers to a chart, we'd need to live beyond age 120 to start from square one again.)

## Experiencing Some of Life's Twists and Turns

## (Mr. Wong's Story)

**Born in Hong Kong December 4, 1958 @ 8:00 a.m.,** Mr. Wong came from a middle-class family, and his father ran a small business. He had a happy childhood and furthered his education abroad. On his return home after graduating from college, he worked in sales and marketing for a number of multinational organizations.

In 1993, at age 36, he tried his hand at starting a business. Raising HK $5 million (US $650,000) mostly from his father, he invested this whole amount. Let's try to deduce from his 10-year chart (age 36-45) whether he would be successful.

### The Self at Age 36-45

Lacking any major stars in his Self house, we shall read those in the opposite sector (Travel). *The Bright Scholar with Wealth $ signifies heirlooms, inheritance, or financial help from the parents. However, Scholar bodes ill for anything having to do with business or money-making ventures.*

Also, *a Brilliant$O$ Intelligence is in retrograde■. This has to do with ideas and the decision-making process; these, alas, will fail to seed. An obstructed Intelligence also brings out the negative traits— the hesitant, doubtful self whereby Intelligence becomes its own enemy.*

In Properties, which also stands for his business, we have a Brilliant$O$ Opportunity with the Wealth$ attachment. *Money coming in from his social contacts.* Furthermore, the Brilliant Commander, a major prosperity star, was trailing Obstruction■, *which represented catastrophic money or liquidity problems. Note that in the Life Chart, this is reflecting the Self.* Under no circumstance should he have started his business within this 10-year phase. It is good to remember this rule: a major prosperity star in obstruction■ means a hemorrhage of money and well-being.

Opposing Properties are the Killing Stars Bell and Void, working against anything to do with wealth. The lucky stars Stardust and Delight are no match against these major Killing Stars.

The story goes that Mr. Wong invested the family fortune in a factory and manufacturing business. *However, these 10 years took him to the brink of ruin (Commander■).* He counted himself very fortunate because his father stepped in again *(Scholar with $)* and saw him out of this crisis.

Mr. Wong's 10-Year Chart 1993-2002 (Age 36-45)

| SELF | OPPOSITE | PROSPERITY | KARMIC |
|---|---|---|---|
| SPINNING TOP | WAIF MOON | RAM LIT. MANAGER | WAIF MOON |

| HEALTH 2063-2072 丁 SPOUSE 巳 | PROSPER 2073-2082 戊 PEERS 午 | MINORS 1963-1972 己 THE SELF 未 | SPOUSE 1973-1982 庚 ELDERS 申 |
|---|---|---|---|
| ◉ EMPER ↗<br>▲ GENRL<br>COMP FIRE<br>6 1<br><br>C T<br>31 C<br>LG BS LD **WS** | RAM<br><br>*LITE*<br><br>T T **T** T F<br>c X **Y** g g<br>DW LS JX BH | DELI BELL VOID<br><br><br><br>G T<br>S D<br>A QL PA TD | HORS<br>7<br><br>ARTS<br><br>T Y T<br>W S k<br>B **XH** SY DK |

| TRAVEL 2053-2062 丙 MINORS 辰 | | | PEERS 1983-1992 辛 KARMIC 酉 |
|---|---|---|---|
| ◉ INTEL ■<br>◉ SCHOL $<br>SPIN<br><br>J T E<br>S x G<br>GD **GF** SP Ys | **Ten Year Chart**<br>**A 10 year analysis**<br><br>**1993-2002**<br>**(36-45)** | | ▲ CRMSN<br>✕ PNEER<br><br><br>S JJ Xs **BF** |

|  |  |  |  |  |
|---|---|---|---|---|
| 1963-1972 (6-15) | 1973-1982 (16-25) | 1983-1992 (26-35) |
| 1993-2002 (36-45) | 2003-2012 (46-55) | 2013-2022 (56-65) |
| 2023-2032 (66-75) | 2033-2042 (76-85) | 2043-2052 (86-95) |
| 2053-2062 (96-105) | 2063-2072 (106-115) | 2073-2082 (116-125) |

| STAFF 2043-2052 乙 PROSP/L 卯 | | | THE SELF 1993-2002 壬 PROPERT 戌 |
|---|---|---|---|
| ✕ MIROR<br><br>PUNI<br>5<br><br>T T C Y<br>f G 32 D<br>MY **FB XH** D46 | Back | | 10<br><br><br>C H T<br>20 G F<br>M Zs SJ HG |

| CAREER 2033-2042 甲 HEALTH 寅 | PROPERT 2023-2032 乙 TRAVEL 丑 | KARMIC 2013-2022 甲 STAFF 子 | ELDERS 2003-2012 癸 CAREER 亥 |
|---|---|---|---|
| ◉ SUN ☼<br>○ MESGR<br><br>3<br><br>B L t<br>Z C s<br>CS **DH Gf ZB** | ○ COMDR ■<br>○ OPPOR $<br>STAR LEFT RIGT<br><br><br>K P T<br>W S S<br>Y **BF GS TS** | ◉ WAIF<br>○ MOON ↗<br><br>9 4<br><br>J S F T<br>L T G L s<br>T XS **SM ZS** | ◉ VAULT ☼<br><br><br>8 2<br><br>T C G<br>K 7 C<br>J FL **HQ JS** |

## Mr. Wong's Next 10-Year Cycle (2003-2012)
### The Self

Mr. Wong is now at age 46-55. A Bright Vault, a major prosperity star from the conservative faction is in his Self House. As The Emperor rules the North, so the Vault rules the South. As the Emperor pioneers, so the Vault guards. Safely trekking paths hewn and hacked by others before him, the Vault quietly builds fortunes. *This star would shine on careers having to do with administration and management.*

At opposite we have a Bright Emperor who has good support from General, Pioneer, Commander, Left & Right Ministers. *As these stars show, a definite improvement in his finances is seen.*
### Stars at 120°

### Karmic

A Brilliant Opportunity with the Wealth$ attachment trails Obstruction■. *Of all the major stars in obstruction, Opportunity carries the least destruction. This star of socializing and flirtation will only have its wings clipped and, therefore, stay grounded—* probably to everyone's relief!

Mr. Wong, at his present phase is definitely enjoying a steadier and more prosperous existence than the last ten years. However, in the Life Chart (gray sub-headings) he has Void in Self together with Bell and Punishment in Prosperity. *He will do well to remember his road to wealth will be difficult throughout life and is definitely not suited to be a business owner.*

*N.B. An afflicted Success Triangle (Self, Career, & Prosperity) weighted down with dark, major stars or in retrograde, especially Commander■ is indicative of business failures and bankruptcy. The Killing Stars which work against wealth are Void and Punishment with Bell delivering a dose of bitterness and more difficulties. It is well to check that these are not in your Success Triangle before venturing into investments of any kind.*

# Vault in the 10-year (46-55) Self AT PIG CHAMBER

*Mr. Wong's 10-Year Chart 2003-2012 (Age 46-55)*

| SELF | OPPOSITE | PROSPERITY | KARMIC |
|---|---|---|---|
| VAULT | EMPEROR GENERAL | DELIGHT BELL & VOID | COMMANDER OPPORTUNITY |

| TRAVEL 2063-2072 丁 SPOUSE 巳 | HEALTH 2073-2082 戊 PEERS 午 | PROSPER 1963-1972 己 THE SELF 未 | MINORS 1973-1982 庚 ELDERS 申 |
|---|---|---|---|
| ⊙ EMPER ▲ GENRL COMP FIRE 6 7 | RAM *LITE* | DELI BELL VOID | HORS ARTS |
| C T 31 C LG BS LD **WS** | T T **T** T F c X **Y** g g DW LS JX BH | G T S D A QL PA TD | T **Y T** W S k B **XH** SY DK |

| STAFF 2053-2062 丙 MINORS 辰 | | | SPOUSE 1983-1992 辛 KARMIC 酉 |
|---|---|---|---|
| O INTEL■ ⊙ SCHOL SPIN 1 | | | ▲ CRMSN ✗ PNEER $ |
| J T E S x G GD **GF** SP Ys | | | S JJ Xs **BF** |

| | | Ten Year Chart A 10 year analysis 2003-2012 (46-55) | |

| 1963-1972 (6-15) | 1973-1982 (16-25) | 1983-1992 (26-35) |
|---|---|---|
| 1993-2002 (36-45) | 2003-2012 (46-55) | 2013-2022 (56-65) |
| 2023-2032 (66-75) | 2033-2042 (76-85) | 2043-2052 (86-95) |
| 2053-2062 (96-105) | 2063-2072 (106-115) | 2073-2082 (116-125) |
| Back | | |

| CAREER 2043-2052 乙 PROSP/L 卯 | | | PEERS 1993-2002 壬 PROPERT 戌 |
|---|---|---|---|
| ✗ MIROR PUNI 5 3 | | | |
| T T C Y f G 32 D MY **FB XH** D46 | | | C H T 20 G F M Zs SJ HG |

| PROPERT 2033-2042 甲 HEALTH 寅 | KARMIC 2023-2032 乙 TRAVEL 丑 | ELDERS 2013-2022 甲 STAFF 子 | THE SELF 2003-2012 癸 CAREER 亥 |
|---|---|---|---|
| ⊙ SUN ○ O MESGR ↗ | O COMDR O OPPOR $ ■ STAR LEFT RIGT 9 | ⊙ WAIF O MOON ↗○ 8 | ⊙ VAULT 10 4 |
| B L t Z C s CS **DH** Gf ZB | K P T W S S Y **BF GS TS** | J S F **F I** L T G **L** s T XS **SM ZS** | T C **G** K 7 C J FL **HQ JS** |

# *Epilogue*

We can neither avoid nor alter our destiny. However, with hindsight, Mr. Wong and his family could have avoided the wasted years of strive and hardships. As parents, we all work towards guiding our children to becoming upright, successful, joyous human beings. Certainly, we don't want them to choose a path or career that would entail worries and hardships over and over again, only to concede defeat after ten or more years and start over again from the beginning.

Now with this tool called the Emperor's Stargate we can know about them in terms of the following Birth Elements:

1. Intelligence quotient;

2. Personality;

3. Emotional quotient;

4. Stress/Volatility tolerance;

5. Linguistic skills;

6. Logical abilities;

7. Kinesthetic/hands-on learning needs;

8. Spatial and artistic inclinations; and last but not the least

9. Yun Chi–the harmony of Heaven and Earth.

Used wisely, Stargate will save you and your family all those unnecessary and at times precarious twists and turns that most of us accept as a part of Life's Journey. Remember: it doesn't have to be like that. Let Stargate light your path.

### *Who Can Change Life's Lessons?*
### *You Can!!*

# The Year Chart

As each New Year approaches, it is a Chinese tradition to seek a yearly forecast to be prepared to face the year ahead with confidence. Some of us might read horoscopes with just twelve signs to try to learn how we will fare.

No one needs to take these overly simplified reports too seriously. The Stargate system, however, fine-tunes its advice down to not only the date-of-birth but also the hour. The Emperor's Stargate is one of the best tools around for helping us plan for the year ahead. It's exciting to have the ability to see whether the foreseeable future will flow easily or not and if not to learn where the difficulty lies.

With such foresight, it would be easy to choose to do the activities which carry good energy and which would work for us and refrain from those that would cause harm or invite disasters.

Remember to always start by reading the Self Chamber and its opposite, Travel. At the same time, refer to your 10-year overall *yun chi* 運氣, the stars, and sub-headings colored blue.

Pay special attention to the red colored Catalysts ($✿↗■). They hold the key to where you stand for the year in question. Since the Obstruction Catalyst■ is the post powerful, it would destroy Wealth$ and turn Fame✿ into Notoriety. Only Power↗ can somewhat withstand and not be poisoned by its presence.

# In bitter snow, a gift of coals brought resurrection~

It is now 1997. Mr. Wong, who lost his family's entire fortune of HK $5M (US $640,000) in his manufacturing business, was facing closure.

## The Self–Commander & Opportunity

That year he had Commander trailing Obstruction■. *The Commander is a prosperity star but when in retrograde dispenses sudden additional management expenses. Carefully worked out financial plans would abruptly get replaced due to circumstances beyond control. There would be great challenges in trying to make ends meet. For a businessman, Commander with Obstruction in the Self is likened to the death knell.*

Also here, we have Opportunity with Wealth $ attached. *Note that the Wealth$ Catalyst attached to Opportunity does not equal a tremendous winning streak. This only means a tremendous amount of money will change hands. It would form a positive liaison if found with Fire or Bell. This dynamic formation would create the circumstance whereby Opportunity could hit the Jackpot. However, if at the same time, it should meet up with Obstruction■, Ram, or Spinning Top, any such winnings would soon be lost again.*

Although Stardust and Delight were also there, these angelic beings were no match against a cacophony of Killing Stars—Bell, Void, Ram, plus other detrimental minor stars. Be particularly wary of the Commander-Void liaison. This is an indication for a major hemorrhaging of wealth.

Add the fact that the 1997 Self and opposite had entered into the 10-year Property and the Life Chart's Self/Travel sectors. With these personal sectors all being afflicted with the above Killing Stars, we are looking at a doubling of Mr. Wong's misfortunes.

Accordingly, orders dropped dramatically. Coupled with faulty production problems with raw materials, loss of revenue and claims, the whole process soon became a vicious circle. At bottom, losses for the worst month reached US $.5 million. Not having deep pockets to see himself through this difficult time, Mr. Wong considered filing for bankruptcy.

*Mr. Wong's 1997 Year-Chart (Age 39)*

| SELF | OPPOSITE | PROSPERITY | KARMIC |
|---|---|---|---|
| COMMANDER OPPORTUNITY | BELL VOID | CRIMSON PIONEER | MIRROR PUNISHMENT |

| CAREER / HEALTH SPOUSE 己 | STAFF / PROSPER 戊 PEERS 午 | TRAVEL / MINORS 己 THE SELF 未 | HEALTH / SPOUSE 庚 ELDERS 申 |
|---|---|---|---|
| ◉ EMPER ↗ | RAM | DELI BELL VOID | HORS |
| ▲ GENRL | 8 | 9 | 7 2 |
| COMP FIRE | LITE | | ARTS |
| 6 1 10 4 | | | |
| C T | T T T F | G T | T Y T |
| 31 C | c X Y g g | S D | W S k |
| LG BS LD WS g f b | DW LS JX BH x c | A QL PA TD d y h s | B XH SY DK l w d s |

| PROPERT / TRAVEL 丙 MINORS 辰 | **Specific Year Chart** | PROSPER / PEERS 辛 KARMIC 酉 |
|---|---|---|
| ◯ INTEL ◼ ☼ | | ▲ CRMSN |
| ◉ SCHOL $ | 丁 丑 年 | ✕ PNEER |
| SPIN | **1997** | 6 3 |
| J T E | | |
| S x G | <1year   Go   >1year | |
| GD GF SP Ys g t s s | | S JJ Xs BF b j h x |

| KARMIC / STAFF 乙 PROSP/L 卯 | <5years       >5years | MINORS / THE SELF 壬 PROPERT 戌 |
|---|---|---|
| ✕ MIROR | | |
| PUNI | Back | 10 |
| 5 | | |
| T T C Y | | C H T |
| f G 32 D | | 20 G F |
| MY FB XH D46 s z m s | | M Zs SJ HG t p d a |

| ELDERS / CAREER 甲 HEALTH 寅 | THE SELF / PROPERT 乙 TRAVEL 丑 | PEERS / KARMIC 甲 STAFF 子 | SPOUSE / ELDERS 癸 CAREER 亥 |
|---|---|---|---|
| ◉ SUN ☼ | ◯ COMDR ◼ | ◉ WAIF ↗ | ◉ VAULT ☼ |
| ◯ MESGR ◼ | ◯ OPPOR $ | ◯ MOON ↗ $ | |
| | STAR LEFT RIGT | | |
| 3 1 | | 9 4 | 8 2 5 7 |
| B L t | K P T | J S F I | T C G |
| Z C s | W S S | L T G L s | K 7 C |
| CS DH Gf ZB h j q l | Y BF GS TS s h j g | T XS SM ZS b z s s | J FL HQ JS d s k y |

YEAR CHART: MR. WONG

It seems it does get darkest just before daybreak. For Mr. Wong, dawn came in the New Year of 1998. Out of the darkness, one of his clients became very interested in his manufacturing business and offered a price tag of HK $ 4M+ to buy the whole set-up from him (deferred over a 3-year period.) Mr. Wong was, of course, more than happy to accept these terms and felt as if a huge weight had been lifted from his shoulders.

Let's take a look at his 1998 chart (>1year) to find out what brought on this sudden turn of events. In the Self Chamber, the major stars included The Sun with double Fame ○ ○ attached, a Brilliant Messenger, and the Literary and (opposite) Arts Ministers.

Of special note is that we do not see any of the Killing Stars within Mr. Wong's Success Triangle. *Comparing this with the previous year's chart, we are seeing a whole universe of difference. Whereas in 1997, the sky was covered with dark, killing stars, in 1998, all of these had moved on.*

## The Self–Sun & Messenger

*The Sun enhanced with the double Fame catalyst indicates his coming into contact with highly positive, benevolent yang energy. This would allude to the prominent (male) client who offered to buy his business.*

*The Sun in the Self in Tiger, Rabbit and Dragon sectors will be basking in the limelight—you will not fail to notice this person. He will love to give a helping hand and is also a careful individual who is prone to extravagance.*

*With Messenger here as well this year, Mr. Wong would have enjoyed some measure of recognition in addressing audiences or congregations. The Messenger also stands for events developing under the surface. Like an undercurrent, things may not be what they seem. Depending on adjacent stars, The Messenger may eradicate bad influences or bring dissatisfaction to the surface.*

Although matters developed rather suddenly and unexpectedly, it worked out to Mr. Wong's complete satisfaction.

## Career & Prosperity–Ram & Spinning Top

The only Killing Stars in his Success Triangle would be Ram and Spinning Top in Career and Prosperity. In this case, it would be expected with the selling of his business that his present career would be "destroyed" as he opened the next chapter of his life path. It can be seen that given different scenarios, the Killing Stars can also work in our favor!

*Mr. Wong's 1998 Year-Chart (Age 40)*

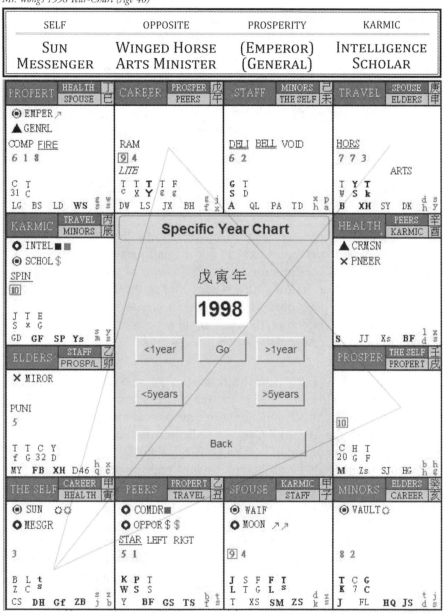

| SELF | OPPOSITE | PROSPERITY | KARMIC |
|------|----------|------------|--------|
| SUN MESSENGER | WINGED HORSE ARTS MINISTER | (EMPEROR) (GENERAL) | INTELLIGENCE SCHOLAR |

| PROPERT HEALTH 丁 SPOUSE 巳 | CAREER PROSPER 戊 PEERS 午 | STAFF MINORS 己 THE SELF 未 | TRAVEL SPOUSE 庚 ELDERS 申 |
|---|---|---|---|
| ⦿ EMPER ↗ ▲ GENRL COMP FIRE 6 1 8 | RAM ⑨ 4 LITE | DELI BELL VOID 6 2 | HORS 7 7 3 ARTS |
| C T 31 C LG BS LD **WS** g w s s | T T **T** T F C X **Y** g g DW LS JX BH g i f x | G T S D A QL PA TD x p h a | T **Y** T W S k B **XH** SY DK d s h y |
| KARMIC TRAVEL 丙 MINORS 辰 | | | HEALTH PEERS 辛 KARMIC 酉 |
| O INTEL■■ ⦿ SCHOL $ SPIN ⑩ | **Specific Year Chart** | | ▲ CRMSN ✕ PNEER |
| J T E S x G GD **GF** SP **Ys** s y m s | 戊寅年 **1998** | | S JJ Xs **BF** l x d |
| ELDERS STAFF 乙 PROSP/L 卯 | ‹1year  Go  ›1year | | PROSPER THE SELF 壬 PROPERT 戌 |
| ✕ MIROR PUNI 5 | ‹5years  ›5years | | ⑩ |
| T T C Y f G 32 D MY **FB XH** D46 h x q c | Back | | C H T 20 G F M Zs SJ HG b h h g |
| THE SELF CAREER 甲 HEALTH 寅 | PEERS PROPERT 乙 TRAVEL 丑 | SPOUSE KARMIC 甲 STAFF 子 | MINORS ELDERS 癸 CAREER 亥 |
| ⦿ SUN ○○ O MESGR 3 | O COMDR■ O OPPOR $ $ STAR LEFT RIGT 5 1 | ⦿ WAIF O MOON ↗↗ ⑨ 4 | ⦿ VAULT○ 8 2 |
| B L t Z C s CS **DH Gf ZB** s z j b | K P T W S S Y **BF GS TS** b t f s | J S F F I L T G L s T XS **SM ZS** d z k s | T C G K 7 C J FL **HQ JS** t j d s |

# The Year Chart—Huge Windfall

## Paradise Lost (Mark's Story)

**Born April 3, 1958, at 12:00 p.m.**, Mark, our son, was so-named after the HK Jockey Club lottery, The Mark 6, which resulted in his winning the first prize jackpot of HK $10m (US $1.3m) in 1990.

### The Self

A Brilliant Emperor at its zenith enriches and banishes evil. Emperor is a star that brings in wealth and prosperity. A leader in every sense of the word, Emperor evokes power and elegance, commands respect, and is so strong that it accommodates more than eradicates. The Killing Star Ram, also here, is altered by the presence of Emperor, which then accounts for a Brilliant Ram that brings in propitious surprises.

Reflecting the Self is a Bright Opportunity$ with Wealth$ attached. Note that Opportunity is not a wealth star in its own right. However, helped by Emperor opposite, this star of gaming and fun is richly rewarded on its own turf. Notice that in the 10-year chart (the sub-headings colored blue), Opportunity $ is sitting squarely in the Self. That it is reflecting the Self in this present year doubles its strength of gaming success.

### Career

Crimson$ with Wealth from Mark's 10-Year shines brightly in his Career sector. This star brings in wealth from a social cause—The Mark 6 makes huge donations to various charities every year. Crimson with the Wealth$ Catalyst indicates that this sociable star is blessing with her prosperity. The Brilliant Vault✿, possessing much wealth within its walls, deals with finance and financial matters. This individual will become famous with Fame attached, and many will hear of his wizardry in managing finance.

### Prosperity

The Winged Horse (7) is not a prosperity star. However, if linked up with propitious Completion (8) in Prosperity and free of any Killing Stars, the pair would have the ability to bring in unlimited wealth. This pair is present both in his 10-year cycle as well as in the current year—a doubling of his fortunes for 1990.

A Brilliant Mirror doubles the winnings of the powerfully wealthy Commander✿↗ with Fame✿ and Power↗ attached.

# THIS IS THE STAR CONFIGURATION
# OF WHAT A HUGE WINDFALL LOOKS LIKE

*Mark's 1990 Year-Chart (Age 35)*

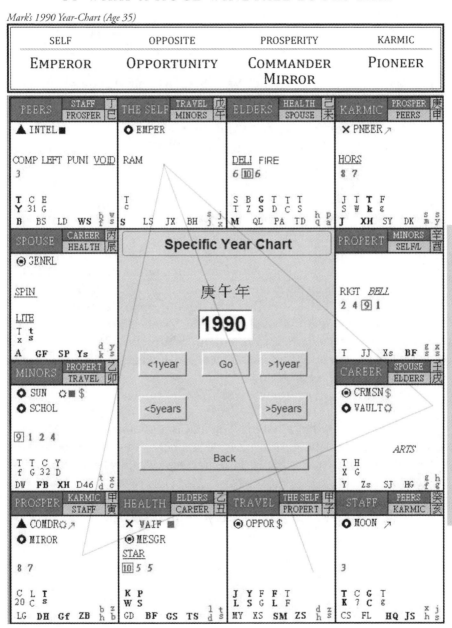

# Paradise Lost (Mark's Story Cont'd)

## 1989 Self & Prosperity Sectors

Click on "<1 year" to 1989. A weak Intelligence■ had Obstacle■ trailing. Moreover, negative stars abound—Punishment, Void, Spinning Top (*both in the Self and Opposing*), Ram and Bell. Prosperity had a dark, erratic Waif. Stardust and Delight were both hemmed in by Ram and Fire. *This was clearly not the bountiful year.*

## Mark's Life Chart's Prosperity Chamber

In Mark's Life Chart (grey headings in the same 1989 chart), the Lucky Completion is in his Prosperity Chamber. This star indicates a rewarding lifetime of wealth and prosperity without the hardships or unsettling changes.

However, a weak Intelligence■ beset with Obstacle■ is also here. Intelligence in prosperity alludes to gambling or someone who is prone to taking chances. With Obstacle■ attached, these would always result in loss. Along with Punishment and Void, these Killing Stars would work against anything to do with Wealth. Bell in Self indicates loneliness. The Brilliant Moon opposite with trailing Power↗ and Fame☼, although a Wealth $ star, is not strong enough against the extremely dark stars in Self. With erratic Waif in Career, there is not enough support from any positive major star. A dark Waif indicates fortunes made would eventually be lost.

In Properties, Opportunity with Wealth$ indicates huge amounts of money changing hands.

Hemmed in by the Spinning Top and Ram before and after, these Killing Stars deplete the Prosperity Chamber, and quashed by these, Completion will never really become very wealthy—spiritually or materially.

Although Mark had an incredibly fortunate year in 1990, whether he could hang on to his bounty very much depended on his overall lifetime fortunes. In his case, it is evident he could not. Within a year, Mark had squandered away the whole of his huge 1990 winning, losing it mostly to gambling and bad speculative investments.

N.B. *However, 1990 is the star configuration of what a huge windfall/winning lottery looks like. You might consider entering the lottery if at any time this pattern comes into your own chart. It is also a matter of interest that the same pattern of stars appears in Mr. Warren Buffett's Life Chart.*

*Mark's 1989 Year-Chart (Age 34)*

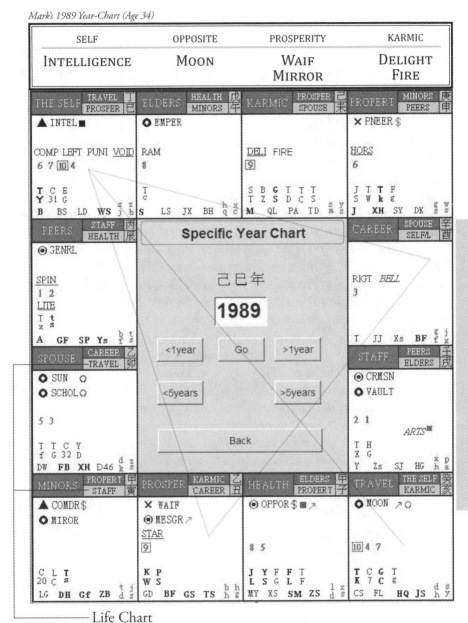

|  | SELF | OPPOSITE | PROSPERITY | KARMIC |
|---|---|---|---|---|
|  | INTELLIGENCE | MOON | WAIF MIRROR | DELIGHT FIRE |

Specific Year Chart

己巳年

**1989**

| <1year | Go | >1year |
| <5years | | >5years |

Back

—— Life Chart

# The Year Chart—Death of Michael Jackson

**Born August 8, 1958 at 10 p.m.**, Michael Jackson died June 25, 2009, after he suffered cardiac arrest at his home in Los Angeles, CA. His personal physician, Conrad Murray, went on trial for administering propofol.

The year 2009 was the last year of Jackson's 5th 10-year cycle (2000-2009). At this point, we are seeing an exact duplication of the stars, i.e., the current year repeats or reinforces whatever the 10-year stars bring in.

*A dark Waif in the Self House brings in emotional volatility. The Messenger, also here, is always on the go—and we're not talking about smooth sailing. Not born with a silver spoon in his mouth, the struggle uphill would have begun early in life.*

The Self is flanked by Fire and Bell. *Fire, if left unchecked in the absence of positive stars brings tragic catastrophes at an early age. Bell beside the Self sector indicates a hard cataclysmic childhood. The Self, flanked by these two stars immediately before and after will be especially weak.* He also had the dark Stardust & Delight. *After age 50, these stars turn retrograde and become the opponent. From this point on, they stagnate and block.*

Opposing the Self is a dark **Ram**. *Often referred to as a flying spear, this star brings life-threatening accidents or attacks. A dangerous star, the Ram destroys or weakens the good stars and at the same time constrains the other Killing Stars with the exception of Fire. The Ram in the Self sector or directly opposite, whether male or female, indicates a serious accident.*

*At 120° in Career he has a weak Intelligence, turned dark by Obstruction■ Catalyst and weighted with money problems. Under dark influences, fear, self-doubt, and despair set in. Spinning Top fuels these dark flames with flagrant gossip and rumor.*

*Moreover, The Arts Minister■ in Karmic is afflicted. This sensitive artisan, underneath all the public glamor and adoration brought on by the Brilliant Sun ✿ and Scholar ✿, was desperately unhappy.*

*Overlapping, the current year's Arts Minister with obstacle■ attached would also affect the 10-year Karmic Sector. Together with Intelligence■ in Career (loss of control) and the afflicted Moon■ (depression) opposite, MJ was under tremendous pressure from his comeback performance.* The resulting insomnia eventually brought about the illegal use of propofol.

*MJ's 2009 Year-Chart (Aged 50)*

| SELF | OPPOSITE | PROSPERITY | KARMIC |
|---|---|---|---|
| WAIF MESSENGER | DELIGHT RAM | LIT. MINISTER | SUN SCHOLAR |

| CAREER | CAREER 丁 / PROSPER 巳 | STAFF | STAFF 戊 / MINORS 午 | TRAVEL | TRAVEL 己 / SPOUS/L 未 | HEALTH | HEALTH 庚 / PEERS 申 |
|---|---|---|---|---|---|---|---|
| ▲ INTEL ■ $ | | ○ EMPER ○ | | | | ✕ PNEER | |
| COMP [10] 4 | | RAM 3 8 | | DELI [9] | | HORS 6 2 4 6 2 | |
| C T T 31 S F | | T c | | C G T T 20 S D C | | T k | |
| B  BS  LD  WS $^g_f$ $^z_b$ | | S  LS  JX  BH $^x_h$ $^x_c$ | | M  QL  PA  TD $^d_h$ $^y_s$ | | J  XH  SY  DK $^l_d$ $^w_s$ | |

| PROPERT | PROPERT 丙 / HEALTH 辰 | | PROSPER | PROSPER 辛 / THE SELF 酉 |
|---|---|---|---|---|
| ◉ GENRL | | | | |
| SPIN  RIGT [9] | | **Specific Year Chart** | 3 | |
| T T t x g s A  GF  SP  Ys $^g_s$ $^t_s$ | | 己丑年 **2009** | T  JJ  Xs  BF $^b_h$ $^j_x$ | |

| KARMIC | KARMIC 乙 / TRAVEL 卯 | | MINORS | MINORS 壬 / ELDERS 戌 |
|---|---|---|---|---|
| ○ SUN ○ ○ SCHOL ↗ ○ | | <1year    Go    >1year | ◉ CRMSN ○ VAULT LEFT PUNI | |
| 8 ARTS ■ | | <5years        >5years | H G | |
| T T T C Y f G X 32 D DW  FB  XH  D46 $^s_m$ $^z_s$ | | Back | Y  Zs  SJ  HG $^t_d$ $^p_a$ | |

| ELDERS | ELDERS 甲 / STAFF 寅 | THE SELF | THE SELF 乙 / CAREER 丑 | PEERS | PEERS 甲 / PROPERT 子 | SPOUSE | SPOUSE 癸 / KARMIC 亥 |
|---|---|---|---|---|---|---|---|
| ▲ COMDR $ ○ MIROR | | ✕ WAIF ◉ MESGR | | ◉ OPPOR $ ↗ | | ○ MOON ↗ ■ | |
| BELL [10] 1 1 | | STAR | | FIRE VOID 5 5 | | 7 7 LITE | |
| B J T Y Y L Z S W S S C LG  DH  Gf  ZB $^h_q$ $^j_s$ | | K P F W S g GD  BF  GS  TS $^s_j$ $^h_g$ | | J  S  F  F  E L  T  G  L  G MY  XS  SM  ZS $^b_f$ $^x_s$ | | T T C G Y K 7 C CS  FL  HQ  JS $^d_k$ $^s_y$ | |

人和 KIND

PEOPLE

# CONFUCIUS

—✦—

By three methods
we may learn WISDOM:
First, by REFLECTION,
which is the noblest;
second, by IMITATION,
which is easiest; and
third, by EXPERIENCE,
which is the bitterest

# Chapter 8

## *The Icons of Our Times*

O ne of the easiest ways to learn is through examples. On the following pages, we have listed our studies of ten iconic personalities who have "made it to the top" in their own ways. They were chosen as subjects for discussion because they are public figures whose life stories, achievements, lessons, and/or failures are well-known and documented. We found it of special interest that the major events that helped shape the person we know today are all laid out in their star charts.

These public figures have influenced our own lives in various ways—some more than others. Whether or not we happen to agree that some of them are indeed "successful" or not is secondary. It is good to keep an open mind and read and analyze the various stages of their lives from the point of view of interpretation.

In studying, we have found a common thread that joins every single one of these individuals, regardless of their life paths, creed, or race—each one lives/lived with total dedication, conviction, and hard work. The rest just followed.

N.B. There is an extraordinary star formation for success that is found with highly successful star-quality individuals. Notice that you will find The Sun-Scholar-Completion-Literary Minister in either the Triangle of Success (Self, Career, Prosperity) and/or the Opposite Chambers.

## Barack Obama ★AUGUST 4, 1961 7:24 P.M. HONOLULU, HAWAII, USA

 Barack Hussein Obama II is the 44th and current President of the United States. He is the first African American to hold the office. Obama previously served as a U.S. Senator from Illinois from January 2005 until he resigned after his election to the Presidency.

### Self House—Completion, Left Minister, Punishment

*Completion in the Self house makes for an upright, honest individual with a big heart. This star indicates a rewarding lifetime of wealth and prosperity without the rigmaroles of toils, hardships, or great changes. Even in the same sector as the Killing Stars, it doesn't quite dry up.*

A native of Honolulu, Hawaii, Obama is a graduate of Columbia University and Harvard Law School where he was the president of the Harvard Law Review. He was a community organizer in Chicago before earning his law degree. He worked as a civil rights attorney in Chicago and taught constitutional law at the University of Chicago Law School from 1992 to 2004.

*Punishment in Self pushes toward a brilliant career in politics. These will be inspired to dedicate their lives to public service, righting wrongs, and bringing about great changes. They are advised not to venture into any kind of business undertaking should their Self Chamber be afflicted with Punishment. Brightened and helped along by Completion in the same house, we are seeing life-long success. It can be seen he made the right career choices early on.*

Obama served three terms in the Illinois Senate from 1997 to 2004. He ran for United States Senate in 2004. Several events brought him to national attention during the campaign, including his victory in the March 2004 Democratic Primary and his keynote address at the Democratic National Convention in July 2004. He won election to the U.S. Senate in November 2004.

*Opposite the Self, Intelligence with a Brilliant Messenger with Wealth $ indicated he was to be richly rewarded with communicating his brilliant thoughts and knowledge. He does not, however, care too much for gains as his Prosperity is dominated by the professionally-inclined Scholar with the elegant Sun in Career. Added to this, L. Minister in Self (the most serene and elegant of stars) emphasizes his public persona.*

*Barack Obama's Life Chart*

| SELF | OPPOSITE | CAREER | PROSPERITY |
|---|---|---|---|
| COMPLETION<br>L. MINISTER | INTELLIGENCE<br>MESSENGER | SUN<br>MOON | SCHOLAR<br>R. MINISTER |

| | | | |
|---|---|---|---|
| PROSP/L 2006-2015癸<br>46-55 巳 | MINORS 1996-2005甲<br>36-45 午 | SPOUSE 1986-1995乙<br>26-35 未 | PEERS 1976-1985丙<br>16-25 申 |
| ✗ SCHOL | ◉ GENRL | | ◘ CRMSN |
| RIGT | STAR | | *SPIN* BELL |
| T K T L<br>f W k C<br>J JJ Gf ZB | T C C Y T<br>c 2032 D S<br>M XH XH D46 | S B T<br>T Z x<br>S QL SP Ys | T C<br>W 7<br>B LS LD WS |
| HEALTH 2016-2025壬<br>56-65 辰 | | | THE SELF 1966-1975丁<br>6-15 酉 |
| ✗ EMPER<br>◉ MIROR | **BARACK OBAMA**<br>———— ✦ ———— | | COMP LEFT PUNI |
| J Y T t<br>L S F s<br>T Zs GS TS | *If you're walking down the*<br>*right path* | | T F F E<br>G G L G<br>A BS JX BH |
| TRAVEL 2026-2035辛<br>66-75 卯 | *and you're willing* | | ELDERS 2076-2085戊<br>116-125 戌 |
| ◉ INTEL<br>◘ MESGR $ | *to keep walking,* | | ◉ PNEER |
| | *eventually* | | RAM |
| T<br>Y<br>Y FL SM ZS | *you'll make progress.* | | G T T<br>S D C<br>DW GF PA TD |
| STAFF 2036-2045庚<br>76-85 寅 | CAREER 2046-2055辛<br>86-95 丑 | PROPERT 2056-2065庚<br>96-105 子 | KARMIC 2066-2075己<br>106-115 亥 |
| ▲ OPPOR | ✗ SUN ↗<br>◘ MOON | ◉ COMDR<br>◘ VAULT | ◘ WAIF |
| DELI | FIRE *VOID* | LITE ∎ | HORS |
| ARTS ☌<br>T T C G T<br>X K 31 C s<br>CS XS HQ JS | P H<br>S G<br>MY BF SJ HG | J F<br>S g<br>GD DH Xs BF | T<br>g<br>LG FB SY DK |

BARACK OBAMA

Obama's presidential campaign began in February 2007, and after a close campaign in the 2008 Democratic Party presidential primaries against Hillary Rodham Clinton, he won his party's nomination. In the 2008 general election, he defeated Republican nominee John McCain and was inaugurated as President on January 20, 2009. Note the extraordinary star formation for success in President Obama's 10-Year Chart (age 46-55): *Sun (in Prosperity), Scholar (in Self), Completion (in Career), and Literary Minister (opposite Career) pattern is found with highly successful, star-quality individuals.*

### The Self—Scholar (Age 46-55)

It can be seen in the present 10-year cycle, *The Self is dominated by the professionally-inclined Scholar and helped by the Brilliant Waif opposite. Scholar is a compassionate, generous, and elegant star. It shines on professionals, i.e., medical doctors, lawyers, etc. Intellectually gifted, it cannot be bothered with business ventures, money-making, etc., that these activities encompass. It is about lofty, humanitarian ideals. Waif, which deals with social issues, is at opposite. A Brilliant Waif has the abilities to build from nothing. Given tenacity, it would regain lost ground or fortunes.*

### Career—Completion, Left Minister, Punishment (Opposite Lit. Minister)

*Punishment in Career pushes toward a brilliant career in politics. These will dedicate their lives to public service, righting wrongs and bringing about great changes. They are advised not to venture into any kind of business undertaking with Punishment here. Helped by Completion in the same house, we are seeing brilliant success. At opposite, Obama also has Messenger $↗ with Wealth and Power attached, plus Literary Minister, which adds to the equation. An eloquent speaker, President Obama's chart indicates he would find power and fortune in the political arena. The L&R Ministers, paired up at Self and Career, are also lending weight to his power and influence.*

### Prosperity—Sun & Moon

*Sun ↗, enhanced with Power here, carries the trait of having the majority or male supporters on his side. Power to the Sun makes for a highly independent mind which gives rise to the pioneering spirit.*

*Of interest is the absence of any major Wealth Star in President Obama's Life and the 10-Year Success Triangle, especially since he is presently (as of the printing 2013) the most influential man in power in the United States. Such is the chart of a brilliant political figure.*

*Barack Obama's 10-Year Chart 2006-2015 (Age 46-55)*

| SELF | OPPOSITE | PROSPERITY | CAREER |
|---|---|---|---|
| SCHOLAR | WAIF | SUN<br>MOON | COMPLETION<br>L. MINISTER |

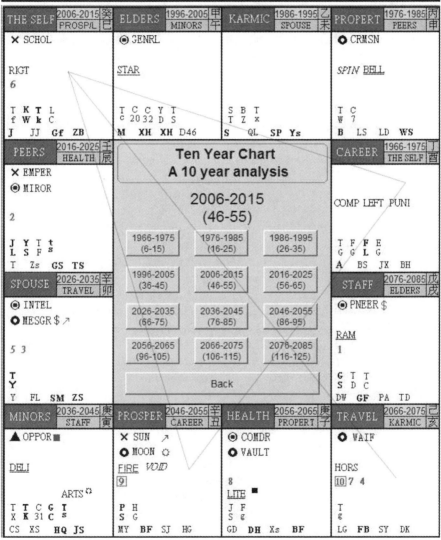

| THE SELF 2006-2015 癸<br>PROSP/L 巳 | ELDERS 1996-2005 甲<br>MINORS 午 | KARMIC 1986-1995 乙<br>SPOUSE 未 | PROPERT 1976-1985 丙<br>PEERS 申 |
|---|---|---|---|
| ✗ SCHOL | ◉ GENRL | | O CRMSN |
| RIGT<br>6 | STAR | | *SPIN* BELL |
| T K T L<br>f W k C<br>J  JJ  Gf  ZB | T C C Y T<br>c 20 32 D S<br>M  XH  XH  D46 | S B T<br>T Z x<br>S  QL  SP  Ys | T C<br>W 7<br>B  LS  LD  WS |

**Ten Year Chart**
**A 10 year analysis**

**2006-2015**
**(46-55)**

| 1966-1975<br>(6-15) | 1976-1985<br>(16-25) | 1986-1995<br>(26-35) |
|---|---|---|
| 1996-2005<br>(36-45) | 2006-2015<br>(46-55) | 2016-2025<br>(56-65) |
| 2026-2035<br>(66-75) | 2036-2045<br>(76-85) | 2046-2055<br>(86-95) |
| 2056-2065<br>(96-105) | 2066-2075<br>(106-115) | 2076-2085<br>(116-125) |

**Back**

(Underlying chart, partly obscured:)

| PEERS 2016-2025 壬<br>HEALTH 辰 | | | CAREER 1966-1975 丁<br>THE SELF 酉 |
|---|---|---|---|
| ✗ EMPER<br>◉ MIROR<br><br>2<br><br>J Y T t<br>L S F s<br>T Zs GS TS | | | COMP LEFT PUNI<br><br>T F F E<br>G G L G<br>A BS JX BH |

| SPOUSE 2026-2035 辛<br>TRAVEL 卯 | | | STAFF 2076-2085 戊<br>ELDERS 戌 |
|---|---|---|---|
| ◉ INTEL<br>O MESGR $ ↗<br><br>5 3<br><br>T<br>Y<br>Y FL SM ZS | | | ◉ PNEER $<br><br>RAM<br>1<br><br>G T T<br>S D C<br>DW GF PA TD |

| MINORS 2036-2045 庚<br>STAFF 寅 | PROSPER 2046-2055 辛<br>CAREER 丑 | HEALTH 2056-2065 庚<br>PROPERT 子 | TRAVEL 2066-2075 己<br>KARMIC 亥 |
|---|---|---|---|
| ▲ OPPOR ■<br><br>DELI<br><br>ARTS ☼<br>T T C G I<br>X K 31 C s<br>CS XS HQ JS | ✗ SUN ↗<br>O MOON ☼<br>FIRE *VOID*<br>[9]<br><br>P H<br>S G<br>MY BF SJ HG | ◉ COMDR<br>O VAULT<br><br>8<br>LITE ■<br>J F<br>S g<br>GD DH Xs BF | O WAIF<br><br>HORS<br>[10] 7 4<br><br>T<br>g<br>LG FB SY DK |

BARACK OBAMA

# Bill Gates ★ OCTOBER 28, 1955 10:00 P.M. SEATTLE, WASHINGTON, USA

 William Henry "Bill" Gates, III, KBE is an American business magnate, philanthropist, author, and chairman of Microsoft, the software company he founded with Paul Allen. He is consistently ranked among the world's wealthiest people (2nd in 2010).

During his career at Microsoft, Gates has been CEO and chief software architect and as of the writing of this book, he remains the largest individual shareholder with more than 8% of the common stock. He has also authored or co-authored several books. Note the extraordinary star formation for success in the Life Chart throughout the whole life: *The Sun-Scholar-Completion-Literary Minister pattern that is found with highly successful star-quality individuals.*

**The Self—Moon, Intelligence, Winged Horse & Literary Minister**
In Gates' Life Chart, he has a Brilliant Moon in Self. *Being Yin (feminine), Moon in the Self people are distinguished by their softer, oval faces. Those in Moon tend to toil late into the night, are extremely patient, and possess the affinity to work with highly detailed, intricate matters.* Such are also the demands of the IT industry.

Whilst the Sun is Elegance, Moon adorns the physical and is the Wealth part of the Chinese characters for Affluence. *Intelligence, the Strategist, is also here, reflecting and supporting the Self with Wealth $. Gates' brilliant innovative ideas and inventions will be richly rewarded.*

Even as a teenager, his programming abilities were legendary. In 1973, he scored 1590 out of 1600 on the SAT (Scholastic Aptitude Test, a standardized test for college admissions in the US) and enrolled at Harvard in the autumn.

*It should be noted that the Moon's wealth is always slowly accumulated. At its brightest hours within the Pig Chamber and trailing Obstruction■, the Brilliant Moon is transformed into its Opposite and becomes a Wealth Giver.*

*Gates' philanthropic side is further confirmed by Intelligence $ opposite Self. Intelligence with Wealth, coupled with an Obstructed Moon equals Robbery or Charity—both being interrelated.* In recent years, Gates has made huge donations to charity and scientific research through the Bill & Melinda Gates Foundation, established in 2000. As of 2007, they were the second most generous philanthropists in the US, having donated over $28 billion.

294

*Bill Gates' Life Chart*

| SELF | OPPOSITE | CAREER | KARMIC |
|------|----------|--------|--------|
| MOON | INTELLIGENCE | SUN SCHOLAR | WAIF MESSENGER |

| | | | |
|---|---|---|---|
| TRAVEL 2019-2028 辛巳 65-74 <br> ▲ INTEL $ <br> HORS <br> T T T <br> X W F <br> LG **FB** SY DK | HEALTH 2009-2018 壬午 55-64 <br> ◐ EMPER☉ <br><br> T J T t <br> c L c s <br> GD **DH** Xs **BF** | PROSPER 1999-2008 癸未 45-54 <br><br> K H <br> W G <br> MY **BF** SJ HG | MINORS 1989-1998 甲申 36-44 <br> ✗ PNEER <br> DELI *FIRE* <br> T T C G <br> f K 31 C <br> CS XS **HQ JS** |
| STAFF 2029-2038 庚辰 75-84 <br> ◉ GENRL <br> RAM <br><br> T J G T T I <br> G S S D S s <br> DW **GF PA** TD | | | SPOUS/L 1979-1988 乙酉 25-34 <br> *BELL* <br><br> C <br> 20 <br> Y FL **SM ZS** |
| CAREER 2039-2048 己卯 85-94 <br> ◐ SUN <br> ◐ SCHOL↗ <br> COMP <br> ARTS <br> F F <br> G L <br> A BS JX BH | | | PEERS 1969-1978 丙戌 15-24 <br> ◉ CRMSN <br> ◐ VAULT <br> PUNI <br><br> Y E <br> S G <br> T Zs **GS TS** |
| PROPERT 2049-2058 戊寅 95-104 <br> ▲ COMDR <br> ◐ MIROR <br> *SPIN* RIGT <br> B T C T <br> Z **Y** 7 g <br> B LS LD **WS** | KARMIC 2059-2068 己丑 105-114 <br> ✗ WAIF <br> ◉ MESGR <br><br> T P F <br> x S g <br> S QL **SP Ys** | ELDERS 2069-2078 戊子 115-124 <br> ◉ OPPOR <br> STAR LEFT VOID <br> S C Y <br> T 32 D <br> M XH XH D46 | THE SELF 1959-1968 丁亥 5-14 <br> ◐ MOON ■ <br> LITE <br> T L <br> k C <br> J JJ **Gf ZB** |

**BILL GATES**

— ✦ —

*It's fine to celebrate success but it is more important to heed the lessons of failure.*

BILL GATES

## Prosperity/Karmic—Waif & Messenger

As an executive, Gates met regularly with Microsoft's senior managers and program managers. First-hand accounts of these meetings describe him as verbally combative and berating managers for perceived holes in their strategies or proposals that placed the company's long-term interests at risk.

*The Messenger here would be engaging in intricate details and thoughts. An eloquent speaker, Messenger is best suited to be in any career that entails speaking for issues close to its heart, for here is where its success lies.*

The target of his outburst then had to defend the proposal until, hopefully, Gates was convinced. When subordinates appeared to be procrastinating, he was known to remark sarcastically, "I'll do it over the weekend."

*The Waif will do well if found in the house of Karmic Wealth. She has the ability to build from nothing, or with the ignition of the (dormant) fire in her, she would develop great tenacity and could even regain fortunes lost.*

## Career—Sun, Scholar, Completion, Literary Minister

He was an active software developer in the early years, particularly on the company's programming language products. He has not officially been on a development team since working on the TRS-80 Model 100 line but wrote code as late as 1989.

*Sun in Career represents light and the transmission of knowledge (the IT industry). Here joined by Literary Minister in Self, he has the perfect but very rare quad-angled star combination for outstanding accomplishments.* The Sun-Scholar-Completion-Literary Minister formation is only found with highly successful star-quality individuals.

## Properties—Commander & Mirror

Since Microsoft's founding in 1975, his business has continued to grow exponentially. Gates is legendary in every sense of the word.

*The action-packed wealthy Commander joins forces with a Brilliant Mirror, which is the stabilizing force. This partnership ensures a smooth running of the business with just the right balance of force and action. Spinning Top, also here, points to highly intricate, repetitive matters— Computer Programming.*

N.B. Note the absence of any of the Killing Stars in the vicinity, whether it be the Life or the 10-Year charts. In sync with all the foregoing auspicious and phenomenal star formations, such is the life of a brilliant philanthropist.

*Bill Gates' Life Chart*

| SELF | OPPOSITE | CAREER | KARMIC |
|------|----------|--------|--------|
| MOON | INTELLIGENCE | SUN | WAIF |
| LIT. MINISTER | | SCHOLAR | MESSENGER |

| TRAVEL 2019-2028 辛 65-74 巳 | HEALTH 2009-2018 壬 55-64 午 | PROSPER 1999-2008 癸 45-54 未 | MINORS 1989-1998 甲 35-44 申 |
|---|---|---|---|
| ▲ INTEL $ | ⊙ EMPER◌ | | ✗ PNEER |
| HORS | | | DELI *FIRE* |
| T T T <br> X W F <br> LG **FB** SY DK | T J T t <br> c L C s <br> GD **DH** Xs **BF** | K H <br> W G <br> MY **BF** SJ HG | T T C G <br> f K 31 C <br> CS XS **HQ JS** |

| STAFF 2029-2038 庚 75-84 辰 | **Life Analysis** | | SPOUS/L 1979-1988 乙 25-34 酉 |
|---|---|---|---|
| ◉ GENRL | Name: Bill Gates | | |
| RAM | 1955/10/28 ▾ :00:00 PM ± ⦿ Male <br> Date of Birth  Time  ◯ Female <br> (yyyy/mm/dd)  (hh:mm:ss) | | *BELL* |
| T J G T T I <br> G S S D S s <br> DW **GF** PA TD | Life \| Ten Years \| Years \| Month \| Day \| T.Z+1 / T.Z-1 \| Record \| Print | | C 20 <br> Y FL **SM ZS** |

| CAREER 2039-2048 己 85-94 卯 | Lunar B.T. (乙未)Y( IX)M(XIII)D(亥)T | | PEERS 1969-1978 丙 15-24 戌 |
|---|---|---|---|
| ⊙ SUN | Solar B.T. (乙未)Y(丙戌)M(壬戌)D(亥)T | | ◉ CRMSN |
| ⊙ SCHOL↗ | 陰陽五行 陰男 土五局 羊人 | | ⊙ VAULT |
| COMP | | | PUNI |
| ARTS | ■ Obstacle ◯ Fame ↗ Power $ Wealth | | |
| F F <br> G L <br> A BS JX BH | ■ Life ■ 10 year ■ Year ■ Month ■ Day | | Y E <br> S G <br> T Zs **GS TS** |

| PROPERT 2049-2058 戊 95-104 寅 | KARMIC 2059-2068 己 105-114 丑 | ELDERS 2069-2078 戊 115-124 子 | THE SELF 1959-1968 丁 5-14 亥 |
|---|---|---|---|
| ▲ COMDR | ✗ WAIF | ◉ OPPOR | ⊙ MOON ■ |
| ⊙ MIROR | ◉ MESGR | | |
| *SPIN* RIGT | | STAR LEFT VOID | |
| | | | LITE |
| B T C T <br> Z Y 7 g <br> B LS LD **WS** | T P F <br> x S g <br> S QL **SP Ys** | S C Y <br> T 32 D <br> M XH XH D46 | T L <br> k C <br> J JJ **Gf ZB** |

BILL GATES

**Bruce Lee** ★NOVEMBER 27, 1940 8:00 A.M. SAN FRANCISCO, CA, USA

Born Li Zhenfan 李小龍, Bruce Lee was an actor, martial arts expert, philosopher, film director and producer, screenwriter, and founder of the Jeet Kun Do concept. He is considered the most influential martial artist of the 20th century, an icon. Lee was born in San Francisco, California, to Hong Kong parents but raised in Hong Kong until his late teens. At eighteen, Lee immigrated to the USA to claim his US citizenship and attend the University of Washington. He began teaching martial arts, which soon lead to film and television roles.

**The Self—Mirror, Delight, Spinning Top,Void**

*Mirror in the Self indicates a careful individual. Upright and blessed with a big heart, he just fits right into everyone's ideal of the Big Brother. Void which is also in Self is a poet by nature, a deep thinker.*

**Karmic—Commander, General**

*Commander↗-General in Karmic, his world revolved around Kung Fu. Commander in Self is strong-willed and a fighter. With Power attached to the Commander, we are seeing an outstanding partnership, which is conducive to a career in the Corps. Chiefs of units and military commanders will usually have this star combination in their charst. For Bruce Lee, this put him among the masters.* His films elevated the traditional HK martial arts film to a new level of popularity and acclaim and sparked the second major surge of interest in Chinese martial arts in the West.

**Opposite Self—Emperor, Pioneer, Left and Right Minister, Stardust**

A Brilliant Emperor opposite Self with his full court of support—Pioneer, Commander↗ and General, Opportunity, Left and Right Ministers, Stardust & Delight! *It was no wonder Lee became the iconic figure known throughout the world!* He also single-handedly changed and elevated the perception of Westerners held towards Chinese people.

**Career—Opposite is Crimson & Opportunity**

*With Crimson & Opportunity reflected in Career, we glimpse into the complicated setting of acting, martial arts, entertainment, and teaching all rolled into one. Such is the twilight world of Crimson-Opportunity in Career.*

While Lee initially trained in Wing Chun, he later rejected well-defined martial art styles, favoring instead to utilize his personal martial arts philosophy he dubbed Jeet Kun Do, The Way of the Intercepting Fist. *Pioneer opposite Self is a strong leader who is also a rebel, constantly opening new frontiers and developing new concepts—the mark of a brave leader. A mover by nature, he is not content to stay put for long.*

*Bruce Lee's Life Chart*

| SELF | OPPOSITE | PROSPERITY | KARMIC |
|---|---|---|---|
| MIRROR | EMPEROR | VAULT | COMMANDER |
| | PIONEER | | GENERAL |

| SPOUSE 2042-2051 辛巳 103-112 | PEERS 2052-2061 壬午 113-122 | THE SELF 1942-1951 癸未 3-12 | ELDERS 1952-1961 甲申 13-22 |
|---|---|---|---|
| ✕ CRMSN<br>✕ OPPOR | ◉ MESGR<br><br>FIRE | ▲ MIROR<br><br>DELI SPIN VOID | ◉ WAIF ■<br>✕ SCHOL<br>COMP |
| | *LITE* | | ARTS |
| T  C  G<br>K  ?  C<br>B   DH  HQ  JS | T  J  T  T  T  F<br>f  L  X  Y  Y  G<br>S    FB  SM  ZS | K  T<br>W  S<br>M    GF  GS  TS | T  Y  L  E<br>W  S  C  G<br>J    BS  Gf  ZB |

| MINORS 2032-2041 庚辰 93-102 | | | KARMIC 1962-1971 乙酉 23-32 |
|---|---|---|---|
| ▲ MOON | | BRUCE LEE | ◉ COMDR↗<br>▲ GENRL |
| | | ───── ✦ ───── | *RAM* |
| S  J  H<br>I  S  G<br>A   BF  SJ  HG | | *If you love life,* | C  Y<br>32 D<br>T   LS  **XH** D46 |

| PROSP/L 2022-2031 己卯 83-92 | | | PROPERT 1972-1981 丙戌 33-42 |
|---|---|---|---|
| ▲ VAULT ◌<br><br>PUNI | | *don't waste time,*<br><br>*for time is what* | ✕ SUN  $ |
| | | *Life* | B  C  T  T<br>Z 20 x g F |
| DW  XS  Xs  **BF** | | *is made up of* | Y    QL  SP Ys |

| HEALTH 2012-2021 戊寅 73-82 | TRAVEL 2002-2011 己丑 63-72 | STAFF 1992-2001 戊子 53-62 | CAREER 1982-1991 丁亥 43-52 |
|---|---|---|---|
| | ◎ EMPER<br>◉ PNEER<br>STAR LEFT RIGT | ◎ INTEL | |
| HORS BELL | | | |
| T  T  t<br>c  k  s<br>LG  FL  SY  DK | G  P  T<br>S  S  D<br>GD  Zs  PA  TD | I<br>s<br>MY  JJ  JX  BH | T  C  T<br>G 31 C<br>CS  **XH**  LD  **WS** |

BRUCE LEE

Lee continued pioneering these new techniques right up to a year before his death. *Literary Minister with Fame✿ in Prosperity in the 10-year chart indicated he was to be hugely rewarded with literary matters, education, the arts, and major tests.*

Although Lee is best known as a martial artist, he also studied drama and philosophy while a student at the University of Washington. *Void in the Self sector individuals very often have their own peculiar outlook on life. They don't say much and perplex people with their often-changing personas. Behind their brooding façade is an active mind that wants to be recognized but at the same time rejects contact. These people are creative and artistic. This Killing Star in the Self sector brings with it at least one major, heart-rending setback.* His eclectic philosophy often mirrored his fighting beliefs though he was quick to claim that his martial arts were solely a metaphor for such teachings. The following quotations reflect his fighting philosophy.

"Be formless—shapeless like water. If you put water into a cup, it becomes the cup. You put water into a bottle, it becomes the bottle. You put it into a teapot, it becomes the teapot. Water can flow, or it can crash. Be water, my friend."

"All kinds of knowledge eventually become self-knowledge."

"Use only that which works, and take it from any place you can find it."

"Do not deny the classical approach simply as a reaction, or you will have created another pattern and trapped yourself there."

"A quick temper will make a fool of you soon enough."

Strangely, an early death was what Lee had contemplated frequently. According to his wife Linda, he had no wish to live to a ripe old age because he could not stand the idea of losing the physical abilities he had strived so hard to achieve. *This had probably to do with his psyche. With the Killing Stars in Self and Void in the Self Sector, individuals very often have their own peculiar outlook on life. Also, in his 10 year ('72-'81) Karmic, there was Intelligence with Power attached that indicated heavy thoughts occupying the Self.* "If I should die tomorrow," he used to say, "I will have no regrets. I did what I wanted to do. You can't expect more from life."

N.B. In the Health Sector of what was to be his last 10 year chart, Crimson had the fearsome ■ Obstacle attached, *relating to diseases of the blood.*

*Bruce Lee's 10-Year Chart 1972-1981 (Aged 33-42)*

| SELF | OPPOSITE | PROSPERITY | KARMIC |
|------|----------|------------|--------|
| SUN | MOON | MESSENGER | INTELLIGENCE |
| | SPINNING TOP | LIT. MINISTER | |

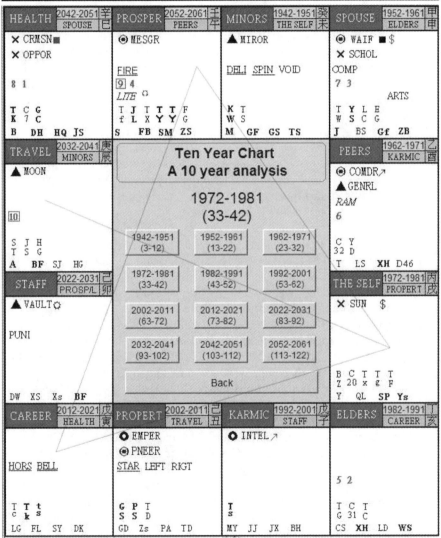

**HEALTH** 2042-2051 辛 SPOUSE 巳
- ✗ CRMSN ■
- ✗ OPPOR

8 1

T C G
K 7 C
B　DH　HQ　JS

**PROSPER** 2052-2061 壬 PEERS 午
- ◉ MESGR

FIRE
⑨ 4
*LITE* ☋

T J　T　T　T F
f L　X　Y　Y G
S　FB　SM ZS

**MINORS** 1942-1951 癸 THE SELF 未
- ▲ MIROR

DELI SPIN VOID

K T
W S
M　GF　GS　TS

**SPOUSE** 1952-1961 甲 ELDERS 申
- ◉ WAIF ■ $
- ✗ SCHOL

COMP
7 3
　　　ARTS

T Y L E
W S C G
J　BS　Gf　ZB

**TRAVEL** 2032-2041 庚 MINORS 辰
- ▲ MOON

⑩

S J H
T S G
A　BF　SJ　HG

**STAFF** 2022-2031 己 PROSP/L 卯
- ▲ VAULT ○

PUNI

DW　XS　Xs　BF

**PEERS** 1962-1971 乙 KARMIC 酉
- ◉ COMDR ↗
- ▲ GENRL

*RAM*
6

C Y
32 D
T　LS　XH　D46

**THE SELF** 1972-1981 丙 PROPERT 戌
- ✗ SUN　$

B C T T
Z 20 x g F
Y　QL　SP　Ys

**Ten Year Chart**
**A 10 year analysis**

**1972-1981**
**(33-42)**

| 1942-1951 (3-12) | 1952-1961 (13-22) | 1962-1971 (23-32) |
| 1972-1981 (33-42) | 1982-1991 (43-52) | 1992-2001 (53-62) |
| 2002-2011 (63-72) | 2012-2021 (73-82) | 2022-2031 (83-92) |
| 2032-2041 (93-102) | 2042-2051 (103-112) | 2052-2061 (113-122) |

Back

**CAREER** 2012-2021 戊 HEALTH 寅

HORS BELL

T T t
c k s
LG　FL　SY　DK

**PROPERT** 2002-2011 己 TRAVEL 丑
- ◉ EMPER
- ◉ PNEER

STAR LEFT RIGT

G P T
S S D
GD　Zs　PA　TD

**KARMIC** 1992-2001 戊 STAFF 子
- ◉ INTEL ↗

I
s
MY　JJ　JX　BH

**ELDERS** 1982-1991 丁 CAREER 亥

5 2

T C T
G 31 C
CS　XH　LD　WS

BRUCE LEE

# Donald Trump ★ *JUNE 14, 1946    8:00 A.M.    QUEENS, NEW YORK, USA*

Donald John Trump is the fourth of five children of a wealthy real estate developer. He is an American business magnate, socialite, author, and television personality. Trump is the Chairman and CEO of the Trump Organization, a U.S.-based real estate development cooperation and founder of Trump Entertainment Resorts, which operates numerous casinos and hotels around the world.

## The Self—Commander, Mirror

Trump is often seen as outspoken and brash, *a trait of Commander in Self. In addition, he is a craftsman and implementer involved with "the nuts and bolts of putting an idea to work."* Starting with the renovation of the Commodore Hotel into the Grand Hyatt with the Pritzker family, Trump continued with Trump Tower and several other residential projects in New York City.

## Opposite Self—Pioneer, Left Minister, Winged Horse, Arts Minister

*Reflecting the Mirror opposite the Self is Pioneer, who tears down and rebuilds. However, the dark Pioneer brings with it a hard lesson to be learned.* Trump would later expand into the airline industry by buying the Eastern Shuttle routes and an Atlantic City casino business that included buying the Taj Mahal Casino from the Crosby family and then taking it into bankruptcy. The personal and business expansion led to mounting debt.

*Interestingly, the Arts Minister here also brings out the actor/performer.* Trump's extravagant lifestyle and outspoken manner have made him a celebrity for years, a status amplified by the success of his NBC reality show, "The Apprentice" where he serves as host and executive producer.

## Properties—Intelligence, Completion, Fire

He has Intelligence↗ in his Properties Chamber, *an early indication of his future power, strengths, and abilities in real estate.* Upon his graduation from Wharton School of the University of Pennsylvania in 1968, Donald Trump joined his father's company, The Trump Organization.

## Career—Emperor, Ram, Right Minister

*In Career is a Brilliant Emperor who is lacking full support and plagued by Ram—signs of huge difficulties.* News about him in the early 1990s involved his much publicized financial problems. Moreover, his affair with Marla Maples resulted in a divorce from his first wife, Ivana. *A Brilliant Vault in Prosperity is weakened by a Bright Crimson■ in retrograde—an indication of females helping themselves to a chunk of his fortune.*

Donald John Trump is the fourth of five children of a wealthy real estate developer. He is an American business magnate, socialite, author, and television personality. Trump is the Chairman and CEO of the Trump Organization, a U.S.-based real estate development cooperation.

# *Commander/Mirror in Self* AT TIGER CHAMBER

*Donald Trump's Life Chart*

| SELF | OPPOSITE | PROSPERITY | KARMIC |
|------|----------|------------|--------|
| **COMMANDER** **MIRROR** | **PIONEER** | **CRIMSON** **VAULT** | **GENERAL** |

| PROPERT 1978-1987 癸 巳 33-42 | CAREER 1988-1997 甲 午 43-52 | STAFF 1998-2007 乙 未 53-62 | TRAVEL 2008-2017 丙 申 63-72 |
|---|---|---|---|
| ▲ INTEL ↗ | ○ EMPER | | ✗ PNEER |
| COMP <u>FIRE</u> | RAM RIGT | <u>BELL</u> VOID | LEFT <u>HORS</u> |
| | *LITE* ☌ | | ARTS |
| T K C T T C<br>G W 20 W W 31<br>B BS LD **WS** | Y F<br>S g<br>S LS JX BH | T G T E T<br>Y S D G s<br>M QL PA TD | T T<br>k S<br>J **XH** SY DK |

| KARMIC 1968-1977 壬 辰 23-32 | | | HEALTH 2018-2027 丁 酉 73-82 |
|---|---|---|---|
| ⊚ GENRL | | | |
| <u>SPIN</u> | **DONALD TRUMP** | | <u>DELI</u> |
| | ✦ | | |
| J B T<br>L Z x<br>A GF SP Ys | *As long as* | | T t<br>g s<br>T JJ Xs **BF** |

| ELDERS 1958-1967 辛 卯 13-22 | *you're going to be* | | PROSP/L 2028-2037 戊 戌 83-92 |
|---|---|---|---|
| ○ SUN<br>○ SCHOL<br>PUNI | *thinking anyway,* | | ⊚ CRMSN ■<br>○ VAULT |
| | *think big.* | | |
| C Y<br>32 D<br>DW **FB XH** D46 | | | S H T<br>T G F<br>Y Zs SJ HG |

| THE SELF 1948-1957 庚 寅 3-12 | PEERS 2058-2067 辛 丑 113-122 | SPOUSE 2048-2057 庚 子 103-112 | MINORS 2038-2047 己 亥 93-102 |
|---|---|---|---|
| ▲ COMDR<br>○ MIROR | ✗ WAIF $<br>⊚ MESGR | ⊚ OPPOR | ○ MOON<br><br>STAR |
| L<br>C<br>LG **DH Gf ZB** | T P<br>X S<br>GD **BF GS TS** | T T J F F T<br>c f S G L C<br>MY XS **SM ZS** | T C G<br>K 7 C<br>CS FL **HQ JS** |

Chapter 8.4 – Donald Trump 303

## Resurgence—The 1998-2007 10-Year Chart

In 2001 Trump completed Trump World Tower, a 72-story residential tower across from the United Nations Headquarters. Also, he began construction on Trump Place, a multi-building development along the Hudson River. Trump owns commercial space in Trump International Hotel and Tower, a 44-story mixed-use (hotel and condominium) tower on Columbus Circle.

*With Bell in his Self Chamber/House, Trump may be feeling quite alone amidst all this real estate. Void, also here, is a major Killing Star that works against anything related to prosperity and wealth. Its characteristic is such that any riches gained will eventually be lost.* Beset with financial woes, Trump's casino empire filed for bankruptcy in 2004.

*However, The Void's contradictory streak comes to the fore if met up by Bell—which is right here in the same sector. This pairing would ignite an explosive development which will have a tremendous up-lifting effect on one's life work. Two evils definitely make a good.* Trump currently owns several million square feet of prime Manhattan real estate and remains a major figure in the field of real estate in the United States.

*This apparent see-sawing of his fortunes may also have to do with a dark Waif reflecting the Self, albeit trailing prosperity$. This erratic star brings emotional and financial volatility; however, she has the ability to build weath from nothing.*

*A Brilliant Sun coupled with Scholar with Power↗ ensure muscle to pull in the cash.* In 2004 Donald Trump filed a trademark application for his catchphrase "You're fired!" used in "The Apprentice" TV show. For the first year of the show, Trump was paid $50,000 per episode (roughly $700,000 for the first season). Following the show's initial success, Trump was paid a reported $3 million per episode, making him one of the highest paid TV personalities.

*However, several dark stars remain to plague his finances (Punishment in Prosperity, Properties with an afflicted Crimson■, and Career's Moon also in retrograde■. Trump will not see his way out of this until the following ten years (2008-2017).*

*Donald Trump's 10-Year Chart 1998-2007 (Age 53-62)*

| SELF | OPPOSITE | PROSPERITY | KARMIC |
|------|----------|------------|--------|
| BELL VOID | WAIF MESSENGER | SUN SCHOLAR | DELIGHT |

| SPOUSE | 1978-1987 癸 PROPERT 巳 | PEERS | 1988-1997 甲 CAREER 午 | THE SELF | 1998-2007 乙 STAFF 未 | ELDERS | 2008-2017 丙 TRAVEL 申 |
|--------|--------|--------|--------|--------|--------|--------|--------|
| ▲ INTEL ↗ $ | | ○ EMPER ○ | | BELL VOID | | ✗ PNEER | |
| COMP FIRE | | RAM RIGT | | | | LEFT HORS | |
| 7 | | 3 | | 6 1 4 | | | |
| | | *LITE* ☼ | | | | | ARTS |
| I K C T T C | | Y F | | T G T E T | | T T | |
| G W 20 ♯ ♯ 31 | | S g | | Y S D G s | | k S | |
| B BS LD WS | | S LS JX BH | | M QL PA TD | | J XH SY DK | |

| MINORS | 1968-1977 壬 KARMIC 辰 | | | | KARMIC | 2018-2027 丁 HEALTH 酉 |
|--------|--------|--------|--------|--------|--------|--------|
| ◉ GENRL | | | **Ten Year Chart** | | | |
| | | | **A 10 year analysis** | | | |
| SPIN | | | | | DELI | |
| 9 | | | **1998-2007** | | | |
| | | | **(53-62)** | | | |
| J B T | | 1948-1957 (3-12) | 1958-1967 (13-22) | 1968-1977 (23-32) | T t | |
| L Z x | | | | | g s | |
| A GF SP Ys | | 1978-1987 (33-42) | 1988-1997 (43-52) | 1998-2007 (53-62) | T JJ Xs BF | |

| PROSPER | 1958-1967 辛 ELDERS 卯 | | | | PROPERT | 2028-2037 戊 PROSP/L 戌 |
|---------|--------|--------|--------|--------|---------|--------|
| ○ SUN | | 2008-2017 (63-72) | 2018-2027 (73-82) | 2028-2037 (83-92) | ◉ CRMSN ■ | |
| ○ SCHOL ↗ | | | | | ○ VAULT | |
| PUNI | | 2038-2047 (93-102) | 2048-2057 (103-112) | 2058-2067 (113-122) | | |
| 8 | | | | | | |
| C Y | | | Back | | S H T | |
| 32 D | | | | | T G F | |
| DW FB XH D46 | | | | | Y Zs SJ HG | |

| HEALTH | 1948-1957 庚 THE SELF 寅 | TRAVEL | 2058-2067 辛 PEERS 丑 | STAFF | 2048-2057 庚 SPOUSE 子 | CAREER | 2038-2047 己 MINORS 亥 |
|--------|--------|--------|--------|--------|--------|--------|--------|
| ▲ COMDR | | ✗ WAIF $ | | ◉ OPPOR | | ○ MOON ■ | |
| ○ MIROR | | ◉ MESGR | | | | | |
| | | | | | | STAR | |
| 10 2 | | | | 5 | | | |
| L | | T P | | T T J F F T | | T C G | |
| C | | X S | | c f S G L C | | K ? C | |
| LG DH Gf ZB | | GD BF GS TS | | MY XS SM ZS | | CS FL HQ JS | |

DONALD TRUMP

# *George Soros* ★ AUGUST 12, 1930 2:00 A.M.  BUDAPEST, HUNGARY

 Born as Schwartz Gyorgy, he is a Hungarian-American currency speculator, stock investor, businessman, philanthropist, and political activist. Soros is chairman of Soros Fund Management and the Open Society Institute.

### The Self—Emperor & Pioneer, Delight, Spinning Top
George Soros has made his mark as an enormously successful speculator, wise enough to largely withdraw when still way ahead of the game. *With a Brilliant Emperor in the Self helped by the strong and positive Pioneer, Soros already has the right stars for a career in Finance.*

### Opposite Self—Mirror, Stardust
*A Brilliant Mirror reflects the Self—The Philanthropist. Mirror ensures that all his returns are doubled.* The bulk of his enormous winnings is now devoted to encouraging emerging nations to become "open societies."

*Mirror signifies Responsibility to those close to him.* He played a significant role in the peaceful transition from Communism to Capitalism in Hungary (1984-89) and provided Europe's largest ever higher education endowment to Central European University in Budapest.

*Mirror is upright and blessed with a big heart; and he just fits right into everyone's ideal of the big brother.*

Later, Soros' funding and organization of Georgia's Rose Revolution was considered by Russian and Western observers to have been crucial to its success. *Mirror goes out of his way to fight for what he believes in. Moreover, we have Delight, Spinning Top and Stardust, all Brilliants in their own right. This, if ever, is the perfect chart befitting a financial wizard!*

### Prosperity and Career
The Dark Commander↗ and General (both of which rule finance) are present in Prosperity. A similar dark Crimson/Opportunity pair is also in Career. Note these allude to the Soros brand of "negative" strategies— well-timed, speculative short-selling. In 1997, the UK Treasury estimated the cost of Black Wednesday (Soros' 1992 shorting of the £) at £3.4 billion.

There are no Killing Stars around, except a Brilliant Spinning Top in Self that brings nothing more than publicity or gossips. But who wouldn't be interested in the exploits of this hugely successful entrepreneur?

*George Soros' Life Chart*

| SELF | OPPOSITE | PROSPERITY | KARMIC |
|---|---|---|---|
| EMPEROR<br>PIONEER | MIRROR<br>STARDUST | COMMANDER<br>GENERAL | VAULT |

| SPOUSE | 2032-2041 辛<br>103-112 巳 | PEERS | 2042-2051 壬<br>113-122 午 | THE SELF | 1932-1941 癸<br>3-12 未 | ELDERS | 1942-1951 甲<br>13-22 申 |
|---|---|---|---|---|---|---|---|
| | | ○ INTEL | | ○ EMPER<br>○ PNEER<br>DELI SPIN | | COMP HORS | |
| | ARTS | | | | | | |
| P<br>S<br>B DH WS BF | | T J<br>f L<br>S FB JX SJ | | K C T I<br>W 20 K F<br>M GF PA HQ | | G<br>C<br>J BS SY SM | |

| MINORS | 2022-2031 庚<br>93-102 辰 | | | | | KARMI/L | 1952-1961 乙<br>23-32 酉 |
|---|---|---|---|---|---|---|---|
| ◉ SUN $ | | | | | | ✕ VAULT ○ | |
| RIGT BELL | | | **GEORGE SOROS** | | | *RAM* | |
| | | | | | | LITE | |
| F G<br>G S<br>A BF Ys DK | | | ──── ✦ ──── | | | C T<br>31 g<br>T LS Xs GS | |

| PROSPER | 2012-2021 己<br>83-92 卯 | | *The financial markets* | | | PROPERT | 1962-1971 丙<br>33-42 戌 |
|---|---|---|---|---|---|---|---|
| ✕ COMDR ↗<br>✕ GENRL | | | *generally are unpredictable.*<br>*So that one has to have*<br>*different scenarios ...*<br>*The idea that you can*<br>*actually predict*<br>*what's going to happen*<br>*contradicts my way of* | | | ◉ MOON<br><br>LEFT *VOID* | |
| S T C C I I<br>T X 7 32 D S<br>DW XS D46 TD | | | *looking at the market.* | | | L H<br>C G<br>Y QL HG Gf | |

| HEALTH | 2002-2011 戊<br>73-82 寅 | TRAVEL | 1992-2001 己<br>63-72 丑 | STAFF | 1982-1991 戊<br>53-62 子 | CAREER | 1972-1981 丁<br>43-52 亥 |
|---|---|---|---|---|---|---|---|
| ▲ WAIF ■<br>○ SCHOL<br>FIRE | | ○ MIROR<br><br>STAR | | ◉ MESGR<br><br>*PUNI* | | ✕ CRMSN<br>✕ OPPOR | |
| I J I Y Y F<br>c S W S S L<br>LG FL ZB BH | | T E<br>C G<br>GD Zs TS LD | | T I I<br>k x s<br>MY JJ ZS SP | | T B T Y<br>G Z Y D<br>CS XH JS XH | |

GEORGE SOROS

**The 10-Year Chart 1992-2001**

Soros instigated two eminent feats—both in the year of the Monkey, exactly twelve years apart. With practically the same star configuration, why did one succeed and the other fail?

*Breaking the Bank of England*

On Black Wednesday (September 16, 1992), Soros' fund sold short more than $10 billion worth of pounds sterling and profited from the Bank of England's reluctance to either raise its interest rates to levels comparable to those of other European Exchange Rate Mechanism countries or to float its currency.

*He had a Brilliant Mirror in Self reflecting and doubling whatever the Brilliant Emperor and Pioneer would spin off. The prosperous Sun$ in his Properties (Business) sector lent strength. As if this wasn't enough, the Vault✿ in Prosperity teamed up with Commander$ and General opposite (the black knights) in his Karmic. He was poised to destroy.*

*Unfortunately for the Bank of England (represented by a weak, erratic Waif■ in retrograde in Elders), the battle was lost before it even began!*

Finally, the Bank of England withdrew the currency from the European Exchange Rate Mechanism, devaluing the pound sterling, and Soros earned an estimated US$1.1 billion in the process. He was dubbed "the man who broke the Bank of England." In 1997, the UK Treasury estimated the cost of Black Wednesday at £3.4 billion.

*Failed Attempt to Topple Bush*

In 2004, exactly twelve years later, Soros donated $23,581,000 to various groups to stop Bush's re-election. *However, the President was a little stronger in Elders, backed by the powerful dark knights Commander↗ and General and helped at Opposite by a dark Vault strengthened by ✿. The President also had the Brilliant Literary Minister opposite—a sign of a victorious government exam!* [That chart is not shown here but is on CD provided.]

Soros had a weak, erratic Waif ■ in his Self House, coupled with Intelligence■ powerfully in retrograde in Career! Obviously, Soros did not succeed, as Bush won by a margin and went on to serve a second term.

# *Mirror/Stardust in 10-year (63-72) Self* AT OX CHAMBER

*George Soros' 10-Year Chart 1992-2001 (Age 63-72)*

| SELF | OPPOSITE | PROSPERITY | KARMIC |
|------|----------|------------|--------|
| **MIRROR** **STARDUST** | **EMPEROR** **PIONEER** | **VAULT** | **COMMANDER** **GENERAL** |

| CAREER 2032-2041 辛<br>SPOUSE 巳 | STAFF 2042-2051 壬<br>PEERS 午 | TRAVEL 1932-1941 癸<br>THE SELF 未 | HEALTH 1942-1951 甲<br>ELDERS 申 |
|---|---|---|---|
| | ○ INTEL | ○ EMPER<br>○ PNEER<br>DELI SPIN | COMP HORS |
| 10 4 | 8 | 9 | 6 2 |
| ARTS ■ | | | |
| P<br>S | I J<br>f L | K C T T<br>W 20 K F | G<br>C |
| B DH WS BF | S FB JX SJ | M GF PA HQ | J BS SY SM |

| PROPERT 2022-2031 庚<br>MINORS 辰 | | | PROSPER 1952-1961 乙<br>KARMI/L 酉 |
|---|---|---|---|
| ⊙ SUN $ | **Ten Year Chart** | | ✕ VAULT ○ |
| RIGT BELL | **A 10 year analysis** | | *RAM* |
| | **1992-2001** | | 3 |
| | **(63-72)** | | LITE |
| F G<br>G S | 1932-1941 (3-12) / 1942-1951 (13-22) / 1952-1961 (23-32) | | C T<br>31 g |
| A BF Ys DK | | | T LS Xs GS |

| KARMIC 2012-2021 己<br>PROSPER 卯 | 1962-1971 (33-42) / 1972-1981 (43-52) / 1982-1991 (53-62) | | MINORS 1962-1971 丙<br>PROPERT 戌 |
|---|---|---|---|
| ✕ COMDR ↗ $<br>✕ GENRL | 1992-2001 (63-72) / 2002-2011 (73-82) / 2012-2021 (83-92) | | ⊙ MOON |
| | 2022-2031 (93-102) / 2032-2041 (103-112) / 2042-2051 (113-122) | | LEFT *VOID* |
| S T C C T T<br>T X 7 32 D S | Back | | L H<br>C G |
| DW XS D46 TD | | | Y QL HG Gf |

| ELDERS 2002-2011 戊<br>HEALTH 寅 | THE SELF 1992-2001 己<br>TRAVEL 丑 | PEERS 1982-1991 戊<br>STAFF 子 | SPOUSE 1972-1981 丁<br>CAREER 亥 |
|---|---|---|---|
| ▲ WAIF ■<br>○ SCHOL ○ | ○ MIROR | ⊙ MESGR | ✕ CRMSN<br>✕ OPPOR ↗ |
| FIRE | STAR | *PUNI* | |
| 1 | | 5 | 7 |
| T J I Y Y F<br>c S W S S L | T E<br>C G | T T I<br>k x s | T B T Y<br>G Z Y D |
| LG FL ZB BH | GD Zs TS LD | MY JJ ZS SP | CS XH JS XH |

**_Madonna_** ★ AUGUST 16, 1958 6:45 A.M. BAY CITY, MICHIGAN, U.S.A.

 Born Madonna Louise Ciccone, Madonna is the third of eight siblings in an American-Italian family. She is a recording artist, actress and entrepreneur. Madonna is currently ranked 4th in the 2010 Forbes Top 20 Richest Women.

### The Self—Vault, Completion

The Vault and Completion are in her Self Chamber at Snake. _It is a characteristic of Vault in the Self that these people will never lack for earthly possessions._

### Karmic—Commander, Opportunity, Delight, Literary and Arts Ministers

_Vault at the Snake chamber is intricately bonded to the Brilliants Commander and Opportunity in Karmic. These stars would lift the lackluster Vault and transform it into a shining spinner—signs of the material girl emerging._

Both the Literary and a Brilliant Arts Ministers are in her Karmic. _She is refined, creative and knowledgeable with emphasis on the performing arts._

### Opposite Self—Emperor, General

Reflecting the Self Sector are Emperor and General. _The strength of this pair makes for a determined and dynamic personality._

### Prosperity—Stardust

_Stardust (in Prosperity) and Delight (in Karmic) is a wonderful couple of stars to have in any sector of the birth chart. Madonna has Stardust in her Prosperity with Delight at opposite (Karmic). As long as the major stars have some measure of brightness, and there are no Killing Stars around, the whole lifetime can be enhanced by this pair._

In 1996, Madonna played the starring role in the film _Evita_, for which she won a Golden Globe Award. To-date, she has sold more than 200 million albums worldwide. She is ranked by the Recording Industry Association of America as the best-selling female rock artist of the 20th century. Guinness World Records listed her as the world's most successful female recording artist of all time. In 2008, Billboard magazine ranked Madonna at number two, behind only The Beatles, making her the most successful solo artist in the history of the chart at that time.

_Such is the power of Vault and Completion in the Self Sector—the combination that produces outstanding and high-ranking administrators and officials. Together with Sun۞ (crowd pleaser) and Messenger (vocal power) in Properties (her business), she raised pop culture to the highest order and honed her craft into a multi-billion dollar industry._

# Vault, Completion in Self AT SNAKE CHAMBER

*Madonna's Life Chart*

| SELF | OPPOSITE | PROSPERITY | KARMIC |
|------|----------|------------|--------|
| VAULT COMPLETION | EMPEROR GENERAL | STARDUST | COMMANDER OPPORTUNITY |

| THE SELF 1962-1971 丁<br>5-14 巳 | ELDERS 2072-2081 戊<br>115-124 午 | KARMIC 2062-2071 己<br>105-114 未 | PROPERT 2052-2061 庚<br>95-104 申 |
|---|---|---|---|
| ▲ VAULT<br><br>COMP | ✕ WAIF<br>✕ MOON ↗<br>RAM BELL | ○ COMDR<br>○ OPPOR $<br>DELI<br><br>LITE          ARTS | ▲ SUN ☼<br>○ MESGR<br>HORS VOID |
| C F<br>31 g<br>LG   BS   LD   WS | T<br>c<br>GD   GF   JX   BH | C G T E T<br>20 S D G g<br>MY   FB   PA   TD | T<br>k<br>CS   DH   SY   DK |

| PEERS 1972-1981 丙<br>15-24 辰 | MADONNA | CAREER 2042-2051 辛<br>85-94 酉 |
|---|---|---|
| SPIN  RIGT  FIRE<br><br>T<br>x<br>DW   LS   SP   Ys | ✦<br><br>*I stand for*<br>*freedom of expression,* | ✕ MIROR<br><br>T   T<br>S   F<br>Y   BF   Xs   BF |

| SPOUSE 1982-1991 乙<br>25-34 卯 | *doing what you* | STAFF 2032-2041 壬<br>75-84 戌 |
|---|---|---|
| ▲ CRMSN<br>◉ PNEER<br><br><br><br>T T B T C<br>f G Z X X 32<br>A   QL   XH   D46 | *believe in,*<br><br>*and going after*<br><br>*your dreams.* | ○ INTEL ■<br>◉ SCHOL<br>LEFT<br><br>H I<br>G s<br>T   XS   SJ   HG |

| MINORS 1992-2001 甲<br>35-44 寅 | PROSPER 2002-2011 乙<br>45-54 丑 | HEALTH 2012-2021 甲<br>55-64 子 | TRAVEL/L 2022-2031 癸<br>65-74 亥 |
|---|---|---|---|
| PUNI<br><br><br>J T Y L<br>S W S C<br>B   XH   Gf   ZB | STAR<br><br><br>K P<br>W S<br>S   JJ   GS   TS | J F F t<br>L G L s<br>M   Zs   SM   ZS | ◉ EMPER<br>▲ GENRL<br><br>S T T C G<br>T Y K ? C<br>J   FL   HQ   JS |

## Madonna's 10-Year Chart—1982-1991—Ages 25-34

Expanding on the use of religious imagery with "Like a Prayer" (1989), Madonna received positive critical reception while at the same time being criticized by religious conservatives and the Vatican.

### The Self—Crimson-Pioneer

*Sex sells! A flirtatious number with a twinkle in her eye! She is an artist by nature and just loves being surrounded by art, music, theatre and the like. A splendidly munificent personality—because she, if anyone, can well afford to be! Joined by Pioneer here, many will find fault with her. But we suspect they all secretly admire this tenacious one who charges on regardless.* Madonna has been known for continually reinventing both her music and image.

### Career—Commander & Opportunity

After performing as a member of the pop musical groups Breakfast Club and Emmy, Madonna released her self-titled debut album, "Madonna" in 1983 on Sire Records. A series of hit singles from her next studio albums, "Like a Virgin" (1984) and "True Blue" (1986) brought her global recognition. They established her as a pop icon that became a fixture on MTV. Her recognition was augmented by the film "Desperately Seeking Susan" (1985) which thrust her further into the spotlight, despite her not playing the lead.

*Commander in the Self Chamber/House people are often slightly built with strong, clear voices. This is a major star of action having to do with wealth. This star will lead its owner to success if found in the Career sector. If aided by Opportunity$, expect entrepreneurial success. Again, flesh sells.*

### Prosperity—Emperor & General

*Presided by a Bright Emperor with ☼ here, The Self deals with or possesses financial prowess. All the qualities of a strong, wise, courageous monarch come forward. With Fame attached, these qualities are enhanced and highlighted. One of the major stars which supports the Emperor, the General, is to be reckoned with. He commands respect and can hold court alone in any sector. With the Ministers and Delight supporting, and none of the Killing Stars around, we are witnessing a perfect Success Triangle here.* Madonna is considered one of the most influential women in contemporary music who has retained a standard of autonomy within the recording industry. She is recognized as an influence and icon among numerous music artists.

# Crimson, Pioneer in Self AT RABBIT CHAMBER

*Madonna's 10-Year Chart 1982-1991 (Age 25-34)*

| SELF | OPPOSITE | PROSPERITY | KARMIC |
|------|----------|------------|--------|
| CRIMSON PIONEER | MIRROR | EMPEROR GENERAL | VAULT COMPLETION |

| | | | |
|---|---|---|---|
| **KARMIC** 1962-1971 丁 / THE SELF 巳 | **PROPERT** 2072-2081 戊 / ELDERS 午 | **CAREER** 2062-2071 己 / KARMIC 未 | **STAFF** 2052-2061 庚 / PROPERT 申 |
| ▲ VAULT | ✗ WAIF<br>✗ MOON ↗ ■ | ⚪ COMDR<br>⚪ OPPOR $ | ▲ SUN ✿<br>⚪ MESGR |
| COMP<br>7 | RAM BELL<br>2 3 | DELI | HORS VOID<br>6 4 |
| | | LITE ARTS | |
| C F<br>31 g | T<br>c | C G T E T<br>20 S D G g | T<br>k |
| LG  BS  LD  **WS** | GD  **GF**  JX  BH | MY  **FB**  PA  TD | CS  **DH**  SY  DK |

**Ten Year Chart**
**A 10 year analysis**
**1982-1991**
**(25-34)**

| | | |
|---|---|---|
| 1962-1971 (5-14) | 1972-1981 (15-24) | 1982-1991 (25-34) |
| 1992-2001 (35-44) | 2002-2011 (45-54) | 2012-2021 (55-64) |
| 2022-2031 (65-74) | 2032-2041 (75-84) | 2042-2051 (85-94) |
| 2052-2061 (95-104) | 2062-2071 (105-114) | 2072-2081 (115-124) |

Back

| | |
|---|---|
| **ELDERS** 1972-1981 丙 / PEERS 辰 | **TRAVEL** 2042-2051 辛 / CAREER 酉 |
| | ✗ MIROR |
| SPIN RIGT FIRE<br>⑨ | |
| T<br>x | T  T<br>S  F |
| DW  LS  **SP**  Ys | Y  **BF**  Xs  **BF** |
| **THE SELF** 1982-1991 乙 / SPOUSE 卯 | **HEALTH** 2032-2041 壬 / STAFF 戌 |
| ▲ CRMSN<br>◉ PNEER | ⚪ INTEL ■ $<br>◉ SCHOL ↗ |
| 8 | LEFT |
| T  T  B  T  T  C<br>f  G  Z  X  X  32<br>A   QL  **XH**  D46 | H  T<br>G  s<br>T  XS  SJ  HG |
| **PEERS** 1992-2001 甲 / MINORS 寅 | **SPOUSE** 2002-2011 乙 / PROSPER 丑 | **MINORS** 2012-2021 甲 / HEALTH 子 | **PROSPER** 2022-2031 癸 / TRAVEL/L 亥 |
| PUNI<br>⑩ | STAR | 5 1 | ◉ EMPER ✿<br>▲ GENRL |
| J  T  Y  L<br>S  W  S  C<br>B  **XH**  Gf  ZB | K  P<br>W  S<br>S   JJ  GS  TS | J  F  F  t<br>L  G  L  s<br>M  Zs  SM  ZS | S  T  T  C  G<br>T  Y  K  7  C<br>J   FL  **HQ** JS |

**MADONNA**

**Michael Jackson** ★AUGUST 29, 1958    10:00 P.M.    BAY CITY, MI, U.S.A.

 Michael Jackson (1958-2009) was an American recording artist, entertainer, and philanthropist. His contribution to music, dance, and fashion, as well as his much publicized personal life made him a global figure in popular culture for over four decades.

**The Self—Blank**
**Opposite—Sun & Scholar, Arts Minister**
Referred to as the King of Pop, Jackson has been recognized as the highest paid and most successful entertainer of all time by Guinness World Records. *Being devoid of major stars in the Self house, we shall look at its Opposite. Note the extraordinary star formation for success in the Life Chart (throughout the whole life): Sun and Scholar (opposite Self); Completion (in Prosperity); Literary Minister (Opposite Prosperity). This pattern is found only with highly successful star-status individuals.*

*The benefactor for the performance arts, Arts Minister, is Brilliant here. Sun with Fame✪ shines on those in the yin, lighting, or broadcasting industries. Note, however, The Sun at Brilliant combined with yin might not have benefitted from an extra mega-dose of the same. A burn-out could result.*

Jackson popularized a number of dance techniques, such as the Robot and the Moonwalk. His distinctive musical sound and vocal style have influenced numerous hip hop, pop, contemporary R&B and rock artists. He was also a notable humanitarian and philanthropist, donating and raising hundreds of millions of dollars supporting more than thirty-nine charities.

*A Brilliant Scholar in Self indicates longevity but alas, a lonesome existence. This star shines on professionals—MJ, as the most successful entertainer of all time, was the master of his profession. The protective, Brilliant Scholar here joins the elegant, benevolent Sun. Being of similar nature, these two stars stand for broadcasting and charity work.*

**Career—Waif, Messenger, Stardust**
*In a sector that is also filled with Auspicious Stars, the Messenger will bear the meaning of fortunes being made by the voice. Here, he had Stardust and Delight (in Opposite—Spouse) shining on him until age 50 when they would turn dark.*

*With having a good time being the order of the day for Waif, when teamed up with Messenger, which stands for vocal abilities, we have the pair in perfect harmony.*

# *(Sun, Scholar) opposite The Self* AT RABBIT CHAMBER

*MJ's Life Chart*

| SELF | CAREER | PROSPERITY | KARMIC |
|---|---|---|---|
| **(SUN)** **(SCHOLAR)** | **WAIF** **MESSENGER** | **INTELLIGENCE** **COMPLETION** | **MOON** **LIT. MNSTR** |

| | | | |
|---|---|---|---|
| PROSPER 2040-2049 丁巳 83-92 | MINORS 2050-2059 戊午 93-102 | SPOUS/L 2060-2069 己未 103-112 | PEERS 2070-2079 庚申 113-122 |
| ▲ INTEL ■ | ○ EMPER | | ✗ PNEER |
| COMP | RAM | DELI | HORS |
| C T T 31 S F B BS LD **WS** | T c S LS JX BH | C G T T 20 S D C M QL PA TD | T k J **XH** SY DK |
| HEALTH 2030-2039 丙辰 73-82 | | | THE SELF 1960-1969 辛酉 3-12 |
| ◉ GENRL | | | |
| SPIN RIGT | **MICHAEL JACKSON** | | |
| T T t x g s A **GF** SP Ys | | | T JJ Xs **BF** |
| TRAVEL 2020-2029 乙卯 63-72 | ✦ | | ELDERS 1970-1979 壬戌 13-22 |
| ○ SUN ◇ ○ SCHOL | *The greatest* | | ◉ CRMSN ○ VAULT LEFT PUNI |
| ARTS T T T C Y f G X 32 D DW **FB XH** D46 | *education in the world* *is watching* *the masters at work.* | | H G Y Zs SJ HG |
| STAFF 2010-2019 甲寅 53-62 | CAREER 2000-2009 乙丑 43-52 | PROPERT 1990-1999 甲子 33-42 | KARMIC 1980-1989 癸亥 23-32 |
| ▲ COMDR ○ MIROR BELL | ✗ WAIF ◉ MESGR STAR | ◉ OPPOR $ FIRE VOID | ○ MOON ↗ LITE |
| B J T Y Y L Z S W S S C LG **DH Gf** ZB | K P F W S g GD **BF GS** TS | J S F F E L T G L G MY XS **SM ZS** | T T C G Y K ? C CS FL **HQ JS** |

## Properties—Opportunity, Fire, Void

Some of Michael Jackson's achievements include multiple Guinness World Records; 13 Grammy Awards (as well as the Grammy Legend Award and the Grammy Lifetime Achievement Award); 13 number-one singles in the United States in his solo career (more than any other male artist in the Hot 100 era); and the estimated sale of over 800 million records worldwide. MJ won hundreds of awards, which have made him the most-awarded recording artist in the history of music.

*MJ had a Bright Opportunity with Wealth $ teamed up in his business/Property sector. His success lies in Entertainment. The best combination with Fire would be with a Brilliant Opportunity. These two stars would jointly create power↗ and prosperity$. He also had Void here. The Void's contradictory streak would come to the fore if met up by Fire. This pairing-up would ignite an explosive development which will have a tremendous up-lifting effect on one's life work.*

## Prosperity—Intelligence & Completion
## Opposite in Karmic—Moon & Literary Minister

Aspects of Michael Jackson's personal life, including his appearance and behavior, have generated controversy, not the least of which—child sexual abuse. *With Intelligence ■ trailing Obstruction, we are seeing major plans being thwarted. It was in 1993 that a planned worldwide tour was cancelled because of these molestation accusations. Hemmed in by Ram in Minors and Spinning Top (gossip), Completion was no match against these Killing Stars.*

In an interview, Michael Jackson said "... And I remember going to the record studio and there was a park across the street, and I'd see all the children playing, and I would cry because it would make me sad that I would have to work instead."

*He had the Brilliant Moon↗ empowered plus the Brilliant Literary Minister. The Self will spend much time in quiet contemplation—a deep, wise individual with unfathomable imagination. At Opposite, Intelligence with ■ indicated feelings of being inadequate and out of control. To compensate, he created his own world—Neverland.*

"...Because I wanted to have a place that I could create everything that I never had as a child. So, you see rides. You see animals. There's a movie theater." *Like many genius artists that went before him, MJ was exploited, misunderstood and ridiculed in life. In death, his legacy will live on forever.*

*MJ's Life Chart*

| SELF | CAREER | PROSPERITY | KARMIC |
|---|---|---|---|
| (SUN) (SCHOLAR) | WAIF MESSENGER | INTELLIGENCE COMPLETION | MOON LIT. MINISTER |

| PROSPER 2040-2049 丁巳 83-92 | MINORS 2050-2059 戊午 93-102 | SPOUS/L 2060-2069 己未 103-112 | PEERS 2070-2079 庚申 113-122 |
|---|---|---|---|
| ▲ INTEL ■ | ⊙ EMPER | | ✗ PNEER |
| COMP | RAM | DELI | HORS |
| C T T 31 S F | T c | C G T T 20 S D C | T k |
| B BS LD **WS** | S LS JX BH | **M** QL PA TD | J **XH** SY DK |

| HEALTH 2030-2039 丙辰 73-82 | **Life Analysis** | | THE SELF 1960-1969 辛酉 3-12 |
|---|---|---|---|
| ◉ GENRL | Name: MJ | | |
| SPIN RIGT | 1958/08/29 ▾  10:00:00 F ⊕ Male | | |
| | Date of Birth (yyyy/mm/dd)   Time (hh:mm:ss)  ○ Female | | |
| I I t x g s | Life \| Ten Years \| Years \| Month \| Day \| TZ+1 TZ-1 \| Record \| Print | | |
| A **GF** SP Ys | | | T JJ Xs **BF** |

| TRAVEL 2020-2029 乙卯 63-72 | Lunar B.T. (戊戌)Y( VII)M(XV)D(亥)T | | ELDERS 1970-1979 壬戌 13-22 |
|---|---|---|---|
| ⊙ SUN ○ | Solar B.T. (戊戌)Y(庚申)M(戊寅)D(亥)T | | ◉ CRMSN |
| ⊙ SCHOL | 陰陽五行 陽男 木三局 狗人 | | ⊙ VAULT |
| | | | LEFT PUNI |
| ARTS I T T C Y f G X 32 D | ■ Obstacle  ○ Fame  ↗ Power  $ Wealth ■ Life ■ 10 year ■ Year ■ Month ■ Day | | H G |
| DW **FB XH** D46 | | | Y Zs SJ HG |

| STAFF 2010-2019 甲寅 53-62 | CAREER 2000-2009 乙丑 43-52 | PROPERT 1990-1999 甲子 33-42 | KARMIC 1980-1989 癸亥 23-32 |
|---|---|---|---|
| ▲ COMDR | ✗ WAIF | ◉ OPPOR $ | ⊙ MOON ↗ |
| ⊙ MIROR | ◉ MESGR | | |
| BELL | STAR | FIRE VOID | |
| | | | LITE |
| B J T Y Y L Z S W S S C | K P F W S g | J S F F E L T G L G | T T C G Y K ? C |
| LG **DH Gf** ZB | GD **BF GS** TS | MY **XS SM** ZS | CS FL **HQ** JS |

MICHAEL JACKSON

**Oprah Winfrey** ★ JANUARY 29, 1954  4:30 A.M.  KOSIUSCO, MS, U.S.A.

Oprah Gail Winfrey is an American television host, producer, and philanthropist, best known for her self-tided multi-award winning talk show. She ranks first in Forbes' list of the richest women in entertainment.

Once upon a time, Oprah was the world's only black billionaire. According to some sources at the time of the printing of this book, she is considered to be the most influential woman on earth.

**The Self—Spinning Top, Right Minister, Winged Horse**
**Opposite—Crimson, Opportunity, Delight, Fire**
Oprah was born into abject poverty in rural Mississippi to a teenage single mother and later raised in an inner city Milwaukee neighborhood. *In her Chamber Opposing Self is a dark Crimson✖—symbolizing hardships having to do with blood or female issues.*

She experienced considerable pain during her childhood, including being raped at the age of nine. *(Opportunity✖■ shows the double curse of a Dark Opportunity, the dark star of vice). Fire also opposed that and together with Ram in Karmic brought tragedies at an early age with possible life-long effects.*

**Karmic—Emperor, Pioneer, Ram, Punishment**
*However, she is blessed with phenomenal strength of mind and tenacity. The Karmic has some very positive stars—Emperor and Pioneer$ that together with the courtiers Commander, General, Opportunity and Delight, saw her through her childhood nightmares.*

**Career—Vault, Stardust, Left Minister**
*Stardust in Career also enhances this sector throughout the life until age 50.* Oprah landed a job in radio while still in high school and began co-anchoring the local evening news at the age of nineteen. *Vault in Career gives groundedness and caution. Free of any Killing Stars, these individuals will become the pillars of the earth. Honesty, integrity, self-help and empowerment are what her shows and life are about.*

**Elders—Intelligence, Completion, Bell**
**Opposite; Health—Messenger, Arts Minister**
Oprah's career choice in media did not surprise her grandmother, who once said. "Ever since Oprah could talk, she was on stage." *This is the result of the vivacious Crimson/Opportunity in Self.* Oprah later acknowledged her grandmother's influence, saying it was Hattie Mae who had encouraged her to speak in public and "gave me a positive sense of myself."

*In Elders (her Grandmother), we have the Brilliant Intelligence—star of Kindness and Motivation, shining on a Bright Messenger⬈ (vocal power) Opposite.*

*Oprah's Life Chart*

| SELF | OPPOSITE | PROSPERITY | KARMIC |
|---|---|---|---|
| SPINNING TOP R. MINISTER | CRIMSON OPPORTUNITY | MIRROR | EMPEROR PIONEER |

| TRAVEL 2015-2024 丁 62-71 巳 | HEALTH 2025-2034 戊 72-81 午 | PROSPER 2035-2044 己 82-91 未 | MINORS 2045-2054 庚 92-101 申 |
|---|---|---|---|
| ✗ CRMSN ✗ OPPOR ■ DELI FIRE | ⊙ MESGR ↗ | ▲ MIROR | ⊙ WAIF ✗ SCHOL |

|  | *ARTS* |  | LITE |
|---|---|---|---|
| T F T f G g J Zs SJ **ZB** | T J T C t G S K 32 s T FL **HQ** D46 | F E L G Y XS **SM Ys** | T G T T X C S F CS **BF GS WS** |

| STAFF 2005-2014 丙 52-61 辰 |  |  | SPOUSE 2055-2064 辛 102-111 酉 |
|---|---|---|---|
| ▲ MOON ☿ | OPRAH ✦ *The whole point of being alive is to evolve into the complete person you were intended to be.* | | ⊙ COMDR ▲ GENRL VOID |
| Y C G T F T S ? S C g s M JJ **TS BF** | | | L P C S MY **DH JX Gf** |

| CAREER/L 1995-2004 乙 42-51 卯 | | | PEERS 2065-2074 壬 112-121 戌 |
|---|---|---|---|
| ▲ VAULT STAR LEFT | | | ✗ SUN |
| S T S **XH ZS DK** | | | C Y 31 D GD **FB PA XH** |

| PROPERT 1985-1994 甲 32-41 寅 | KARMIC 1975-1984 乙 22-31 丑 | ELDERS 1965-1974 甲 12-21 子 | THE SELF 1955-1964 癸 2-11 亥 |
|---|---|---|---|
| | ○ EMPER ⊙ PNEER $ RAM *PUNI* | ○ INTEL COMP *BELL* | *SPIN* RIGT HORS |
| T T Y D B QL **JS TD** | K T H W k G A LS HG BH | J C L 20 DW BS Xs LD | T B T T c Z W x LG **GF SY SP** |

**Oprah's 10-Year Chart (age 12-21)**

*Note the Success Formation projected from Career: Completion in Self, Scholar and Literary Minister in Prosperity, and Sun opposite Career. The Sun-Scholar-Completion-Literary Minister pattern is found with highly successful star-quality persons. She'll be having a few more of these successful 10-Year Charts.*

At fourteen, her mother sent her to live with her father in Nashville, Tennessee. Vernon was strict but encouraging and made her education a priority. Oprah became an honors student, was voted Most Popular Girl, joined her high school speech team at East Nashville High School, and placed second in the nation in dramatic interpretation *(Waif at Prosperity; Arts Minister opposite Self Literary Minister at 120°).*

She won an oratory contest that secured her a full scholarship to Tennessee State University, a historically black institution, where she studied communication *(The Messenger⊅ shining brightly Opposite).*

At age seventeen, Oprah won the Miss Black Tennessee beauty pageant *(Completion in Self with the beauty-and-brains Arts Minister opposite).* She also attracted the attention of the local black radio station which hired her to do the news part-time. *The Moon✿ in Career enlightened her plight on issues regarding women, homosexuals, Blacks and the Disadvantaged. The Sun with Obstruction■ Opposite indicates her broadcasting choice to deal with dark issues.*

At nineteen, her emotional ad-lib delivery on radio eventually got her transferred to the daytime talk show arena. After boosting a third-rated Chicago talk show to first place, she launched her own production company and became internationally syndicated.

By the mid-1990s, she had reinvented her show with a focus on literature, self-improvement, and spirituality. *(Arts Minister reflecting the Self sector, indicates a refined person who also has other-worldly spiritual leanings. She will find herself dabbling in astrology or other forms of divination).*

Though criticized for unleashing confession culture and promoting controversial self-help fads, she is generally admired for overcoming adversity to become a benefactor to others *(The Life Chart: Emperor and Pioneer $ in Karmic).* In 2006, she became an early supporter of Barack Obama and one analysis estimated she delivered over a million votes *(the workings of vivacious, people-oriented Crimson and Opportunity in Self),* for which the governor of Illinois considered offering her a seat in the U.S. Senate.

# Intelligence, Pioneer in Self AT RAT CHAMBER

*Oprah's 10-Year Chart 1965-1974 (Age 12-21)*

| SELF | OPPOSITE | PROSPERITY | KARMIC |
|---|---|---|---|
| INTELLIGENCE COMPLETION | MESSENGER ARTS MINISTER | WAIF SCHOLAR | COMPLETION WINGED HORSE |

| STAFF 2015-2024 丁 TRAVEL 巳 | TRAVEL 2025-2034 戊 HEALTH 午 | HEALTH 2035-2044 己 PROSPER 未 | PROSPER 2045-2054 庚 MINORS 申 |
|---|---|---|---|
| ✗ CRMSN $ <br> ✗ OPPOR ■ <br> DELI FIRE <br> 3 | ⊚ MESGR ↗ | ▲ MIROR <br><br> 6 | ⊚ WAIF <br> ✗ SCHOL |

*ARTS*

| T F T <br> f G g <br> J  Zs  SJ  ZB | T J T C t <br> G S K 32 s <br> T  FL  HQ D46 | F E <br> L G <br> Y  XS  SM  Ys | LITE <br> J G T T <br> X C S F <br> CS  BF  GS  WS |

| CAREER 2005-2014 丙 STAFF 辰 | | | MINORS 2055-2064 辛 SPOUSE 酉 |
|---|---|---|---|
| ▲ MOON ○ | | | ⊚ COMDR ○ <br> ▲ GENRL <br> VOID <br> 2 4 |

**Ten Year Chart**
**A 10 year analysis**
**1965-1974**
**(12-21)**

| 1955-1964 (2-11) | 1965-1974 (12-21) | 1975-1984 (22-31) |
|---|---|---|
| 1985-1994 (32-41) | 1995-2004 (42-51) | 2005-2014 (52-61) |
| 2015-2024 (62-71) | 2025-2034 (72-81) | 2035-2044 (82-91) |
| 2045-2054 (92-101) | 2055-2064 (102-111) | 2065-2074 (112-121) |

Back

| Y C G T F T <br> S 7 S C g s <br> M  JJ  TS  BF | | | L P <br> C S <br> MY  DH  JX  Gf |

| PROPERT 1995-2004 乙 CAREER/L 卯 | | | SPOUSE 2065-2074 壬 PEERS 戌 |
|---|---|---|---|
| ▲ VAULT <br><br> STAR LEFT <br> 9 1 | | | ✗ SUN ■ |

| S <br> T <br> S  XH  ZS  DK | | | C Y <br> 31 D <br> GD  FB  PA  XH |

| KARMIC 1985-1994 甲 PROPERT 寅 | ELDERS 1975-1984 乙 KARMIC 丑 | THE SELF 1965-1974 甲 ELDERS 子 | PEERS 1955-1964 癸 THE SELF 亥 |
|---|---|---|---|
| | ○ EMPER <br> ⊚ PNEER $ ↗ <br> RAM *PUNI* <br> 10 5 | ○ INTEL <br><br> COMP *BELL* | *SPIN* RIGT HORS |
| 8 7 | | | |

| T T <br> Y D <br> B  QL  JS  TD | K T H <br> W k G <br> A  LS  HG  BH | J C <br> L 20 <br> DW  BS  Xs  LD | T B T T <br> c Z W x <br> LG  GF  SY  SP |

OPRAH

**Princess Diana** ★ JULY 1 1961 6:45 P.M. SANDRINGHAM, NORFOLK U.K.

 Diana Frances née Spencer was a popular international media icon of the late 20th century as the first wife of Charles, Prince of Wales. The wedding, which was held at St. Paul's Cathedral, was televised and watched by a global audience of over 750 million people.

### The Self—Sun, Scholar & Completion

*Note the extraordinary star formation for success in the Life Chart (throughout the whole life): The Sun-Scholar-Completion-Literary Minister pattern is only found with highly successful star-quality individuals.* Diana was born into an old, aristocratic English family with royal connections and remained the focus of worldwide media scrutiny before, during and after her marriage, which ended in divorce in August 1996. *The presence of Scholar indicates a profession in teaching or administration, as well as represents benevolence, heirlooms and inheritance. This is also a longevity star—pointing the way to a long, albeit lonesome existence. The Scholar works with medicines, hospitals or healing. Completion in the Self house makes for an upright, honest individual with a big heart. This star indicates a rewarding lifetime of wealth and prosperity without the rigmaroles of toils, hardships or great changes. The wealth that Completion brings carries its own peculiarity in that it never stops for it is a glowing, lucky star that brings material and spiritual wealth.*

At the same time, she was admired for her groundbreaking charity work, in particular, her work with AIDS patients and supporting the campaign for banning landmines. *She also had the Sun↗ empowered in her Self chamber. Elegance would be the jewel on The Sun's gleaming golden crown, his position being second to none but the Emperor. The Sun stands for all that is fiery, cleansing and positive. The Sun with the Power↗ catalyst carries the obvious trait of having the crown or male supporters on your side. Power to the Sun makes for a highly independent mind which gives rise to the pioneering spirit.* After her death, the Ottawa Treaty was signed banning the use of anti-personnel landmines. Many agree that her support and role in the campaign played an important role in influencing this decision.

At its brightest, none would fail to be appreciative and warmed by the Sun's powerful rays. A Brilliant Sun would just leave good fortune at its wake and wouldn't even notice it had done that; thus, it would not expect to be thanked.

*Princess Diana's Life Chart*

| SELF | CAREER | PROSPERITY | KARMIC |
|---|---|---|---|
| SUN SCHOLAR | (WAIF) (MESSENGER) | MOON | INTELLIGENCE |

| PROSPER 2046-2055 癸 86-95 巳 | MINORS 2056-2065 甲 96-105 午 | SPOUSE 2066-2075 乙 106-115 未 | PEERS 2076-2085 丙 116-125 申 |
|---|---|---|---|
| ✗ MOON | ◉ OPPOR | ✗ WAIF | ▲ COMDR |
| | | ✗ MESGR $ | ◯ MIROR |
| | STAR RIGT | BELL | *SPIN* LEFT PUNI |
| T K C T T **T** | T Y C Y E T | T T | C |
| f **W** 20 W W **k** | c S 32 D G g | Y x | 7 |
| LG **BF Gf ZB** | DW **DH XH** D46 | A FB SP Ys | B GF LD WS |

| HEALTH 2036-2045 壬 76-85 辰 | PRINCESS DIANA | | THE SELF 1966-1975 丁 6-15 酉 |
|---|---|---|---|
| ◉ CRMSN | | | ▲ SUN ↗ |
| ◯ VAULT | *They say it is better to be* | | ▲ SCHOL |
| | | | COMP |
| J T t | *poor and happy* | | T F **F** |
| L S s | *than rich and miserable,* | | G G **L** |
| GD XS **GS TS** | *but how about* | | S BS JX BH |

| TRAVEL/L 2026-2035 辛 66-75 卯 | *a compromise* | | ELDERS 1976-1985 戊 16-25 戌 |
|---|---|---|---|
| | *like moderately rich* | | ◯ GENRL |
| | *and just moody?* | | RAM |
| T | | | G T T |
| F | | | S D C |
| MY FL **SM ZS** | | | M LS PA TD |

| STAFF 2016-2025 庚 56-65 寅 | CAREER 2006-2015 辛 46-55 丑 | PROPERT 1996-2005 庚 36-45 子 | KARMIC 1986-1995 己 26-35 亥 |
|---|---|---|---|
| ✗ PNEER | | ▲ EMPER | ▲ INTEL |
| DELI *VOID* | | FIRE | HORS |
| | LITE ■ ARTS ◊ | | |
| S T C G **I** | T P H | B J | F |
| T K 31 C s | X S G | Z S | g |
| CS Zs **HQ JS** | Y JJ SJ HG | T **XH** Xs **BF** | J QL SY DK |

**Career—Literary and Arts Ministers**
**Opposite in Spouse—Waif, Messenger, Bell**
A public figure from the moment of the announcement of her engagement to Prince Charles, Diana remained the focus of worldwide media scrutiny before, during and after her marriage that ended in divorce in August 1996. This adoration put her at the forefront of many humanitarian causes close to her heart.

*The best pairing up for the Literary Minister would be with The Sun or Scholar. If joined by Completion, the perfect but very rare quad-angled star combination of beauty, brains and outstanding accomplishment will be formed. Such a combination would be in the birth chart of star-quality high-profile individuals. The opposite sex's attraction to them is inevitable. She will have many admirers throughout life.*

**Prosperity—Moon**
**Karmic—Intelligence, Winged Horse**
*The Moon here is in darkness. A dark moon would take on the qualities of the Brilliant sun. It will be basking in the limelight—you won't fail to notice this person who will enjoy helping others. This is further testament to her charitable work and public persona.*

*Intelligence has the balanced, strong mind of a kind leader who is calm but motivated. This person will thirst for knowledge. Also, Intelligence here ensures a quick mind and agile body. Alas, intrigued by anything that is new and pioneering, these individuals may spread themselves too thin and become jacks-of-all-Trades but Masters of None. This star is a strategist by nature and is mechanically inclined. Its presence indicates lateral movements—the pursuit of new or challenging opportunities as opposed to moving up the corporate ladder.*

Her natural sympathy and oneness with patients was much admired. In 1987, Princess Diana was one of the first well-known celebrities to be photographed with, touching or hugging a victim of AIDS.

*Moon with Intelligence applies kindness and patience to strategy. These are hands-on people who would take on responsibilities or tasks that others shun.*

Princess Diana once said, "I'd like to be a queen in people's hearts, but I don't see myself being queen of this country."

*Intelligence▲ in retrograde carries the meaning of a "planning or implementation error that had gone unnoticed for a long time, suddenly being exposed, resulting in loss. This can also take the form of an erroneous job change." This was contrary to public expectations. However, it seems the powerful rays of her Sun↗ will always be shining in the hearts of many.*

*Princess Diana's Life Chart*

| SELF | CAREER | PROSPERITY | KARMIC |
|---|---|---|---|
| SUN SCHOLAR | LIT. MINISTER | MOON | INTELLIGENCE |

| PROSPER 2046-2055 癸巳 86-95 | MINORS 2056-2065 甲午 96-105 | SPOUSE 2066-2075 乙未 106-115 | PEERS 2076-2085 丙申 116-125 |
|---|---|---|---|
| ✕ MOON | ◉ OPPOR  STAR RIGT | ✕ WAIF  ✕ MESGR $  BELL | ▲ COMDR  ◯ MIROR  *SPIN* LEFT PUNI |
| T K C T T T f W 20 W W k LG BF Gf ZB | T Y C Y E T c S 32 D G g DW DH XH D46 | T T Y x A FB SP Ys | C ? B GF LD WS |

| HEALTH 2036-2045 壬辰 76-85 | | | THE SELF 1966-1975 丁酉 6-15 |
|---|---|---|---|
| ◉ CRMSN  ◯ VAULT | **Life Analysis** | | ▲ SUN ↗  ▲ SCHOL  COMP |

Name: Princess Di

1961/07/01  :00:00 PM  ◯ Male

Date of Birth (yyyy/mm/dd)  Time (hh:mm:ss)  ◉ Female

Life | Ten Years | Years | Month | Day | T.Z+1 / T.Z-1 | Record | Print

Lunar B.T. (辛丑)Y( V )M( X IX )D(酉)T

Solar B.T. (辛丑)Y(甲午)M(乙未)D(酉)T

陰陽五行 陰女 火六局 牛人

■ Obstacle  ☼ Fame  ↗ Power  $ Wealth
■ Life  ■ 10 year  ■ Year  ■ Month  ■ Day

| J T t L S s GD XS GS TS | | | T F F G G L S BS JX BH |
|---|---|---|---|

| TRAVEL/L 2026-2035 辛卯 66-75 | | | ELDERS 1976-1985 戊戌 16-25 |
|---|---|---|---|
| | | | ◯ GENRL  RAM |
| T F MY FL SM ZS | | | G T T S D C M LS PA ID |

| STAFF 2016-2025 庚寅 56-65 | CAREER 2006-2015 辛丑 46-55 | PROPERT 1996-2005 庚子 36-45 | KARMIC 1986-1995 己亥 26-35 |
|---|---|---|---|
| ✕ PNEER  DELI *VOID* | LITE ■ ARTS ♎ | ▲ EMPER  FIRE | ▲ INTEL  HORS |
| S T C G T T K 31 C s CS Zs HQ JS | T P H X S G Y JJ SJ HG | B J Z S T XH Xs BF | F g J QL SY DK |

## Warren Buffett ★ AUGUST 30, 1930; 4:00 A.M. OMAHA, NEBRASKA, U.S.A.

Warren Edward Buffett is an American investor, industrialist, and philanthropist. Being one of the most successful investors in the world, he is consistently ranked as one of its wealthiest people, and is the third wealthiest person in 2010.

### The Self—Emperor

Often called the "Legendary Investor," Warren Buffett is the primary shareholder, chairman and CEO of Berkshire Hathaway. Buffett's interest in the stock market and investing dated to his childhood and the days he spent in the customers' lounge of a regional stock brokerage near the office of his father's brokerage company.

*The Brilliant Emperor in Self is in the Horse Chamber and will display all its positive strengths as an investment genius— opinionated, willful, and confident. Opposite is Opportunity, which adds flair and creativity to the Emperor's stability and wisdom. The result will be responsible and wise decision-making and exciting, new leadership.*

### Career—Vault & Crimson

Even as a child, Buffett displayed an interest in making and saving money. He went door to door selling chewing gum, Coca-Cola, or weekly magazines and newspapers. By the time he finished college, Buffett had accumulated more than $90,000 in savings (as measured in 2009 dollars).

*Vault, a major prosperity star, is Brilliant and has fame♡ attached. As the Emperor pioneers, so the Vault guards. The Vault, possessing much wealth within its walls, deals with finance and financial matters. This individual has far to go with Fame attached. Many will hear of his wizardry in managing finance. Crimson, also here, will add flair and excitement.*

### Prosperity—Commander & Mirror

While his long term investment strategy may not be for everyone, The Buffett Portfolio has been the subject of countless books and discussions. Without a doubt, Buffett is recognized globally as a wizard investor. *A prosperous star in its own right, the Commander↗ is our action hero. With Power to boost, you can be sure to see him rewarded for his relentless efforts. The Brilliant Mirror then reflects and doubles his earnings.*

*Warren Buffett's Life Chart*

| SELF | OPPOSITE | PROSPERITY | KARMIC |
|------|----------|------------|--------|
| EMPEROR | OPPORTUNITY | COMMANDER MIRROR | PIONEER |

| PEERS 2042-2051 辛巳 113-122 | THE SELF 1932-1941 壬午 3-12 | ELDERS 1942-1951 癸未 13-22 | KARMIC 1952-1961 甲申 23-32 |
|---|---|---|---|
| ▲ INTEL | ◇ EMPER | | ✕ PNEER |
| BELL | | DELI SPIN | COMP HORS |
| | *ARTS* | | LITE |
| P | T J | K C T | G T |
| S | f L | W 20 K | C F |
| B   DH  WS  BF | S   FB  JX  SJ | M   GF  PA  HQ | J   BS  SY  SM |

| SPOUSE 2032-2041 庚辰 103-112 | | | PROPERT 1962-1971 乙酉 33-42 |
|---|---|---|---|
| ◉ GENRL | | | |
| RIGT | **WARREN BUFFETT** | | *RAM* VOID |
| | ✦ | | |
| | *Look at market* | | C |
| S F G T F | *fluctuations* | | 31 |
| T G S S g | *as your friend rather than* | | T   LS  Xs  GS |
| A   BF  Ys   DK | *your enemy;* | | |

| MINORS 2022-2031 己卯 93-102 | *profit from folly* | | CAREER/L 1972-1981 丙戌 43-52 |
|---|---|---|---|
| ◉ SUN  $ | *rather than* | | ◉ CRMSN |
| ◇ SCHOL | *participate in it.* | | ◇ VAULT ⟡ |
| FIRE | | | LEFT |
| T C C T | | | B L H |
| X 7 32 D | | | Z C G |
| DW  XS  D46 TD | | | Y   QL  HG  Gf |

| PROSPER 2012-2021 戊寅 83-92 | HEALTH 2002-2011 己丑 73-82 | TRAVEL 1992-2001 戊子 63-72 | STAFF 1982-1991 丁亥 53-62 |
|---|---|---|---|
| ▲ COMDR ↗ | ✕ WAIF ■ | ◉ OPPOR | ◇ MOON |
| ◇ MIROR | ◉ MESGR | | |
| | STAR *PUNI* | | |
| T J T Y Y F | E t | T I I | T I Y I I |
| C S W S S L | G s | k x C | G Y D g s |
| LG  FL  ZB  BH | GD  Zs  TS  LD | MY  JJ  ZS  SP | CS  XH  JS  XH |

WARREN BUFFETT

## Buffett's 10-Year Chart (age 73-82)

Perhaps Buffett's most noteworthy feat regarding his karma with wealth is not in its making but rather in its giving away. Buffett, whose personal wealth was estimated at US$47 billion in 2010, personally pledged that "more than 99 percent of my wealth will go to philanthropy during my lifetime or at my death." In 2010, he hand-picked other renowned billionaires and persuaded them to also pledge their billions to charitable causes.

*The Obstruction■ Catalyst and Killing Stars all work against wealth, especially when around the major prosperity stars. Wealth loss can be through business loss or closure, stealth, robbery etc., or charity as in Buffett's case:*

### The Self—Waif & Messenger

*With the dark Waif becoming more erratic with Obstruction■, we are seeing the opposite of its abilities—the eschewing of fortunes gained, i.e., donations. Messenger, also here, then makes its intentions known to the world.*

### Karmic — Sun & Scholar

*The benevolent Sun at Brilliant, has wealth $ attached. Being of similar nature, the Brilliant Scholar with Fame✿ attached, joins forces, and the pair gives forth unimaginable amounts of wealth and good fortune. Note that the Sun-Scholar pair is also in Minors in the Life Chart. This very likely points to Buffett's partnership with Bill Gates, the other great philanthropist of our times.*

### Prosperity—Ram & Void

*With Punishment in Self (and Spinning Top opposite), Bell in Career, Ram and Void in Prosperity (and Fire opposite), all the Personal Wealth Sectors are afflicted. Coupled with Obstruction■ in Self, we should be seeing huge losses.* Indeed, these Killing Stars had Buffett acknowledging, "I've been dead wrong," referring to some of his decisions during the economic downturn that cost Berkshire Hathaway a 77% drop in earnings during 2007.

However, these setbacks did not dampen his pioneering spirit nor put an end to his philanthropy. Indeed, he gave even more. Nor did he lose the Midas touch when it came to investing. Notwithstanding his colossal donations every year, Buffett is still currently ranked 3rd richest man in the world.

*Such is the power of Emperor in Self at Horse in the Life Chart. This and the absence of any Killing Star or Obstruction■ all around ensured that a bad 10- year cycle became only a dent in the larger picture of Buffett's life path.*

Warren Buffett's 10-Year Chart  (Age 73-82)

| SELF | KARMIC | PROSPERITY | CAREER |
|---|---|---|---|
| WAIF MESSENGER | SUN SCHOLAR | RAM VOID | INTELLIGENCE BELL |

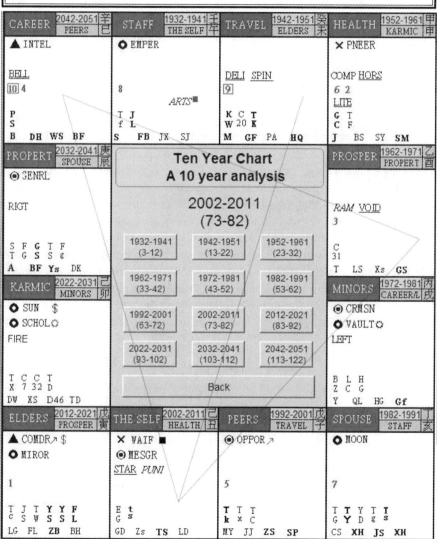

| CAREER 2042-2051 辛巳<br>PEERS | STAFF 1932-1941 壬午<br>THE SELF | TRAVEL 1942-1951 癸未<br>ELDERS | HEALTH 1952-1961 甲申<br>KARMIC |
|---|---|---|---|
| ▲ INTEL | ○ EMPER | | ✕ PNEER |
| BELL | 8 | DELI SPIN | COMP HORS |
| 10 4 | | 9 | 6 2 |
| | ARTS■ | | LITE |
| P | I J | K C T | G T |
| S | f L | W 20 K | C F |
| B  DH WS BF | S  FB JX SJ | M  GF PA HQ | J  BS SY SM |

**Ten Year Chart**
**A 10 year analysis**

**2002-2011**
**(73-82)**

| | | |
|---|---|---|
| 1932-1941 (3-12) | 1942-1951 (13-22) | 1952-1961 (23-32) |
| 1962-1971 (33-42) | 1972-1981 (43-52) | 1982-1991 (53-62) |
| 1992-2001 (63-72) | 2002-2011 (73-82) | 2012-2021 (83-92) |
| 2022-2031 (93-102) | 2032-2041 (103-112) | 2042-2051 (113-122) |

Back

| PROPERT 2032-2041 庚辰<br>SPOUSE | | PROSPER 1962-1971 乙酉<br>PROPERT |
|---|---|---|
| ◉ GENRL | | |
| RIGT | | RAM VOID |
| | | 3 |
| S F G I F | | C |
| T G S S g | | 31 |
| A  BF Ys  DK | | T  LS Xs GS |

| KARMIC 2022-2031 己卯<br>MINORS | | MINORS 1972-1981 丙戌<br>CAREER/L |
|---|---|---|
| ○ SUN $ | | ◉ CRMSN |
| ○ SCHOL○ | | ○ VAULT○ |
| FIRE | | LEFT |
| T C C T | | B L H |
| X 7 32 D | | Z C G |
| DW XS D46 TD | | Y  QL HG Gf |

| ELDERS 2012-2021 戊寅<br>PROSPER | THE SELF 2002-2011 己丑<br>HEALTH | PEERS 1992-2001 戊子<br>TRAVEL | SPOUSE 1982-1991 丁亥<br>STAFF |
|---|---|---|---|
| ▲ COMDR↗ $ | ✕ WAIF ■ | ◉ OPPOR ↗ | ○ MOON |
| ○ MIROR | ◉ MESGR | | |
| | STAR *PUNI* | | |
| 1 | | 5 | 7 |
| I J I Y Y F | E t | T T T | T T Y T I |
| C S W S S L | G s | k x C | G Y D g s |
| LG FL ZB BH | GD Zs TS LD | MY JJ ZS SP | CS XH JS XH |

WARREN BUFFETT

# EPILOGUE

How accurate is The Emperor's Stargate? At this point, we hope you have seen that it is over 90% correct in describing personality and life path. With over 1,000 years of history and fine-tuning, that is to be expected. We might emphasize that Stargate is not fortune-telling. We have delivered its wisdom and that of the Ancients and present-day leaders as a guide to discovering our own strengths and challenges. In understanding, we can become the best that we can be. It must not be expected that someone sharing the same birth chart as say, Warren Buffett, would also be an investment genius. Remember the prerequisites: family, social, cultural, and geographical background: Heaven, Earth & People—this is the Harmony Equation. If an individual with Buffett's chart was born in a small village in the middle of nowhere, he would hardly be able to access the global equity markets, let alone play them. That said, he would have the same Buffett dispositions and should do well in finance in his own capacity.

Expanding on this, let's ponder on the fact that over 80% of our lives is formed by our parents. Studies have shown that the parental influence in the life of the child had never been stronger. It is important to realize that because this is the developmental stage, this is a time of preparation. Making sure that a strong foundation is laid can help ease the transition from childhood to adolescence and later on in life. Our children's Stargate chart can be the guiding light to steer them towards the path that is uniquely theirs, sidestepping the pitfalls and moving toward their goals.

In closing, we offer this Lao Zhi thought:
A great tree that you can't put your arms around
grew from a small seed.
A nine-story tower rose from a paltry heap of earth.
A journey of a thousand miles must begin with a single step.
Chapter 64 of The Book of the Great Integrity

The Emperor's Stargate offers an expanded view of what can be expected and shows us the tools we possess as we embark on this remarkable journey called Life. It is not about shortcuts or cutting corners. Instead, one must keep an open mind. This plus the total dedication to one's Life Path WILL reap SUCCESS.

# ABOUT THE AUTHORS

**Master Albert Cheung** is a scholar and teacher on the subject of Chinese Metaphysics. His interest in the subject dates back to early school days when he discovered that scientific phenomena go much deeper than causality: the day to day cause and effect of things in life. Because of his passion and keen interest in the subject of Chinese ancient wisdom and culture, he has made it a lifetime mission in sharing, promoting and spreading various applicable subjects like the I-Ching, Astrology, the Art of War, and Feng Shui in the form of simple tools to be easily applied in our everyday life.

To share his knowledge and skills on the subjects with the world, he has created and designed a wide range of useful tools, including books: the I-Ching tarot, the I-Ching pictorial guide, the Strategy and Tactics (card and book set), and the Emperor's Stargate. In 2002, Master Albert was awarded the Innovative Entrepreneur Award (by the Junior Chamber of commerce) for his innovative design of the I-Ching Tarot (innovative creation of the 64 I-Ching pictures on tarot cards as a tool of divination as well as inspiration and enlightenment).

He is currently a visiting lecturer at the Hong Kong Polytechnic University, a Chinese University teaching subjects on I-Ching, the Art of War, Astrology and Creativity Methods. He also writes articles for magazines, periodicals and is frequently interviewed on television for prediction of events and views on things in the aspect of Chinese ancient wisdom. Master Albert was interviewed on CNN for 2 consecutive years - 2006 and 2007 - to give his prediction on local and world events. And recently (2011), he was on CNN again for an interview on Prince William's wedding.

**Alexandra Harteam** is a professional writer and editor and devotes her time writing and researching Middle Eastern and Asian Art and Culture.

# Other Books By Ozark Mountain Publishing, Inc.

**Dolores Cannon**
Conversations with Nostradamus,
  Volume I, II, III
Jesus and the Essenes
They Walked with Jesus
Between Death and Life
A Soul Remembers Hiroshima
Keepers of the Garden.
The Legend of Starcrash
The Custodians
The Convoluted Universe - Book One,
  Two, Three, Four
Five Lives Remembered
The Three Waves of Volunteers and the
  New Earth
**Stuart Wilson & Joanna Prentis**
The Essenes - Children of the Light
Power of the Magdalene
Beyond Limitations
Atlantis and the New Consciousness
The Magdalene Version
**O.T. Bonnett, M.D./Greg Satre**
Reincarnation: The View from Eternity
What I Learned After Medical School
Why Healing Happens
**M. Don Schorn**
Elder Gods of Antiquity
Legacy of the Elder Gods
Gardens of the Elder Gods
Reincarnation...Stepping Stones of Life
**Aron Abrahamsen**
Holiday in Heaven
Out of the Archives – Earth Changes
**Sherri Cortland**
Windows of Opportunity
Raising Our Vibrations for the New Age
The Spiritual Toolbox
**Michael Dennis**
Morning Coffee with God
God's Many Mansions
**Nikki Pattillo**
Children of the Stars
A Spiritual Evolution
**Rev. Grant H. Pealer**
Worlds Beyond Death
A Funny Thing Happened on the Way to
  Heaven
**Maiya & Geoff Gray-Cobb**
Angels - The Guardians of Your Destiny
**Maiya Gray-Cobb**
Seeds of the Soul
**Sture Lönnerstrand**
I Have Lived Before
**Arun & Sunanda Gandhi**
The Forgotten Woman
**Claire Doyle Beland**
Luck Doesn't Happen by Chance

**James H. Kent**
Past Life Memories As A Confederate
  Soldier
**Dorothy Leon**
Is Jehovah An E.T
**Justine Alessi & M. E. McMillan**
Rebirth of the Oracle
**Donald L. Hicks**
The Divinity Factor
**Christine Ramos, RN**
A Journey Into Being
**Mary Letorney**
Discover The Universe Within You
**Debra Rayburn**
Let's Get Natural With Herbs
**Jodi Felice**
The Enchanted Garden
**Susan Mack & Natalia Krawetz**
My Teachers Wear Fur Coats
**Ronald Chapman**
Seeing True
**Rev. Keith Bender**
The Despiritualized Church
**Vara Humphreys**
The Science of Knowledge
**Karen Peebles**
The Other Side of Suicide
**Antoinette Lee Howard**
Journey Through Fear
**Julia Hanson**
Awakening To Your Creation
**Irene Lucas**
Thirty Miracles in Thirty Days
**Mandeep Khera**
Why?
**Robert Winterhalter**
The Healing Christ
**James Wawro**
Ask Your Inner Voice
**Tom Arbino**
You Were Destined to be Together
**Maureen McGill & Nola Davis**
Live From the Other Side
**Anita Holmes**
TWIDDERS
**Walter Pullen**
Evolution of the Spirit
**Cinnamon Crow**
Teen Oracle
Chakra Zodiac Healing Oracle
**Jack Churchward**
Lifting the Veil on the Lost Continent of
  Mu

For more information about any of the above titles, soon to be released titles,
or other items in our catalog, write or visit our website:

# Other Books By Ozark Mountain Publishing, Inc.

**Guy Needler**
The History of God
Beyond the Source – Book 1,2
**Dee Wallace/Jarred Hewett**
The Big E
**Dee Wallace**
Conscious Creation
**Natalie Sudman**
Application of Impossible Things
**Henry Michaelson**
And Jesus Said – A Conversation
**Victoria Pendragon**
SleepMagic
**Riet Okken**
The Liberating Power of Emotions
**Janie Wells**
Payment for Passage
**Dennis Wheatley/ Maria Wheatley**
The Essential Dowsing Guide
**Dennis Milner**
Kosmos
**Garnet Schulhauser**
Dancing on a Stamp
**Julia Cannon**
Soul Speak – The Language of Your
    Body
**Charmian Redwood**
Coming Home to Lemuria
**Kathryn Andries**
Soul Choices – 6 Paths to Find Your Life
    Purpose

For more information about any of the above titles, soon to be released titles,
or other items in our catalog, write or visit our website: